"In a field saturated with codes, standards, and regulatory language, this book stands apart by teaching clinicians and counselors how to reason ethically in real time. Dr. Reynolds moves beyond black-and-white rule adherence to illuminate the interplay between legal mandates, aspirational ethics, therapist cognition, and practical decision-making. The clinical vignettes—ranging from multiple relationships to romantic transference and complex termination dilemmas —are nuanced, realistic, and pedagogically powerful.

Particularly compelling is the framework of identifying what feels "sticky" and then learning to "boil it down" into actionable ethical steps. This practical heuristic offers therapists something many ethics texts lack: a usable decision-making compass. Grounded in beneficence, non-maleficence, autonomy, and veracity, the book consistently returns to its central thesis—the protection of the therapeutic relationship as an ethical mandate.

This is an invaluable resource for graduate students, supervisors, and seasoned clinicians alike."

William Hutter, PsyD, LMFT, **Clinical Psychotherapist and Licensed Marriage and Family Therapist**

"Ethics books often aim to maximize clarity, using simplistic examples that bear no resemblance to the real world. A therapist does something that clearly violates a rule; the client gets angry and complains. But real professional ethics are filled with gray areas and difficult choices that go beyond mandates and prohibitions. This book honors the complexity and messiness of trying to discern what's best in real-world ethical decision-making. As therapists, we're called upon to manage multiple issues and concerns at once; this book will help you think through more than just what you can and can't do. It will help you decide — and act on — what's best."

Benjamin E. Caldwell, PsyD, LMFT, **Author of Basics of California Law for LMFTs, LPCCs, and LCSWs**

The Ethical Therapist

This practical guide transforms complex therapeutic codes of ethics from organizations like AAMFT and APA into accessible, everyday guidance for navigating ethically challenging cases in clinical practice.

Rather than presenting ethics as abstract concepts, Dr. Lisa René Reynolds illustrates key ethical themes through relatable, real-world scenarios that therapists encounter in their daily work. This book offers rich, detailed discussions stemming from each ethical principle, complemented by illuminating clinical case examples of best (and worst) practices in therapeutic settings. Readers will develop a deeper understanding of what it means to be an ethical practitioner, moving beyond surface-level familiarity with terms like competence, non-abandonment, and informed consent to be able to make informed decisions about treatment and therapeutic approaches. Chapters discuss core ethical principles and their application across diverse contexts and scenarios such as professional obligations and responsibilities, relationships with professional colleagues, technology and social media, self-of-the-therapist, and evaluation and assessment.

This book is essential reading for practicing therapists, counselors, clinical supervisors, and behavioral specialists across all therapeutic disciplines. It is also designed to be a valuable resource for graduate students in therapy and counseling programs.

Lisa René Reynolds, Ph.D., is faculty at The Family Institute at Northwestern University. She is a Clinical Member and Approved Supervisor at the American Association for Marriage and Family Therapy (AAMFT), where she has served as chair of the Ethics Committee and is currently serving on the Judicial Committee.

The Ethical Therapist

A Guide to Confident Decision-Making in Clinical Practice

Lisa René Reynolds

Routledge
Taylor & Francis Group
NEW YORK AND LONDON

Designed cover image: Getty Images

First published 2027
by Routledge
605 Third Avenue, New York, NY 10158

and by Routledge
4 Park Square, Milton Park, Abingdon, Oxon OX14 4RN

Routledge is an imprint of the Taylor & Francis Group, an informa business

Library of Congress Cataloging-in-Publication Data
A catalog record for this title has been requested

ISBN: 978-1-041-25106-4 (hbk)
ISBN: 978-1-041-24921-4 (pbk)
ISBN: 978-1-003-74513-6 (ebk)

DOI: 10.4324/9781003745136

Typeset in Sabon
by Taylor & Francis Books

Contents

Acknowledgments

My eternal thanks to the wonderful graduate students who fuel my passion for writing therapy texts. Thanks especially to my very competent "reference queen," an incredible "almost" therapist in her own right, Kimberly Fuller. Also, my deepest gratitude to dear colleagues who I am blessed to call friends, for their various supports of my writing this book—Dr. Sam Allen, Dr. Will Hutter, Dr. Mudita Rastogi, and Dr. Ben Caldwell. My greatest thank you goes *always* to my parents (for supporting my writing from the very youngest childhood), and to my beloved daughters, granddaughter, and best partner in life—your love and patience with another book is appreciated more than you will ever know.

Introduction

Why write another text on ethics? There is an abundance of books on the topic, but despite this, why do so many therapists still find ethics difficult to navigate in practice? The following chapters are the culmination of many years of teaching graduate ethics classes and supervising therapists.

The book takes on the "nuts and bolts" of traditional ethical frameworks and breaks them down into meaningful, understandable ways of thinking. The text and examples in the book highlight four ways of thinking ethically. First is ***legal***. Since I am not an attorney, nor am I familiar with the state and province regulations of the readers of this book, I cannot include specifics here from this perspective. Throughout the book, I refer *often* to the need for therapists and counselors to utilize their state and province resources, as well as legal counsel (via their professional organization affiliation or malpractice insurers) when appropriate.

Next is ***aspirational***. Some ethical specifics are not delineated in the code of ethics, or in state or province laws and rules. This leaves some "gray area" when navigating ethical situations. In cases where there is no clear "right or wrong," therapists and counselors should *aspire* to act ethically. This means they will follow all the pathways to ensure they have done their due diligence. They strive for the correct actions that will result in a favorable outcome for their clients. ***Aspirational*** ethics are things that may not be enforceable by any single law or rule or ethic, but should be included in therapists' and counselors' practice.

One example would be when we consider a code of ethics that states, "Marriage and Family Therapists maintain high standards of professional competence and integrity" (Standard III, AAMFT, 2026). This standard has a general, broad, overarching, and ***aspirational*** expectation. All therapists practicing under this code should strive to do as the standard instructs. However, a specific violation of this standard would be more enforceable via one of the sub-standards.

For example, let's say that a therapist's daily alcohol use results in impairment of work performance (not showing up for scheduled sessions, forgetting to bill for sessions in a timely fashion, neglecting to complete progress notes, falling asleep in sessions, etc.). The therapist would certainly

DOI: 10.4324/9781003745136-1

not be maintaining a "high standard of professional competence and integrity" (aspirational), but they would be in violation of the specific sub-standard here of "Marriage and Family Therapists seek appropriate professional assistance for issues that may impair work performance or clinical judgment."

Next is ***mental***. The "how" therapists and counselors think about things is imperative to ethical practice. The book focuses on things like assumptions, cultural lenses, value systems, and traits such as conflict avoidance or lack of confidence, and how they can influence ethical decision-making. Where might there be "blocks" or defenses in therapists' or counselors' thinking?

Last is ***practical***. Therapists and counselors are always looking for practical, tangible ways to manage ethical situations. The book focuses most heavily on this area, offering many specific thoughts and strategies to help assist in maintaining ethical practice.

For this book, I referenced the codes of ethics for the following mental health fields: Ethical Principles of Psychologists and Code of Ethics (American Psychological Association, 2017), the American Association of Marriage and Family Therapy (AAMFT) Code of Ethics (2026), The American Counseling Association (ACA) Code of Ethics (2014), and the National Association of Social Workers (NASW) Code of Ethics (2021). Due to the differences in requirements of the different codes of ethics, no single code or profession is used in any of the content here; rather, there are general discussions on the themes that exist across the codes. The terms "therapist" or "client" are used interchangeably throughout the text, and the content is applicable to *all* mental health professionals. Therapists and counselors should always refer to their own professional codes for the specific requirements, as well as to the state or province laws and rules that exist where they practice, for the most thorough understanding of ethical practice. This guide is not meant to replace any code; instead, it is intended to be a valuable addition to all of the codes, to help cement the clinical understanding of them for therapists and counselors alike.

Lastly, all cases are either fictional or based on real-life cases and situations where identifying details have been significantly changed. On many occasions, several scenarios are morphed into one for learning purposes. Through these examples and vignettes, therapists and counselors will have the chance to think through ethical decision-making in clinical situations.

Therapists and counselors have laws, rules, and regulations that govern many things when practicing therapy. These things may be formal or informal, but they offer clear directives, and tell therapists and counselors what to do or not do. One example is that all U.S. states have mandated reporting laws. This means that therapists and counselors are required to report suspected child abuse to their state's child protection services. However, states vary in their rules on what *types* of abuse and neglect must be reported, or *who* is required to report. So although spanking a child—assuming it does not lead to physical injury—may be allowable as a form of discipline in your state, you may be required to report it if it leaves a mark on the child's body. In cases like this, the laws and rules are generally pretty clear and straightforward, and thus easy to follow.

Knowing the laws and rules in one's state of practice is imperative to being an ethical therapist or counselor. But this is the *easy* part. State laws and rules can be looked up. They can be printed out for regular reference. They are black and white in their instruction. It's the *rest* of ethical practice—the part that is *not* defined by straightforward laws and rules—that is far more complicated. Codes of ethics instruct us *what* to do or not do, but not *how* to do or not do those things.

Codes of ethics are both thorough and far-reaching in the areas that they cover, yet at the same time, they can lack specificity. This can lead therapists and counselors to feel confused. Often, the complexity of clinical situations, coupled with the varying interpretations that can be made, leave therapists and counselors searching for simple and straightforward answers to their ethical dilemmas. Many of my graduate students over the years have reported feeling worried, stressed, guilty, and "dumb" over navigating ethical issues in their clinical work. Therapists and counselors may hold the expectation that their code of ethics will tell them *exactly* how to navigate ethical situations, and come away feeling frustrated and hazy on what to do.

An important reminder—even when clear and straightforward answers to ethical dilemmas cannot be found in the state or province laws and rules, or in a profession's code of ethics, ***therapists and counselors are still responsible for making correct ethical decisions.***

In a study by Mullen et al. (2017), the authors found that having a higher occurrence of clinical ethical dilemmas related to a higher level of therapist and counselor burnout and stress among their research participants. However, they also found that therapists and counselors who had higher rates of *reflecting* on the ethical dilemmas, did *not* have an increase in participants' burnout and stress. For this reason, this book will focus on in-depth discussions of ethical dilemmas, with the aim to better prepare therapists and counselors for how to deal more easily with the ethical issues they will inevitably encounter. The need for more therapists and counselors remains high, and these fields need to prevent burnout of these valued folks whenever possible!

There is a term that is often heard in systemic therapy—***equifinality.*** Equifinality was first described by von Bertalanffy (1968), and is defined by Ciccheti and Rogosch (1996) as the way that the same end state may be reached from different starting points and via multiple intervening processes. For example, a therapist or counselor might choose not to take on a potential client and refer to someone else, because they feel the potential client needs a more intensive type of treatment. Alternatively, another therapist or counselor might agree to see a client, but then refer to a more intensive type of treatment a few weeks later, after it is clear the client needs a higher level of care. Both decisions—to refer the potential client out right away, and to see the client for treatment first, and refer out if it becomes clear that the client is not progressing—can be considered ethical practice. I like how equifinality fits with the way that we can view ethics. In many cases, there is not one singular way to be ethical.

Ethics are not "things," but ways of thinking. I like to tell my graduate students that codes of ethics are really just a set of ***boundaries***. Therapists and counselors are very familiar with the concept and importance of boundaries, so it's only natural that ethical standards can be seen in the same way. A therapist or counselor would never cross the physical boundary of the therapeutic relationship by embracing a client upon first meeting them, or sitting on their lap on the therapy couch. Similarly, codes of ethics would mandate such things as not having a sexual relationship or friendship with a client.

If we can wire ourselves with a strong foundational understanding of the basic tenets, ethical practice becomes much easier. It's important to remember that ethics evolve over time, and are influenced by many things, including the political, sociocultural, and relational environments in which therapists, counselors, and clients exist. *Context* matters.

Good, caring, competent therapists and counselors across the world make ethical errors every day. In my time on the American Association of Marriage and Family Therapy (AAMFT) Ethics Committee, I saw this happen far too many times. Despite the many books and resources available to them, therapists and counselors still fail to always "do the right thing." This book's aim is to provide a resource that fills the gaps where others do not, helping therapists and counselors to truly understand themselves, what ethical rules actually mean, especially when encountered in clinical settings rather than in textbooks, and how errors occur. Lastly, the book will offer copious clinical examples that demonstrate what to do and not to do in ethical situations, but more importantly, discussions on how these choices can impact the client, the therapist or counselor, the therapeutic relationship, and one's own practice.

So, let's start with two important foundational pieces to our "ethical wiring" journey. First, a brief exploration of the "why" of ethics, and remembering the central importance of it in clinical practice. Again, not the dry tenets of ethics, but more of a discussion of how ethical practice potentially influences both clients and therapists or counselors and the therapeutic experience and outcome.

Second, there is a simple and practical takeaway for how to navigate ethical situations in therapy. Therapists and counselors may find this key concept useful to carry with them in all clinical cases. Understanding "sticky" and "boil it down" are strategies that can simplify managing difficult situations that require ethical decision-making.

The "Why" of Ethics

Why are ethics important? There are several reasons that having an ethical framework or code is vital. First of all, ethics are meant to primarily protect the vulnerable clients that therapists or counselors treat. However, ethics can also ensure the protection and safety of the therapists and counselors.

For example, most codes state that therapists and counselors should refrain from working with clients who present with issues they are not adequately trained in or experienced with. This protects clients by ensuring that they are getting treatment from folks who know what they are doing. The same code can protect therapists and counselors as well. Consider the following clinical vignette:

THERAPIST: So, you're telling me that your [13-year-old] son doesn't want to come to therapy with me anymore?

CLIENT'S MOTHER: That's right. You told me you worked with teens in your practice, but I feel like there are so many things you missed with him.

THERAPIST: Can you explain a bit more what you mean?

CLIENT'S MOTHER: Well, you have never even asked him about stuff that happens frequently to teens. Why wouldn't you have asked him more about bullying at school? Drug use? You just took him at face value when he said "No" to those questions the first time we met. He said he doesn't feel comfortable talking to you. He said you scolded him when he swore in session and told him swear words were bad for him to use. But did you think about his friends and social groups who all use that language before shaming him for something that doesn't seem "bad" in his world?

THERAPIST: Okay, I'm sorry that's how he took what I said. That's not how I recall things going, but I'd love to discuss this with him.

CLIENT'S MOTHER: It just makes me really mad that you don't seem to have any training or experience with teens, and frankly, it doesn't seem like anything has gotten better with him since he's been seeing you. I'm going to report you to the state board to make sure you don't see any teenagers for therapy again.It is clear in this vignette that the mother is frustrated and distressed by the lack of improvement in the behavioral issues she brought her son in to see the therapist for. It is also clear that the mother feels that the therapist was not truthful about his therapeutic ability. However, the therapist cannot disclose the details of what he did or did not discuss with his client when the mother was not present. Now, consider the following conversation between that 13-year-old client and his best friend later that night:

CLIENT: Guess what? I don't have to go to therapy anymore.

BEST FRIEND: How'd you get out of that?

CLIENT: I told my mother that the therapist sucked and didn't know anything about kids my age. I told her that I didn't feel comfortable talking to him and that he told me I was bad for swearing. I told her that he kept saying how my mother didn't understand me, and that he obviously doesn't know how to work with kids at all. And so she said I didn't need to go anymore.

BEST FRIEND: Wow! Lucky you! My mom is still making me go.

CLIENT: Yup. I'm so smart!

The code that requires therapists and counselors to only treat where they have experience and training works here to help *them*, as well as the client. In the vignette, the therapist was absolutely trained and experienced in working with teens. The client was attempting to manipulate his mother into getting his way and not going to therapy by creating a narrative of the therapist not being skilled.

This therapist was indeed experienced in treating teens, having interned at a child and adolescent agency for several years, and having many continuing education credits from workshops on adolescent issues and treatment. In addition, the therapist had documented the many topic areas he had explored with the client in the session notes, as well as the client's adamance that he had no issues, and that he had not seemed invested in treatment.

The client's mother can certainly file a complaint, but this ethical therapist would not be in violation of what she accused him of—having no training or experience with teens. If this therapist had *not* actually had a history of working with this age group, the therapist might have ended up needing to defend himself and prove that the "failed" case was not due to his lack of experience. This is why it's important for ethical therapists and counselors to ensure they can provide evidence that demonstrates their ability to treat a given population.

What sorts of things might be considered "proof" that the therapist or counselor has enough experience and training in the case with the 13-year old client and his mother above? Unfortunately, most codes use terms like "adequate" or "appropriate" when they describe things like having sufficient training. They do not offer a list of specifics of what would "count" as adequate or appropriate experience or training. The responsibility is on the therapist or counselor to demonstrate sufficiency. Often, the state or province in which they practice will offer clear requirements—things like a certain number of clock hours of training, and on particular topic areas. There is however, a lot of autonomy and flexibility for therapists and counselors to acquire "sufficient" experience. The following are some tangible things therapists can do in this case to flesh out experience and training:

- Use supervision to fill in any gaps on client treatment issues and document accordingly.
- Attend continuing education (CE) trainings.
- Check in with colleagues about how they trained in certain areas.
- Read and research particular clinical issues and populations.
- Have a solid referral list handy in the case that someone with a higher level of experience is needed.
- Be open and check in with clients.

This last bullet point, "Be open and check in with clients," is arguably the most important one, since therapists and counselors often forget that one of the biggest resources they have is the clients that are right in front of them.

They aren't bound by releases of information, privacy, and confidentiality when exploring, asking, collaborating, or checking in with clients. Clients are perhaps the biggest experts therapists and counselors have on how the therapy is going. Clients might best be seen as the most important "consultants"!

In the next chapter, we will explore the several foundational principles in ethics, including ***Autonomy*** (clients have the right to make decisions for themselves) and ***Veracity*** (truthfulness). When thinking about choices in the case above, we can incorporate these two concepts into ethical decision-making. For example, the therapist can share his credentials and experience with the client and the mother from the onset of therapy (Veracity). He can also share that he will check in with them along the way to see if the fit and progress of the therapy is what they expected, and if they'd like to continue treatment with him (Autonomy). These are two ethical ways to work *with* clients to ensure the therapist's experience and training are sufficient to treat them, as well as to create a collaborative relationship that honors the ethical principles of Autonomy and Veracity.

There are other reasons why ethics are important in the therapy field. Not only do they protect clients and therapists or counselors, but they also encourage the trust of the public. When people look to therapy or counseling for help, they should know that the folks they will see for treatment are held to certain regulations and expectations. Therapists and counselors follow guidelines. Perhaps most importantly, they are *governed* in practice by a regulatory board that is tasked with enforcing a code of ethics.

Therapists and counselors who make the effort to ethically "wire" themselves before going into practice will find it easier to navigate difficult ethical situations. This is because, oftentimes, ethical situations crop up quickly, and therapists and counselors might not have time to think things through. Better to have the ethical wiring figured out, so it's easier to navigate the situations quickly as they come up.

Ethics also serve as a space for "best practices." This means that the creators and monitors of codes are incorporating all the current research, societal environment, and trends into the continually updated codes that they publish. Individual therapists and counselors can lean on their field's codes to get the most up-to-date standards of practice.

The Practical: "Sticky" and "Boil it Down"

As you will see in this book's text and many vignettes, clinical situations can crop up that have lots of levels to consider when navigating them. However, if therapists and counselors fail to *recognize* the "stickiness" of situations, then they won't recognize the need for ethical consideration at all. However, if they *can* recognize "sticky," there are ways to "boil it down" to simple steps that will guide their decisions. Consider the following scenario with a client (Raymond) and the client's fiancée (Rebecca):

> Rebecca accompanies Raymond to his therapy unexpectedly one day. The therapist has never met Rebecca before. Raymond says he brought her with him because he's concerned that she has been increasingly depressed lately and wants her to see how therapy works and to get some strategies for feeling better. He says that Rebecca has been reluctant to "try" therapy, and he is certain that if she could see how wonderful and helpful the therapist is, she would agree to get help for herself.

What would you do in this situation? Many therapists and counselors go into this field because they are "bleeding hearts." In other words, they care deeply, and want to be helpful, sometimes at an ethical cost. Some would embrace the situation and immediately invite the fiancée into the session. However, in doing this, they might be ignoring the potential "stickiness" of the situation. Here are some things to consider before making the decision on the client and his fiancée:

The Potential "Sticky"

If the Therapist Agrees to Allow Rebecca in the Session

- Has Rebecca completed the required paperwork (e.g., HIPAA, Informed Consent) before being seen by the therapist?
- Does the therapist have time to adequately explain the limits of confidentiality, etc., in session?
- Does the therapist have time to adequately assess Rebecca for depression, or possible suicidal or homicidal ideation?
- Is it fair to Rebecca to meet with the therapist once and then be transferred to someone else, especially if she connects really well with the therapist?

Remember, the therapist might not be able to begin any kind of assessment or treatment in an outpatient facility or practice without completing a thorough intake that includes explanations from the therapist and signatures from Rebecca. In a single session, it is unlikely that the therapist will have time to do all of this.

There are other things to consider here as well. Is it ethical to use Raymond's original session time to assess and work with Rebecca? Whose insurance will the therapist bill for the meeting? And what procedural code will the therapist use (intake, individual, or couple)?

Lastly, is it ethical to see both your client *and* his fiancée for individual therapy at the same time? What if part of the depression of the fiancée is because she is having an affair with someone else? Will she feel comfortable telling the therapist this or not, given that the therapist sees her fiancée as a client as well?

If the Therapist Does Not *Allow the Fiancée in the Session*

- What will the impact be on the therapeutic relationship between the therapist and client if the therapist refuses to let the fiancée join the session?
- What is the liability, if any, of the therapist on knowing that there is a person who is struggling with mental health issues and not seeing them once they are in the office?

There are some things to consider in *not* seeing the Rebecca here as well. First, how will the therapist say no to Raymond? What rationale will the therapist use to explain why Rebecca can't join?

Next, what about the ethical clause on non-abandonment? Would refusing to see Rebecca be abandoning her? If the therapist works at an agency, are there any rules on "walk-ins" or seeing both parts of a couple individually?

Now that we've identified some potentially sticky areas, how does the ethical therapist navigate the above scenario? Let's use the "boil it down" concept to create a possible course of action after employing some ethical decision-making. Considering laws, rules, policies, codes of ethics, ethical decision-making, and self-of-the-therapist influences, the following might be a few ethical courses of action:

1 **Therapist:** It's a great idea to help Rebecca feel more comfortable with the experience of therapy. That's being a really supportive partner. I'm not able to do an individual intake for her today—there just wouldn't be enough time for me to do what I need to. And since we scheduled for you today, Raymond, maybe I can just spend a few minutes seeing if there are any questions that Rebecca would like to ask me before you and I start today? That might help her understand what therapy is all about.
2 **Therapist:** So, Rebecca, how do you feel about going up to the front desk with me for a few minutes so we can talk about setting you up for an intake with someone here at the agency? If you're comfortable with that, we can ask the receptionist to see if any of the therapists are free between now and when Raymond's session with me is done, so you can meet them for a couple of minutes and see how you feel?
3 **Therapist:** So, in order for Rebecca to join us today, Raymond, we'd need her to fill out a bunch of paperwork and forms before we meet. If we can get those done, we could have her join the session just this once to work on the relational ways you can best support Rebecca during this tough time. How do you feel about giving up your individual session today to focus more on how you can best navigate this with Rebecca? Meanwhile, let's get her set up at the front desk for a therapy session of her own as soon as possible. And, Rebecca, if you change your mind after we all meet, you can always cancel that appointment.

4 **Therapist:** I'm not going to be able to get all the paperwork complete and have you in for the session for today, but I do want to make sure that you are feeling as though the depression is something you have a handle on for now. If it's okay, I'd like to ask you a couple of questions, Rebecca? (Possible lines of questioning: Have you ever felt like maybe you couldn't deal with the depression anymore? Are you feeling safe? Has it ever gotten so bad that you thought about hurting yourself? Have you ever had any suicidal thoughts?)

There is some leeway in what the therapist chooses to do here, while still staying within ethical bounds. Many things are covered here, like including the client (Raymond) in the decisions about how to use his therapy session, adhering to laws on signing forms, assessing for the possibility of Rebecca's need for a more urgent or intensive level of care, following agency policies on who therapists can see, etc. This is all done with mindfulness about how to *both* follow policies and act in ethical ways *and* try to attend to the support needs of Raymond and Rebecca.

In summary, developing a sense of what feels sticky is such an important part of being an ethical therapist or counselor. Attending to their own personal feelings of discomfort or uncertainty, as well as those "gut feelings" that something just doesn't feel right, is key. This should be followed by boiling the situation down to the pieces that therapists and counselors *do* know, like ensuring that paperwork is properly explained and signed before meeting with someone new. When there are pieces that therapists and counselors *don't* know, it will be easier to make decisions based on the building blocks that they *do* know.

The next chapter will give an overview of six main principles in ethics, with thorough discussions of clinical vignettes for each. These principles can help inform the rest of the chapters, the ones that will get into more specific areas of therapist and counselor codes of ethics.

Chapter Takeaways for Therapists and Counselors

1 Codes of ethics tell therapists and counselors *what* to do, but not *how* to do it.
2 It's imperative that therapists and counselors understand *both* the code of ethics standards of their specific profession *and* the laws and rules of the state or province they live in.
3 Having a higher occurrence of clinical ethical dilemmas is related to a higher level of therapist and counselor burnout and stress, while those who have higher rates of *reflecting* on the ethical dilemmas do *not* have an increase in burnout and stress.
4 Recognizing the "stickiness" in clinical situations is imperative to making ethical decisions, while employing the "boiling it down" concept can simplify the actions needed for a complicated situation.

1 Six Main Principles of Ethics

When considering ethical scenarios, therapists and counselors must strike an ethical balance by considering morals and ethics, while still maintaining focus on what's in the best interests of clients. Both ethics and the "warm heart" of caring professionals are vital parts of the therapeutic process. The following principles will help guide therapists and counselors towards striking this important balance in their treatment of clients.

First, an overview of six main principles in ethics—Autonomy, Beneficence, Non-Maleficence, Justice, Fidelity, and Veracity. These are presented not just as words or concepts, but fleshed out in practical ways that simplify adhering to them. Short descriptions of the principles, as they pertain to clients and therapy, are as follows:

Autonomy—clients have the right to make their own, uncoerced decisions.
Beneficence—therapists should do what is in the best interests of their clients.
Non-Maleficence—therapists "shall do no harm," or avoid doing anything that will be hurtful to clients.
Justice—therapists should treat each client they see equally.
Fidelity—therapists should do what they say they will do.
Veracity—therapists should be genuine and truthful with clients.

The next sections will break down each principle via more meaningful discussion of sticky clinical situations and cases.

Autonomy

In short, clients have the right to make their own, uncoerced decisions. So if a therapist or counselor is seeing a couple for treatment, and the couple decides that they want to get divorced, the therapist or counselor should not tell them that they should or shouldn't do that. I have heard from so many couples that prior therapists or counselors have told them, after a lack of "sufficient" progress, that they shouldn't be together. Autonomy supports that the *clients*, not the *therapist or counselor*, have the right to choose whether to stay together or to split up.

DOI: 10.4324/9781003745136-2

What if the therapist or counselor thinks that the couple truly *is* at a dysfunctional crossroads, and might be happier and healthier if they are *not* together? First, they certainly are allowed to have a thought or opinion on this. They may also share their rationale for thinking this with the clients if it seems helpful to treatment. However, how do they adhere to the principle of ***Autonomy*** when feeling these doubts about the couple's relationship?

Read the following possible responses from a fictional therapist to a couple who continues to be stuck in problematic and unhealthy patterns, despite having been in therapy for some time. In each case below, consider whether the therapist is showing up genuinely and therapeutically, while still allowing the clients to make their own choices for themselves (Autonomy). Which of the options do you like best/least? Which one fits the best for your personal style of doing therapy? Does any option make you uncomfortable? Why or why not?

1 **Therapist:** We've been working together for some time now, and I can see the growing frustration you both have with not feeling like anything is getting better between you. I'm wondering if either of you have ideas on what we might be missing here? Are there things we should be talking more or differently about that might help us get on top of some of these issues a bit better? I'm feeling a little stuck on what we might be missing here.

In the above scenario, the therapist is attempting to shift the possible "cause" of the "stuckness" to a constraint, or something that they are collectively missing that's in the way of change. If they can discover it, it might help the couple interact in more healthy ways. This message lets the clients know the therapist has not "given up" on them, while being open to collaboration on possible ideas. This approach may open a whole new area for discussion. It may also yield a "brick wall." Remember that therapists can only know what is knowable.

There is a concept of "wholeness" in systemic therapy that is written like this: 1 + 1 = 3. This means that sometimes all the things we "know" don't equal the total sum of what seems to be going on. What if one of the spouses in the above scenario had been having a long-term, secret affair for several years? What if that partner wanted, and was invested in, the couples' counseling failing so that they would get divorced, and the cheating partner could be with the new love?

One way the therapist in this situation might address the possibility of a secret affair or something else being the stuck point is to use a general statement based on prior clinical experience. The therapist could say, "In my experience, there are many reasons why one or both partners might themselves feel unable to move forward. Maybe they are just tired and burned out and can't fight for the relationship anymore. Or maybe they don't think their partner is the right one for them anymore. Or maybe they've met someone else who makes things seem so much easier. Or maybe there are just non-negotiables for one of them that stop them from moving forward."

In clinical practice, I always like to layer the cause I might suspect in between other things. This is so that if one of these resonates with a partner, they don't feel like I'm "outing" them. This is important in keeping the therapeutic alliance intact in couples' work.

2 **Therapist:** Sometimes, when couples get really entrenched in these unhealthy patterns, they start to think about what it would be like to not be together anymore. I'm wondering if either of you have thought about this? Is this something you have considered or would entertain?

In the above scenario, the therapist is attempting to share clinical experience that may help the couple know that whatever they may have been thinking is a common response. They are not alone. It's also gives permission for them to make that decision if they have been considering it. Additionally, carrying doubts like this, that are not verbalized, can be a heavy burden. Freeing the possible "elephant in the room" can be therapeutic for clients and the therapist alike.

Some couples I have worked with have told me that they always assumed that the therapist or counselor would both know and tell them when it was time to break up. This assumption can lead clients to perhaps want to break up, but believe that the therapist or counselor knows better, and thinks they should stay together. This centers on the ***referent power*** that therapists and counselors can have. Referent power means that clients place power or expectations or authority on the therapist or counselor, often unbeknownst to the therapist or counselor. This would also be a good place for the therapist above, to add, "I hope it is okay that I poke around a bit and challenge you and ask some hard questions. I do this so that we can find a pathway that is helpful to you. Although I may ask difficult questions, it is not my place to decide for either of you when this relationship is not something you want anymore. If either of you are feeling like this, I invite you to share it so I can support you in those tough conversations here."

3 **Therapist:** Given how long we've been working on these issues, with so little progress, it seems, I'm wondering if you think there would be any benefit in having a few sessions with another therapist who is trained and practices in a different type of therapy? Perhaps someone else might have some different ideas on things, or different interventions based on the models they use?

Many codes of ethics have some reference to only practicing when it's beneficial to the client (see *Beneficence* section below), or when the therapist or counselor feels they are competent to do the work they are doing. This may be especially true for therapists and counselors who are just starting out, or those who may be further along in practice but lack experience in working with certain populations (like couples in this case). If a therapist or counselor feels that the clinical stuckness may be caused by a lack of experience or limitations of their training or models, it's a good idea to open up this conversation.

Again, sharing thoughts with clients allows them to have the information that they need to make their own decisions. In this case, the therapist is respecting the tenet of ***Autonomy***, or ensuring that clients get to ultimately make their own decisions. This also touches on the ethical concept on ***non-abandonment*** (covered in Chapter 3), where the therapist should be able to offer a range of resources to clients, should they feel that they are appropriate. Ethical therapists and counselors should always have some resources in the community. They should at least be able to help clients navigate an online directory of providers and help them understand who they might be looking for. In this example with difficult couples' work, helping them find a clinician who advertises experience with couples, an "LMFT" (Licensed Marriage and Family Therapist), or a Gottman-, Imago-, or EFT-trained provider might be helpful.

4 **Therapist:** Given how long we've been working on things, and how you are reporting things just getting worse, I feel like I can't ignore the continued toll that I can see this taking on the both of you. If things continued on just like they are now, if they never got any better than they are right now, would you both be able to stay in this relationship? Would it be tolerable and "good enough" for you?

These aforementioned discussions highlight an important occurrence—what happens when a therapist or counselor is caught between two different levels of ethical consideration? For example, how do they act when they are bound by *both* the principle of Beneficence (Is it in the best interest of the client?) *and* the principle of Autonomy (Clients have the right to their own, uncoerced decision-making)? Here are two examples of clinical scenarios that center on this:

1 Does a client have the right to continue to see a therapist or counselor for 25 years if they find it helpful, even if the therapist or counselor thinks that the issues are gone and now they are just a "paid friend"?
2 Does a client have the right to see a particular therapist or counselor, even when there is a far better skilled and expert provider in the particular issue that the client is seeking therapy for?

Both of these situations pit the therapist or counselor between the two principles of Autonomy and Beneficence. If the client wants to see a particular therapist or counselor, regardless of the specific training or experience that that provider has, should the client be allowed to do so? If viewing this situation from solely an Autonomy lens, the answer would be yes, clients are allowed to see whomever they wish. When adding the principle of Beneficence to the situation, therapists and counselors need to consider whether the client seeing them will be in the client's best interests. There is no clear-cut map for how to gauge this. This is why practicing ethically can be tricky.

Consider the following ideas on how to balance Autonomy and Beneficence in the #1 and #2 questions above:

1 Keeping Autonomy in mind, the therapist or counselor should respect clients' desire to continue therapy if they report it helpful to them. However, keeping Beneficence as a key consideration, the therapist or counselor should check in with the client to see if the therapy is still helpful on a regular basis, and document these conversations in the notes. Some models of therapy will guide the therapist or counselor, by encouraging shorter- or longer-term treatment. The therapist or counselor can check in by asking, "So we've been meeting for about six months now, and it seems that most of your original treatment goals have been met. I wanted to check in with you to see if therapy still feels helpful to you?" *If* the client reports that it is still helpful, the therapist or counselor should dig into understanding the specific ways that therapy is working—"Can you tell me more about *how* therapy is still helping you?" From what the client reports, the therapist or counselor can create new goals. For example, if the client says, "I find it helpful to have check-ins and support about sticking to the promises I made to myself on how I will allow others to treat me," the therapist or counselor might create a new treatment goal of "maintaining follow-through on boundaries in interpersonal relationships."

There are two special considerations related to the aforementioned section. First, the therapist or counselor should assess for the possibility that the client has become dependent on them, especially if it is in an unhealthy or obsessive way. Or perhaps the client has used the therapist or counselor as a replacement for friends or other social interactions. Maybe the therapist or counselor has become a parent figure. In this case, it may *not* be beneficial for the therapy to continue, or, at very least, it may warrant a discussion about the therapeutic relationship and treatment. These can be tricky conversations to have, but they are imperative for practicing ethically. Therapists and counselors can talk to clients about what termination looks like, or what they might fear. Also, a helpful plan can be cutting back on the frequency of meetings in order to make the termination a bit slower and easier on the client.

In my years of clinical work, I have found it helpful to keep a central theme in sessions with all clients whenever appropriate. With the exception of mandated therapy clients who are *required* to attend sessions, I tell my "voluntary" clients, "You don't *need* therapy. You are making a wise, informed choice to *seek* therapy to help in (fill in the blank here—for example, feeling better, being treated more respectfully, reducing stress, getting sober)."

The second special consideration here is in terms of insurance billing. Most insurers require treatment plans with regular reviews, and many offer a limited number of sessions. If this is the case with clients a therapist or counselor is seeing, then they *must* adhere to ethical billing and reporting, and being truthful about treatment.

2 According to the Autonomy principle, clients can choose the therapist or counselor they feel is the best fit and works for them. Similar to the discussion above in #1, ethical therapists and counselors need to also assess whether the treatment they are offering the client is effective. Checking in with clients along the way to see if the therapist's or counselor's limited experience and skill set with a particular issue will help gauge Beneficence (if the treatment is in the best interests of the client). The following is one way a therapist or counselor might address concerns about a trained-enough provider for a client, especially when there are far more trained and specialized therapists in the area who work with a particular issue:

- **Therapist:** When we met for the first time and discussed what you wanted to get out of therapy, you listed the main issue as not being able to get over the loss of your beloved aunt a few years ago. As I mentioned to you, I don't specialize or have specific training in grief work, but given that we had worked together well on different issues in the past, I was willing to see you for therapy. I wanted to check in with you and talk about whether you might consider trying out a few sessions with another local provider. I'm concerned because you are reporting no improvement in your depression and loss since we first starting meeting several months ago. I obviously want you to get the right treatment to help you heal and grieve your aunt, and I'd be remiss if I just looked the other way and kept doing what I'm doing. There are some grief and loss specialists in the area that I've heard great things about. I'm wondering how you'd feel about contacting one of them to see if their methods might help you a bit more than I've been able to. And, of course, you and I will continue to meet weekly until we can be sure you can get an appointment and start therapy with one of the other providers.

One important thing to consider in this scenario is that although the therapist is acting ethically in opening the discussion of whether there might be a different/more effective kind of treatment for the client, this may bring up something else. Might the client feel rejected by the therapist, or feel that the therapist has given up on and doesn't want to work with them anymore?

Beneficence could also be applied here, in that it focuses on the best interests of the client. Again, the therapist may feel caught between two principles—respecting the client's desire to work with the therapist (Autonomy), while ensuring the treatment is working, and therefore in the best interests of the client (Beneficence). Only this time, doing "the right thing" here may leave the client feeling bad or hopeless or rejected, which may *not* be beneficent. Therefore, it's the ethical responsibility of the therapist to *attempt* to address and alleviate any signs of this from the client. The following is an example of what the therapist might say if there is suspicion that the client feels rejected:

- **Therapist:** I want to address the comment you just made about me thinking you are "hopeless." I want to be very clear that I do not, in any way, think you are hopeless. In fact, I feel exactly the opposite. You are a resilient person who has survived many things and gotten through difficult things in your lifetime with strength and grace. Me bringing up the possibility of another provider is not about you at all—it's about me and my ethical responsibility to be sure you are getting the most appropriate treatment I know is available for you. It's also about still seeing you suffer hugely with a loss that has continued to have negative effects on your functioning and relationships and life while we've been working together. I need to be sure that there isn't a provider with a different skill set who would be more effective with grief work. Not doing that would be selfish of me and not in your best interests.

Beneficence

In short, therapists and counselors should do what is in the best interests of the clients. However, it can be difficult sometimes to figure out if something is in the best interests of the client. How does the therapist or counselor know?

As trained therapists and counselors, we can make an educated and informed *guess* at what is best for a client, but we cannot be sure. The postmodern influence on many providers today, leads them to adhere to the principle that there is no one universal truth or understanding. This belief helps them understand how clients are different from one another, and prompts them to treat clients from a ***collaborative***, rather than ***directive*** modality. How can it be in the best interest of a client for another person (the therapist or counselor), one who has different life experiences, values, and lenses from which to view the world, to tell clients what is best for them? How is it ***beneficent*** to make decisions for clients? The following are some basic foundations that can help therapists and counselors strive to act in beneficent ways when treating clients:

1. Work Collaboratively With Clients

Therapists and counselors should include clients' thoughts, opinions, and feelings in therapeutic discussions. They should also attend to the power differential, or hierarchical misalignment, that may be present during these discussions. Working collaboratively may be difficult if clients feel that the therapist or counselor is more knowledgeable. I often share with clients that, indeed, I have lots of knowledge and training and experience, but what I am sorely lacking are the specifics of their unique experiences. Clients are an integral part of the discussion and decisions, an irreplaceable part of the therapy "team."

2. *Use Tentative Language With Clients*

One way to ensure that clients' thoughts, opinions, and decisions are being included in the therapeutic discourse, is for the therapists and counselors to use tentative language. Anyone who has ever been my graduate student will tell you that I'm a big fan of adding a question mark to the end of statements with clients. What I mean by this is that when therapists or counselors want to say something to a client that may come off as directive, ***asking***, rather than ***telling***, results in a more collaborative discourse. For example, instead of a therapist or counselor ***telling*** their client, Mary, that "you shouldn't tolerate your daughter talking to you like that," the therapist or counselor could *ask*, "So, Mary, have you thought about finding a way to not tolerate your daughter talking to you like that anymore?" This subtle shift from telling to asking results in the therapist or counselor highlighting the importance of the client in the decision-making process.

3. *View Clients as Experts on Their Own Lives*

If therapists and counselors believe *both* that clients and their providers have unique and useful views and understanding *and* that they are both "experts" in certain areas, then it should be easy for them to value their clients' thoughts, opinions, and feelings. Therapists and counselors can be direct in how they let clients know they are experts on their own lives. From the very first meeting with clients at intake, I share my belief and stance that there will always be *two* "experts" in the room, and that it is within the collaboration of the two that we can best find answers and solutions and change that is in their best interests.

4. *Regularly Check In With Clients*

It is easy for therapists and counselors to "forget" that their clients are right there with them every week for treatment. When in doubt, *check in*! The check-ins can be peppered in throughout treatment. For example, after sharing a thought or idea with a client, the therapist or counselor can ask, "I don't know how you feel about this, but it was something I noticed today and wanted to see if you agree with it." Another example would be if the therapist or counselor said, "How do you feel about taking our conversation today home with you and sharing it with your husband? There were so many things that we explored today that I'm wondering if he might be very interested and grateful to understand a bit more about how you're feeling?"

Working collaboratively with clients, including their thoughts, opinions, and feelings in therapeutic discussions, and checking in with them to see what they think are all integral parts of maintaining Beneficence in treatment of clients.

Let's take the clinical case of Yvonne, a 38-year-old, Latinx female. Yvonne was assigned male at birth, but transitioned five years ago and, in doing so, lost the support and involvement of her entire family in her life. Yvonne begins therapy to help her deal with pressure from her current girlfriend, Ingrid, who is insistent that Yvonne must reach out and fix things with her family. Ingrid explains that family is so important to her personally, and that Yvonne is making a disastrous mistake in not working to repair the rupture in her relationships with her mother and siblings.

Keeping the basic foundations (listed above) in mind, here is one possible way an ethical therapist or counselor, who is attempting to keep Beneficence at the forefront of the treatment, approaches the topic with Yvonne:

THERAPIST: So you've told me a lot about how Ingrid feels about family, but I haven't heard much from you on how you feel.

YVONNE: Well, in theory I feel the same. But I don't have the kind of family that Ingrid has, so it's different.

THERAPIST: Do you feel like Ingrid understands that?

YVONNE: No, not really. She thinks it's fixable with my family.

THERAPIST: Is it? And more importantly, do you want to fix it?

YVONNE: I don't know. Maybe. What do you think I should do?

THERAPIST: I'd love to say I know the "right" decision here for you, Yvonne. But the decision I would make, or Ingrid would make, or anyone would make, might be different from the decision that's right for you here.

YVONNE: But I trust your opinion. And I don't know what to do.

THERAPIST: I'm glad you trust me. That's important. But trust still doesn't make me able to make a very big decision for you. How about if we try to work through this together? You trust me, right?

YVONNE: I do. And yes, I'm willing. Where do we start?

THERAPIST: Well, let's start with exploring what Ingrid thinks. When Ingrid first told you that you needed to fix your family-of-origin dynamics, what was your initial reaction?

Instead of the aforementioned discussion, the therapist here could have easily told Yvonne, "Ingrid doesn't know what's best for you. She doesn't understand the very serious dynamics that exist in your family. And it might be opening you up to a lot of judgment and abandonment and hurt if you take that chance." The therapist's suggestion *may* be beneficent, or the right decision for the client. But how would the therapist know? If the therapist believes this is the best course of action for Yvonne, that's okay. But what the therapist would be *missing* in this approach is gathering the client's thoughts and feelings *first*, before making a statement or suggestion.

Instead, the therapist's communication in the vignette above highlights an ethical and collaborative approach that seeks to operate from a beneficent stance in working with the client to discover what is in the client's best interests.

Non-Maleficence

In short, this means that therapists and counselors "shall do no harm," or avoid doing anything that will be hurtful to clients. Most therapists and counselors respond to this principle with, "Oh, of *course* I'd never do anything to intentionally cause harm to my client!" So, what sorts of things might a well-intentioned therapist or counselor do that might be considered harmful to a client? Read the following client statements from a 34-year-old Black male with a history of Bipolar II disorder, and the responses from Therapist #1 and Therapist #2. Consider which therapist's responses might cause more potential harm to the client:

CLIENT: I'm just feeling really down this week. I feel like I can't deal with my life anymore. Everything is just shit. I'm sorry, I just don't have the energy to talk about stuff with you today. Just not feeling motivated or hopeful enough to try to figure it all out. I just need to go distract myself and not deal with all this today.

THERAPIST #1 POSSIBLE RESPONSES: That's okay, I understand, and want to respect where you are today. Do you want to talk about something else today? Is there anything exciting you have to look forward to? Or would you like to just cancel for today, and reschedule for next week when you're feeling more up to working on some of the things we've been addressing in our sessions? I want to honor your wishes, and the last thing I ever want to do is add more stress or negativity to you when you are already feeling bad.

THERAPIST #2 POSSIBLE RESPONSES: I'm so sorry to hear how down you're feeling this week. Can you tell me a little more about how this week has been? I'm a little concerned about whether your feelings of not being able to deal with your life have gotten bad enough to make you think about hurting or killing yourself at all? I know you don't feel like talking today, but given how you are feeling, I want to be sure I don't let you leave here today without a plan. What do you think we could do today to help make you feel better? Let's talk about what extra supports we can put in place for you until you're feeling better.

Therapist #1 strives to "meet the client where he is," by wanting to respect how the client feels, and not pushing him outside of his stated comfort zone. The therapist attempts to divert the conversation to lighter topics, and even gives the client the option of not meeting that day. Although this may be *easier* for the client in the state that he's in, is it a good example of not doing harm?

Therapist #1 is making two vital mistakes here. First, the therapist is taking the client at his word, even though he is in a very negative emotional place. The client might truly be fine and just need a break to chill out and try not to think about the bad stuff in his life. However, the therapist did not ask any questions to explore or confirm this. Second, the therapist *assumes* that letting the client cancel the session or only talk about positive things will make the client feel better. Perhaps the client would feel better by talking with the therapist and, in doing so, gain a different perspective, strategies for coping, or support? Again, the therapist failed to ask questions that might have ensured Non-Maleficence here.

The therapist's worry about making things worse for the client by pushing on more info about how he's feeling, coupled with her well-intentioned attempt at honoring his wishes, has left an opening for possible harm. The therapist was given sensitive information by the client, did not adequately explore how he felt, and jumped to the assumption that the best thing to do was let him leave or distract him with positive thoughts.

Therapist #2 "meets the client where he is" as well, but chooses to probe a bit more and have the difficult discussions that the client may not want to have. By softly approaching the client's stated mood that week, while still challenging the client with the important questions, the therapist attempts to ensure the client is both safe and has the appropriate supports in place. Additionally, the therapist has shown up in a supportive way, giving the client the opportunity to talk about things he may not have told anyone else. This is an example of non-maleficent efforts by the therapist.

After the therapist acknowledges the client's emotional state and lends support and questions to assess what's in the best interests of the client, there may be an appropriate option of letting the client end the session early. Likewise, having a "lighter" session if the client finds that more helpful may be appropriate as well. These two options allow for the ***Autonomy*** of the client, while also allowing for assessment, support, and overall caretaking for the client in a non-maleficent manner.

A couple of other non-maleficent errors therapists or counselors can make are as follows:

1 The therapist or counselor encourages the client to work out a deal where they charge a higher hourly rate to insurance so that the client's deductible is met more quickly. For the time that they are charging a higher rate to the insurance, they allow the client to pay less than the charged amount. When the deductible is met, insurance will begin reimbursing the therapist or counselor at the full rate. In this case, the therapist or counselor is doing harm to the client because the agreement has made the client an accomplice to insurance fraud.
2 A therapist discovers that a client (Gloria) has been recently diagnosed with a variety of new sexually transmitted infections after she had several drunken, unprotected hook-ups with a coworker. The client works

at a small site where the therapist has other clients. The employees at this site are known to party a lot together after work. The therapist is concerned about the sexual safety of her other clients, after the one client disclosed their sexual health issues. The therapist decides to do a blanket "warning" to each of her clients who work there about how important it is to "use protection" when engaging in sexual activities. One of the clients challenges the therapist and says, "Why are you so concerned about this now? Are you talking about Gloria? Did you hear about the shit going down with her?" In this case, the therapist attempting to "do good" by warning the other clients, without alluding to Gloria specifically, ends up shining light on Gloria. Additionally, if one of the clients told Gloria that their therapist warned them about safe sex, Gloria might be very embarrassed and hurt and wonder if her therapist told anyone. This, too, does harm to clients.

Justice

In short, this means that therapists and counselors should treat each client that they see in a fair and equitable way. Most therapists and counselors I know would say, "Well, of *course* I treat every client I see in an equitable way. Everybody matters the same to me." But what exactly does practicing Justice look like in clinical action?

At the very root of Justice is the notion of ***inclusion***. The Oxford Dictionary's definition of inclusion is "the practice or policy of providing equal access to opportunities and resources for people who might otherwise be excluded or marginalized, such as those who have physical or intellectual disabilities and members of other minority groups." This means things like striving for a practice that allows access to as many people as possible. The following are some broad-stroke examples of how therapists and counselors can make their practice more inclusive:

- Have an office that has wheelchair ramps in the parking lot, is on the first floor or has an elevator, and is overall ADA compliant.
- Be aware of resources in your local community that exist for a wide range of clients' identities, such as LGBTQ+, HIV+, and Spanish-speaking new mothers support groups.
- Offer sliding-scale or pro bono spots, so that those who are uninsured or cannot afford an insurance co-pay can receive services. Additionally, some communities offer subsidy programs through local agencies that can help reduce costs for potential clients.
- Consider having a practice in an area that is close to a train or bus line, or is accessible by walking.
- Consider maintaining a teletherapy practice to accommodate those whose geographical location, work or childcare schedule, or transportation status makes traditional therapy difficult or impossible.

This list is not at all exhaustive, but contains some solid starts for a Justice-infused practice. Now, let's get into some of the stickier, more layered clinical situations where Justice needs to be considered by the ethical therapist or counselor.

A brand-new therapist, Gianna, wants to make her practice as inclusive and accessible as possible. Considering the ethical principle of Justice, she decides to have a generous range of sliding-scale fees in her payment options so that everyone, regardless of finances, would be able to access her care. She creates a form that intends to capture income and costs of clients, so that she can be equitable in assigning fees. Soon, Gianna is overwhelmed by calls and emails, and quickly fills her schedule.

A few months later, Gianna gets a call from a potential client, Fawn. Fawn explains that they are cousins with one of Gianna's other clients, and asks if Gianna would see them for therapy at the same reduced rate that Gianna charged for seeing Fawn's cousin. Gianna agrees, as she is trying to build her ethical practice, and wants to help potential clients with access to care.

A couple of weeks later, Gianna gets a request for treatment from a brand-new couple. After meeting with them a few times, the couple shares with Gianna that they are feeling unhappy because they just found out that neighbors of theirs are also seeing Gianna, and that couple pays $30 less than they do for sessions. The couple goes on to explain that the paperwork they filled out had the same financials as the other couple, because they both worked at the same company and got hired at the same time, in the same job. Gianna, feeling bad that the couple thinks she is overcharging them, attempts to repair the therapeutic rupture:

> I'm so sorry that you are unhappy, and feel like I'm overcharging you. My intention was always to have a fair and equitable range of fees, so that everyone, no matter their finances or circumstances, would be able to access care with me. I want you to know that I take my payment scales and treating all my clients justly very seriously. Although you both filled out the same income on the sliding-scale form, there were other things to consider there, like childcare fees, and debt, and mortgage amounts, etc. So I'm really sorry you're feeling this way, and given the circumstances, I'm willing to make an exception and see you at the same fee as your neighbors. Are you okay with that?

Keeping the principle of Justice and inclusion in mind, what did Gianna do ethically here? And what did she do that may *not* have been ethical?

Gianna did indeed consider the principle of Justice as she created a practice that attended to potential clients' needs, inclusion, fairness, and access. She also did a nice job of explaining the motives for, and care she took in considering, her sliding fee scales to the couple.

However, Gianna did several things that could be considered unethical. Were her policies on fees fair and transparent? Not really. It appears that

Gianna made up the "rules" of change as she encountered issues. In her attempts at fairness (giving clients what seems appropriate for their unique circumstances), she ended up not treating everyone the same. Ultimately, Gianna gave in to offering the couple the same fee as their neighbors, even though they technically did not qualify for that reduced rate. Would Gianna do this same things for every client who requested it? If not, then she wouldn't be acting justly.

More importantly—and perhaps Gianna's biggest ethical error here—she inadvertently disclosed protected information about her clients. Even in *acknowledging* that she saw the couple's neighbors for therapy was a misstep. Furthermore, she gave personal details, like housing and childcare costs, and debt, being considered in the decision. This admission of details lets the couple know that their neighbors have debt.

Gianna is a wonderful example of well-meaning therapists and counselors who can easily get onto the slippery slope of unethical behavior.

Fidelity

In short, this means that therapists and counselors should do what they say they will do. Another way for them to think of Fidelity is that they follow through on their word. There are many simple ways that therapists and counselors can adhere to this principle.

Let's take one example of a therapist, Carla, who advertises and bills at a 50-minute session rate. She schedules clients on the hour, to ensure she has ten minutes in between sessions to use the bathroom, do a session note, check her personal texts and email messages, or make a phone call.

One day, Carla goes over her 50 minutes with a young client who is struggling with the recent loss of her grandmother and her childhood dog in the same week. This is Carla's first client of the day each Friday. For several weeks, Carla spends over 60 minutes with the client, working overtime to help the young client stabilize and feel better.

Feeling bad for the young client, Carla offers extra time and effort to help her. In doing this, she cuts into her allotted between-session time to complete notes and run to the restroom. Carla then finds that the rest of her day is running behind because she went over in that earlier session. She hasn't been able to find time to eat or catch up on messages. She starts the subsequent sessions late, and tries to end them a minute or two earlier so she can fit in a bathroom break and get back on track. By the end of the day, Carla finds herself feeling irritable and is annoyed when her final session isn't wrapping up a bit early. She is short with the client she is seeing, and chalks it up to being hungry.

At first glance, this seems like Carla's well-meaning and kind gesture towards the young client who has had difficult losses, and has few resources for support, is appropriate ethically. However, in attending so gallantly and selflessly to the young client, Carla is not showing up fairly, and as promised, to her other clients. Carla not adhering to her own "rule" of ending sessions on time to give herself a few minutes to manage other tasks. She is also not keeping her standard of care with other clients, including things like sticking to 50-minute sessions, full attention to clients' needs, and not letting personal issues (like irritation or feeling hungry) get in the way of treatment.

Another way to view Fidelity is through the lens of ***treatment fidelity***. Bellg et al. (2004) describe how this term first appeared in our professional literature in the late 1970s and early 1980s. This means that therapists and counselors should treat their clients by delivering interventions and assessments according to the way they were intended to be administered. This might include the therapist or counselor ensuring they are trained in the tools, methods, models, or techniques. It also means that things like an assessment measure will be given as is instructed, and in the same way to every client. The resulting information should be utilized as directed. The consistent way that therapists and counselors show up in the room and utilize the models, tools, assessments, and techniques in the way they were intended is vital for the clients' comfort. The therapeutic setting and experience should be dependable and safe for clients.

So, how do therapists and counselors ensure treatment fidelity? First, they should be competent to perform the things they do or administer in the session. Next, they should make their intentions and protocols overt to the client. This can include detailing policies in the informed consent, thoroughly explaining assessments they are using, including clients in the decisions to try certain things, and making sure results or opinions are clarified. Lastly, they should show up in ways that the client expects. A client should consistently experience a therapeutic setting that has boundaries, a certain cadence, rules of engagement, and non-judgment. Consider Alexander's description of his current therapist to a friend who is asking about and considering seeking out therapy for himself:

ALEXANDER: My therapist is awesome! I've been seeing him for about nine months now, I think.

FRIEND: Is it weird talking to your therapist? I'm kind of nervous about talking to a stranger and not being sure what the therapist is thinking about what I'm sharing.

ALEXANDER: I feel really comfortable talking to my therapist! He has this really calm demeanor, and he never makes me feel judged by what I'm saying. We kind of do a variation of the same thing every time we meet.

FRIEND: Really? Do you like that? Doesn't it get boring?

ALEXANDER: No! I really enjoy the consistency, actually. I know what to expect. He always starts by asking me about my week. I usually tell him all the bad stuff first, and then he tends to poke around a bit and help me see what wasn't going so bad. He uses a couple of different models of therapy, and he tells me about some of the interventions he's using. Like cognitive reframes. He explains it to me. By the end, we usually have a good plan for how to show up and deal with stuff the next week, and he gives me some ideas for homework that I might do to help some of the things I told him.

FRIEND: Okay, so sounds pretty predictable...

ALEXANDER: Exactly! His degrees are on the wall, he's always calm and non-judgmental, he explains stuff, and he tells me why he wants to try certain things with me and explains it all when he gets the results. He makes sure we are on the same page and I'm part of the process. It's really very comfortable. I hope you find a great therapist too...

This is a very good sign that Alexander and his therapist have a solid therapeutic relationship, in part due to the therapist's treatment fidelity. But how can therapists and counselors assure treatment fidelity, when the clients they see have diverse presentations, personalities, and needs? This is where some flexibility may be needed.

Although there are some assessment tools that need to be utilized in very specific and standardized ways, therapeutic models and techniques offer much more variability in how they are delivered. The growing popularity of integrative therapy, rather than focusing on one single model, offers therapists and counselors a more flexible framework for treatment. Zarbo et al. (2016) describe "integrative psychotherapy" as an approach that is more flexible, collaborative, and inclusive of the various different parts of therapy models.

One of the tasks for ethical therapists and counselors adhering to Fidelity in practice is to find the balance between using evidence-based treatments and still remaining flexible with stances and interventions that are tailored to the unique needs of individual clients. Katz et al. (2019) note that recent studies suggest that:

> Adherence flexibility (the capacity of the therapist to flexibly adapt treatment to the patient, which may involve using interventions from other treatment approaches and modalities) may be associated with superior outcomes.

In short, the principle of Fidelity is an important part of ethical practice. It requires therapists and counselors to keep a central focus on delivering treatment in a way that is consistent and ensures the same quality across sessions, regardless of the various models or interventions they use. This not only maintains the integrity of the profession but also helps support the therapeutic relationship.

Veracity

In short, the word depicts honesty or truthfulness. According to this foundational principle, therapists and counselors should be genuine and truthful with clients. For example, consider the following vignette between a therapist and the client, Vivienne, who is going through a difficult divorce:

VIVIENNE: I've been hiding my drinking problem from my husband for the last few months because I'm afraid he'll go to court and get my son taken away from me.

THERAPIST: Oh my gosh, Vivienne, that will NEVER happen. You are a good mother, and he can't just take your child away from you.

VIVIENNE: Oh yes he can. He would do that to me if he knew.

THERAPIST: But you are in therapy now and going to AA and doing all the right things, Vivienne.

VIVIENNE: I know, but I relapsed twice, and I'm so ashamed.

THERAPIST: Vivienne, STOP worrying about this. You are a good mom who loves her child, and you are making every effort to get sober. If your husband finds out about any of this, he can try whatever he wants, but no court is just going to snap their fingers and take your son away.

The therapist in the above vignette sees all the great strides the client is making, how motivated she is to get sober, how much she loves her son, and how honest she is in therapy sessions. For these reasons, the therapist attempts to support the client, build her up, and assuage her fears. But in doing so, the therapist is not being completely truthful. There are more things the therapist needs to help the client explore. For example, Vivienne's husband might, in fact, try to file for sole custody given her history with alcohol. Is it true that no court is just going to snap their fingers and take a person's child away?

In addition to not embracing honesty in the session, albeit for the reason that the therapist wants to make Vivienne feel better, the therapist is doing something else here. While attempting to assuage Vivienne's fears, the therapist is neglecting to focus on important therapeutic interventions like helping her develop strong coping skills and strategies to remain sober and avoid triggers that may lead to relapse.

Let's complicate things a bit now. Consider the following case of Maria, a client who has been seeing the therapist, Marcel, for six months. She began therapy to help her deal with her long-term girlfriend (Jezebel) ending their relationship. When Jezebel reaches out to Maria for help with her relationship with her son, Maria readily suggests they go to therapy, and provides her with contact information for her own therapist, Marcel.

Sometimes, honesty is simply sharing the things therapists *can* say, while being truthful about the things they *can't* say. From the vignette described above, consider the following response from the therapist, Marcel:

MARCEL: Hi, Maria. How was your week?

MARIA: Crappy! To say the LEAST.

MARCEL: Do you want to talk about it?

MARIA: I'm so pissed off! You know how Jezebel left me almost six months ago? And do you remember how I told you she always seemed to have issues with her grown son? They got in these fights all the time and wouldn't talk to each other for months, and Jezebel would be so upset by this.

MARCEL: Yup. I do recall that you said she had a difficult relationship with her son.

MARIA: Well, Jezebel texted me a few weeks ago and asked for help. I told her she should call you to see if you would see her and her son. I told her you are a really great therapist and that if anyone could help them, it would be you.

MARCEL: Well, thank you for the vote of confidence. I'm really glad you've found our work together helpful to you.

MARIA: Of course! You're the best, Marcel. You've helped me so much. But you see, I gave your name and contact to Jezebel to reach out to you for her relationship with her son, not for her to give your number to her new girlfriend!

THERAPIST: I'm confused, Maria...

MARIA: I wanted Jezebel and her son to see you for therapy. But I found out that she gave your info to her new girlfriend. And I know you now see her for therapy! Last week after my session with you ended, I was walking down the hallway, and I thought I saw the new girlfriend walking down that other hallway to the bathroom. But I wasn't sure, so I waited a few minutes and saw her leave the bathroom and go into your office. I did NOT give Jezebel your number so that her new girlfriend could share MY awesome therapist!

THERAPIST: Maria, you know I cannot disclose who I see or don't see...

MARIA: You don't have to disclose it. I already know you see her. I drove by an hour later and saw her leave your office.

THERAPIST: Maria, I can see how distressed you are about this, and it seems like you should talk to Jezebel about how you feel.

MARIA: I don't know why you just won't admit you see her. I already know anyway... Tell her you can't see her for therapy anymore. Tell her it's a conflict of interest.

THERAPIST: Maria, I protect all my clients' privacy. I simply cannot tell any client who I see or don't see.

MARIA: But I already told you—I know you see her. I'm not asking you to confirm it. I KNOW you do. I'm asking you to tell the new girlfriend client you can't see her.

THERAPIST: I cannot disclose if I see this person, whether or not you suspect that I do. If this were the case, I can understand how you'd feel betrayed. So it seems like the first step is for you to talk to Jezebel and tell her how you feel. I think that's an important conversation to have.

Did Marcel demonstrate Veracity here? Was he genuine and truthful with Maria in everything he said? Marcel was both honest with Maria about the things he was allowed to share, but also honest with her about what he couldn't. This is an example of the essence of what the principle of Veracity looks like in clinical action.

In this case, the next question might be whether or not it's ethical for Marcel to continue to see both Maria and Jezebel's new girlfriend. So far, Marcel has acted ethically. He has demonstrated taking care to treat both Maria and Jezebel's new girlfriend with the same protection (Justice), and been truthful where he can be (Veracity), and shows follow-through on what he has said he cannot do by not disclosing information even after Maria asks repeatedly for it (Fidelity). Beneficence and Non-Maleficence are considered by Marcel, but now he needs to decide if it's in the best interests of both clients to continue to see both of them, while still navigating it through the ethical means of not disclosing protected information to either of them. The situation is sticky. The ethical decision on this depends on a few things. The following are a few pathways for navigation and outcomes that allow Marcel to remain ethical:

1 Maria takes Marcel's advice and talks to Jezebel, and Jezebel asks her new girlfriend to find another therapist because Maria is upset with the both of them seeing Marcel. "Problem" solved!
2 Marcel explores with Maria if she can still see him for therapy, given that she seems annoyed at his insistence on adhering to ethics and not breaking rules. Does Maria feel that she can still trust Marcel and refocus on the therapy they are doing? Marcel should be armed with appropriate referrals should Maria feel that she cannot work through this incident with him.
3 Marcel gently explains how his adherence to privacy and ethics, etc. is there to protect Maria as well, and therapeutically explores with Maria the reasons for her concern about the situation. They (successfully) incorporate her experience into broader themes that Maria is experiencing from the breakup, including hurt, disappointment, frustration, anger, and lack of control.

Which pathways feel most comfortable for you? Which one would you choose and why?

One additional thing for Marcel to consider here is his self-of-the-therapist (SOTT) work. How does Marcel feel about the decision he makes? How easy was it for him to figure out how to handle the situation? Repeated sticky ethical situations, and the way that the context lands on the therapist or counselor, can contribute to stress and burnout (Mullen et al., 2017). It is important that therapists and counselors develop an ethical wiring that simplifies decision-making for them, and that they have adequate personal and professional supports intact. After all, therapists and counselors are simple humans too, and can bear the same stress that people who work in different careers can carry. Self-care and support is of the utmost importance in being an ethical therapist or counselor.

The ethical principle of Veracity centers on therapists' and counselors' truthfulness and showing up in an honest and genuine way with clients. Not only does this help protect the soundness of treatment, but it also helps support the therapeutic relationship.

Chapter Takeaways for Therapists and Counselors:

1. The six foundational principles of ethics (Autonomy, Beneficence, Non-Maleficence, Fidelity, Justice, and Veracity) are especially important to integrate into the clinical framework in order to maintain an ethical practice.
2. "Referent Power" is an important factor to consider in ethical practice. It means that, unbeknownst to the therapist or counselor, clients can inadvertently place power or expectations or authority on them.
3. "Treatment Fidelity" is an important ethical concept to keep central to all clinical work. This means that therapists and counselors should treat their clients by delivering interventions and assessments according to the way they were intended to be administered.

2 The (Ethical) Therapeutic Relationship

It is very important to listen before one speaks. When thinking about the therapeutic relationship, we can see how listening to the client(s) can guide the therapist or counselor towards ethical choices. These sound choices can only be made by considering and including the clients' thoughts, feelings, and needs. And how can therapists and counselors know what these things are? ***Listen.***

Consider the following dialogue between a therapist and their 15-year-old client, Aña:

THERAPIST: Thank you for sharing all of that at our first meeting, Aña. Especially that your mother passed away unexpectedly a few months ago.

AÑA: Well, everybody tells me that if I want therapy to work, I need to be honest and tell you everything.

THERAPIST: I think that's very true. And I'm glad you feel comfortable enough to be so open with me. Please let me know along the way if there are things I can do or not do that will continue to make you comfortable sharing with me, okay?

AÑA: Okay. I guess I felt like you should know that my mom died. I don't think that's what the average 15-year-old is dealing with.

THERAPIST: Oh, Aña, I'm so very sorry to hear of the loss of your mom. I can't even imagine how hard that must be for you.

AÑA: Actually, it's not really that hard. Except that everybody wants to ask me about it. I get tired of talking about it.

THERAPIST: Of course, I can understand that, but I also understand how everybody wants to check on you. It's such a terrible thing to lose a mother so young. I cannot even imagine…

AÑA: But actually, it's not hard. Life is so much easier without her now. When she was alive, there was so much drama. The cops were always at our house trying to arrest her or take us kids away. It was stressful. She was always high and angry, didn't make us food, and brought really sketchy men over to the house. One of them…did some bad things to me, and I got taken from my home for a while because of that. So, you see how life is calmer now for me? I'm actually relieved that she's gone.

DOI: 10.4324/9781003745136-3

THERAPIST: I'm so sorry to hear about all of that—that must have been so difficult to have all that going on, when all you probably wanted to do was be a 15-year-old, huh?

AÑA: Pretty much.

THERAPIST: But, Aña, even though all that bad stuff happened when your mom was alive, there is still a profound loss in losing one's mother so young. Do you feel sad about your mom dying?

AÑA: No, I probably *should* feel sad, but I already told you that I feel *relief*.

THERAPIST: Let's see if we can try to dig deep and find that sadness, that loss, buried inside of you.

AÑA: Why can't I just feel relieved? That's the truth. So what's wrong with not feeling sad?

THERAPIST: Well, people experience grief in lots of different ways, but trust me, one day the sadness will bubble up for you, and it's a good idea to try to find places for all of the mixed emotions if we can.

In this vignette, the therapist's focus was flowing from their own thoughts and assumptions about the loss of a parent. Although well meaning, and intending to help the client, the therapist neglected to ***listen*** to Aña's experience, and thereby wasn't meeting her where she was on the loss of her mother. A better option here, especially given that it was their first meeting, would be for the therapist to focus on the therapeutic relationship and simply listen, validate, and seek to understand Aña's experience.

The Art of Being Wrong

The dialogue between therapist and the client, Aña, above, highlights an example of the therapist "getting it wrong." One of the most important skills a therapist or counselor can develop is the "art" of being wrong. Given the discussion above on differing experiences, feelings, family or cultural lenses, and our own unique worldviews, it is expected that therapists and counselors can "get it wrong" at times. Consider the following vignette between a therapist and a couple client, Max and Renaldo:

THERAPIST: So, how do the two of you plan to arbitrate the terms of this together?

MAX: Arbitrate? I don't know what that word means! Sorry, but that sounds like a fancy S.A.T. word that I *definitely* don't know.

RENALDO: Me either!

THERAPIST: I'm sorry! You're right—it *is* an S.A.T. word and I remember it and use it a lot because I had a college law professor who *always* said it in class lectures. Let me try this again, in a non-college-law-lecture way! I'm wondering how the two of you plan to figure out the details of the household chores that you said you were going to work on splitting more fairly?

In this vignette, the therapist chooses a "big" word that the clients do not know. The therapist shouldn't feel bad or embarrassed by this; it was a simple word choice. First of all, it's great that the clients felt that the therapist was approachable, and that they could say that they didn't understand the word that was used. Next, the therapist was able to own the "mistake" of using a word they did not know, and easily transition into a more understandable description. Letting *listening* guide the therapeutic interactions and relationship helps therapists and counselors remain ethical in their treatment of clients.

Multiple Relationships

All of the mental health professional codes generally reference the importance of *avoiding* "multiple relationships" whenever possible. Multiple relationships are relationships that therapists or counselors may have at the same time that they are in a therapeutic relationship with a person(s). These may be *prohibited*, when the multiple relationship could impair the therapist's or counselor's judgment, objectivity, or competency in the therapy room.

So, how might multiple relationships be unethical? If ethical therapists and counselors adhere to the main ethical principles, then the concept of Beneficence should be paramount. Consider the following scenario and ask yourself: Is the potential multiple relationship that will be created between therapist or counselor and client beneficial to the client? In the following example, the therapist is Dr. Adams, and the possible client is Marie:

> Dr. Adams plays poker with some of his male friends every Thursday night, and they alternate whose home they play at each week. One of his friends asks Dr. Adams to see his wife, Marie, for therapy, as he is worried that she has been feeling depressed lately. Dr. Adams agrees to see Marie for individual therapy. Is this multiple relationship helpful to her?

Sticky: There are several things to think about here. What does Dr. Adams do with any information about Marie that her husband shares with the group at poker? Does he share that with her? This may cause Marie to be angry with her husband, and her husband may confront Dr. Adams about telling his wife what he said. Or does he ask the husband not to talk about Marie at poker anymore, now that she is his client? Dr. Adams is not allowed to share with any of the other poker players that he is seeing Marie. Therefore, if any of them talk about her or pose other related questions, Dr. Adams is not able to respond freely. He is also not allowed to say, "I'm sorry, but I'm not allowed to talk about Marie, since she is my therapy client." How does Marie feel about having Dr. Adams at her home once a month? How do they interact with one another? Is it uncomfortable or awkward? And do the others notice this? What does Dr. Adams do if Marie discloses personal or unflattering things about her husband to him? Do these disclosures about the husband change the way Dr. Adams views his poker friend? And does Marie know her husband is asking Dr. Adams to see her? Does she even want or feel comfortable with Dr. Adams seeing her for therapy? Has anyone checked in with her on this?

Boil it Down: Ideally, Dr. Adams would simply tell his poker friend that although he'd love to be helpful to Marie, the overlap of his personal and professional relationships with her makes him feel that he wouldn't be the best provider. Dr. Adams can share that he has concerns about seeing Marie and how his social involvement with his poker friends might negatively impact his therapeutic relationship with her. Lines can easily be blurred when Dr. Adams is drinking whiskey and fraternizing with his poker friends in Marie's home. Dr. Adams could simply say that he doesn't want to make anyone uncomfortable, or compromise the social relationships he has with both his poker buddy *and* his wife. *Before* Marie becomes a client, Dr. Adams has the liberty to say any of this to his poker friend. Once she has become a client of Dr. Adams, he is far more limited, and it is impossible to "undo" whatever has occurred.

In this case, you can see that there is a lot of risk of discomfort or impact on everyone involved. If any of the discomfort is on Marie, then it is clearly not beneficent, or in her own best interests. It might turn out to be just fine, but Dr. Adams cannot know that going into it. It seems far safer, and ethically sound, to simply refer Marie to a trusted colleague.

Let's look at another example of a possible multiple relationship between a therapist and client. Should the therapist proceed in using the client as the seller in this scenario?

> A (female) therapist's aunt passes away after a long battle with cancer. The aunt leaves the therapist and her wife her house and everything in it. The aunt had mentioned to the therapist that she had a collection of original, antique toys that were worth a lot of money. The therapist and her wife decide to hire an estate management company to go through the aunt's house and make them an offer on the things that they can buy and resell. The company also agrees to dispose of the other items that are not worth anything, as part of their clean-out service. The company tells the therapist that the antique toys, however, are a very niche, specialized market that they are not familiar with. They recommend that the therapist and her wife seek out the services of an antique toy specialist to gauge the market and worth of those items. After a lengthy search, the therapist and her wife can only find one expert anywhere near where they live, and that specialist is one of the therapist's current clients.

Being a therapist shouldn't preclude us from being able to seek certain services in our area. Of course, *avoiding* is best at all costs, because with risk, may come *sticky*. In this case, the therapist has a number of options in how to proceed. Consider the following choices, and ask yourself which one resonates most with you.

1 The therapist does not consult her client about the toys; rather, she tries to sell them herself on eBay™ for significantly less money than they are worth. There is no sticky with this option.
2 The therapist asks the client if she could take on the selling of the specialty antiques, and carefully explores the client's comfort with the multiple relationship. The client shares that it will be a 50/50 for all proceeds, and that he thinks he can get her close to $250,000 for the lot. The sticky here might be if the therapist feels disappointment with the client's lack of aggressive or timely selling of the items. Additionally, the client might feel some judgment of the client regarding the 50/50 split, or might have expected the client to be more generous in the split given the therapeutic relationship. What if the therapist finds out that the client wasn't truthful about some of the items' worth? Or that the client kept more of the money than he was supposed to?
3 The therapist decides to stay out of the transactional relationship with the client and instead sends her wife to make the contact and connection for selling with the client. The sticky here might be that the therapist is forced to "secret-keep" and not mention anything regarding the transactions of the toys. Additionally, the therapist's wife cannot know that the toy seller is the therapist's client. This might be difficult for the therapist to navigate, in that she must ensure that she is never part of any of the interactions regarding the toys. Lastly, what if the therapist's wife unknowingly mentions her wife is a therapist, and the client inquires about this in session with the therapist? What if the client is homophobic, and the therapist has now unintentionally outed herself? Might this new knowledge impact how the client views the therapist, thus impacting the dynamics of the therapy?

Lots of things to think about here. Although there is not one singular "right" answer, it's imperative that all therapists and counselors practice due diligence in considering all the facets of the situation before deciding on a course of action.

Perhaps the safest course of action here is to not use the client as the toy seller. However, if the therapist does decide to strike up a seller agreement with the client, the following should be considered first.

1 It's obviously in the best interests of the therapist to have the client be the toy seller, but is it in the best interests of the client (Beneficence)?
2 Could the toy-selling arrangement cause harm to the client (Non-Maleficence)?
3 Will the toy-selling arrangement alter the dynamics of the therapeutic relationship? For example, will part of the client's session be used to discuss the selling updates?
4 Is the therapist prepared for the additional layers that may crop up in the toy-selling arrangement with the client? For example, will the client

have to come out to the aunt's house to look at the items first? Will the client meet the therapist's wife?

5 Did the therapist adequately explore the possibility of the toy-selling arrangement with the client before agreeing to it? Were the potential risks discussed? Did the client prepare a release or informed consent or other written agreement for the client to sign before making the agreement? Did the therapist document the decision, rationale, and protection of the client's best interests in the client's chart notes?

What if therapists or counselors find themselves in a multiple relationship with a client *after* they are well into the therapeutic relationship? This can easily happen to any therapist or counselor. How do they include Beneficence, Veracity, the various code standards on avoiding multiple relationships, and non-abandonment in their decision, once they've found out about the multiple relationship? Preventative boundaries are best (Reynolds, 2016), but there may be occasions when this is not possible. Read the following clinical scenario, and think about what your course of action would be after discovering the multiple relationship:

> A therapist, Hassan, has a client, Denise, who messages to let the therapist know that she will need to cancel her appointment later that week, due to her brother passing away. Hassan sends his condolences and then reschedules the appointment with Denise for the following week. When Hassan gets home, his son tells him that he's really upset because his girlfriend's father passed away suddenly. The son is nervous about going to the services with her, but he wants to be supportive. As Hassan talks to his son about what the services might be like, he realizes that his son's girlfriend's father is likely the brother of his client.

The therapist cannot say or ask anything of his son that may expose his therapeutic relationship with Denise. However, the therapist *can* ask Denise about the possibility that they share a different relationship, outside of the therapeutic one that they are both aware of. This would be prudent, as the two need to discuss how they will navigate the possible personal overlap, should that come up.

When Denise returns to therapy the following week, Hassan might say to her, "It's come to my attention that we may have an overlap in personal relationships outside of the therapy room, and I wanted to discuss this with you." After this discussion, Hassan should explore with Denise whether this outside overlap may cause awkwardness for either of them that would negatively influence their therapeutic relationship. Additionally, if they choose to continue the therapeutic relationship, Hassan and Denise should explore how they will handle situations that may come up. For example, what if Hassan's son's girlfriend's mother invites Hassan to attend their daughters high school graduation bash at their house? Considering it is likely that Denise would be invited as well, is it appropriate for Hassan to attend? What will he tell his wife or son about why he has chosen not to attend? If Hassan does choose to attend, has he talked to Denise about limits to their interactions, what to say about them knowing each other, etc.?

Keep in mind that *Denise*, however, may talk to anyone about anything. Denise can talk to her sister (Hassan's son's girlfriend's mother) and explain that she sees Hassan for therapy. She may choose to tell her not to invite Hassan and his wife to the party. In turn, Hassan's son's girlfriend's mother may choose to tell her daughter and Hassan's son that she knows of the situation and that they are all welcome to visit anytime that they feel comfortable doing so. Denise is the only one who has the ability to let everything out in the open.

It should be pretty clear from the prior discussion that multiple relationships are best to avoid whenever possible. If there are unavoidable situations, and ones that are deemed not likely to impact the client negatively in any way, they should be navigated with an abundance of caution, clear communication, and collaboration with clients, and be documented. Additionally, it is the therapist's or counselor's responsibility to track and assess the impact of the multiple relationship in an ongoing manner, throughout the course of the relationship.

There are a few things that may contribute to a higher risk of the therapist or counselor encountering multiple relationships in their practice. The following are some of the situations that may increase the probability of multiple relationships.

1 **Practicing in a small town:** Practicing in a small town, especially when the therapist or counselor is one of the only professionals in the locale specializing in a certain area or population (e.g., play therapy, couples' work, addiction), may yield a wider overlap with personal and professional relationships. For example, perhaps the local pediatrician regularly refers to a particular therapist or counselor in the community. What happens when the pediatrician is in need of couples' counseling? Or when the therapist or counselor has a baby and needs to use the pediatrician as their own baby's doctor? Or when the pediatrician's child is experiencing depression and that child then becomes the therapist or counselor's client? The widespread availability of teletherapy now has been very helpful in giving additional resources for situations like the one described above. However, especially for young children, in-person therapy may be preferable. Amount of screen time, technological ability, privacy issues, and attention spans may be constraints for effective online therapy for young children.

   Much like practicing in a small town can lead to "muddier pools," so too can practicing within more insular communities. Especially if the therapist or counselor is personally part of these communities (e.g., LGBTQ+, specific cultures or religions, 12-step programs), it may be easier for multiple relationships to exist.

2. **Personal involvement in community events or causes:** Therapists and counselors who partake in political and activist endeavors in their community may interact publicly with like-minded folks. This may increase the chances of therapists or counselors having clients in those same community circles, thereby potentially blurring boundaries. Additionally, given the sensitive and divided nature of some of these causes, therapists or counselors may find that multiple relationships with some clients may lead to assumptions or misconceptions that may add a problematic layer to the therapeutic relationship.
3. **Personal involvement in community support groups like AA or NA:** Therapists and counselors who are involved in their own recovery work may find themselves overlapping personal and professional lines when attending meetings where clients may be present. This may be very tricky, as many folks in recovery prefer in-person meetings. Some of the reasons cited for the preference of attending in-person meetings include more intimacy, computer fatigue, and not trusting the security and privacy of the internet (Hassett-Walker, 2025). Especially in smaller communities, where there are extremely limited choices on meetings, this can cause an increase in potential multiple relationships.
4. **Personal involvement in activities in a faith-based community:** Therapists or counselors who are part of a religious community and participate in religious services or events may find themselves in multiple relationships with clients who are part of this same community. Similar to all of the others listed above, participation by therapists or counselors in faith-based community events where clients also attend may lead to personal and professional line blurring.

In all of the scenarios above, there are a few ethical things therapists and counselors should keep in mind. First, whenever possible, multiple relationships should be avoided. This helps the therapist or counselor prevent risky and sticky altogether. If the multiple relationship might be harmful to, or exploitative of a client, the therapist or counselor must refer the client out.

Next, if the multiple relationship is unavoidable (like a therapist or counselor seeing a client in the rooms at a 12-step meeting, or if both of their children attend the same school), or deemed to be not hurtful to the client, best practice is *always* to be up front about how seeing each other outside of a therapy session will be handled (Reynolds, 2016). This ensures that all parties involved are clear on what the boundaries will be.

Next, therapists and counselors *must* be continually assessing the foundational principles of ethics (e.g., Beneficence, or is the relationship set-up in the best interests of the client?) to ensure the appropriateness of care. If the relationship ever shifts in a way that it may create something more risky or have a negative impact on the client (e.g., if the therapist or counselor discovers that a client's teenager is dating their own teen), there should be a discussion on whether referring out might be prudent.

Lastly, therapists' and counselors' codes of ethics require that they not "abandon" a client. This means that if the therapist or counselor makes the decision to refer out a client with whom the existence of a multiple relationship would not be appropriate or beneficial, they must facilitate that process. It is expected that therapists and counselors will assist in a referral to another provider, and work with the client to make a seamless transition.

Romantic/Sexual Relationships

One specific type of multiple relationship is a *sexual* relationship. The various therapist and counselor codes have different standards on *when* it might be appropriate for these relationships to occur after the end of treatment, but *all* codes prohibit sexual relationships *while* the client is in therapy. Individual codes will guide therapists and counselors on the specifics here, but let's explore *why* the sexual relationship is unethical. Additionally, we will look at the preceding "hints" of romantic or sexual interest or attraction, and both how to navigate them, as well as how to decide if the therapeutic relationship can continue.

So why is a romantic or sexual relationship inappropriate for a therapist or counselor and client? This particular type of multiple relationship—a romantic or sexual one—can be very powerful. And *dangerous*. But how does the therapeutic relationship go astray? In a piece on the intimate experience of the client in therapy, by Joanna Briscoe in *The Guardian* (2020), she writes:

> There's nothing quite like it. You sit together, in hushed intimacy, just the two of you, finally revealing lifelong secrets. The atmosphere is exquisitely calm, the tranquility shot through with alertness as the world shifts, brilliantly refigured, and relief floods in. You have the certainty that you are protected and profoundly understood by someone who is on your side.

It's a "slippery slope." It is easy to see how the proverbial stage can be set for the entrance of romantic feelings within the therapeutic relationship. The therapist or counselor feels helpful and supportive and appreciated, while the client feels safe and protected and heard. When a therapist or counselor shows up for the client with listening, attention, validation, support, alliance, positivity, kindness, understanding, etc., they are also showing up in the same ways that many people would report as desirable traits in a romantic or sexual partner.

The most notable issue with a romantic or sexual relationship with a client is that they are necessarily built on differential positions of power. For example, the client seeks therapy with the assumption that the therapist or counselor knows more than they do about the things they may be struggling with—depression, anxiety, relationship issues, communication, work stress, or parenting. Additionally, the structure of the therapy allows for the therapist or counselor to know a lot about the client's personal life, but the client will know very little about the therapist's or counselor's private life. In short, any romantic or sexual relationship that begins within the therapeutic relationship is based on unnatural circumstances, and has the potential to cause harm to both the client and the therapist.

Now, consider the following possibilities that might occur if a romantic relationship has begun between a therapist or counselor and client:

- **Complicate:** The therapeutic relationship is not pure anymore. It may become complicated. Will they keep the relationship a secret for a while? What will others say when they eventually see them together? Are both the therapist or counselor and client single, or are there significant others who will be affected? Will their families judge them? Will someone report the therapist or counselor to a licensing board?
- **Vulnerable:** The client came to therapy for a reason. That reason may make them vulnerable and susceptible to making decisions under duress or desperation. The relationship between therapist or counselor and client can never be equal when it begins under therapeutic circumstances.
- **Distraction:** Any relationship, other than a healthy therapeutic one, can distract the therapist or counselor and client away from important therapeutic goals they had established. Instead of focusing on therapy, the client may be thinking about recent interactions with, or fantasizing about, the therapist.
- **False views:** The client who begins a romantic or sexual relationship with a therapist or counselor may feel better, excited, hopeful. These improvements in the client's presentation may be falsely attributed to successful therapy, when, in reality, perhaps they are just the result of a new, illicit, exciting relationship. Additionally, even if the therapist or counselor and client decide to end the therapeutic relationship in order to pursue a romantic or sexual one, there may be issues. For example, the client may still see the therapist as their therapist, despite ending that relationship. This might include expectations, continued power differentials, or illusions about who the therapist is as a person.
- **Desire to impress:** When most people engage in a new romantic or sexual relationship, they want the new partner to like them and think highly of them. This desire to impress the therapist or counselor may interfere with a client's ability to be honest about how they are doing and feeling. They may intentionally not disclose things to the therapist or counselor that they may deem embarrassing or might disappoint the therapist or counselor.
- **Impact the ability to receive feedback:** A client may feel hurt or resistant to receiving feedback from the therapist or counselor. Likewise, the therapist may be reluctant to give important feedback or challenges to the client for fear of how it would land on the client.

- **Quarrels:** During the process of any romantic or sexual relationship, there will inevitably be disagreements or quarrels about any number of things. This is normal during the growth process of "getting to know you." How might those quarrels impact the therapeutic process? Therapy works best when there are not "attitudes" and "cold shoulders" or resentment in the room!
- **Feelings of being taken advantage of:** Especially if the romantic or sexual relationship *doesn't* work out, clients may reflect on how they became intimate with the therapist or counselor, and feel that they were taken advantage of. Not only can this lead to things like self-loathing, embarrassment, and anger, but it can also lead the client to report the therapist to the licensing board. Additionally, the client may share the information about the affair with the therapist publicly and destroy their practice and their reputation.

Are the above possibilities things that contribute to a healthy and trusting therapeutic relationship? Do they reflect Beneficence towards the client? Non-Maleficence?

After the aforementioned discussion, it should be clear why the romantic or sexual versions of multiple relationships are completely prohibited in every mental health profession. It is the therapist's or counselor's responsibility to ensure that this sort of relationship *never* creeps over into the therapeutic one. The repercussions of these relationships may be drastic and far-reaching for the client. Likewise, the penalty for the therapist or counselor who gets caught engaging in this is severe, with good reason. Be mindful, be honest with yourself, get support or supervision, and learn to notice *sticky* before it goes too far.

Next, let's look at the precursors to a romantic or sexual interest within the therapeutic relationship, and how to assess and navigate whether they require an end to the therapeutic relationship. There are no hard and fast rules that provide the exact details of when an overture of interest of one person in the therapeutic relationship might occur. However, they do need to be noticed, addressed, and managed, to be sure they don't become inappropriate.

Read the following scenarios and think about (1) whether the therapy can continue, given the situation, and (2) how the therapist could ethically navigate the situation:

> A female therapist is seeing a couple, Luis and Linda, for couples' work. A few months into the therapy, Luis says that their marriage is over, and he wants to end therapy. He plans on moving in with his mother for a while, as they decide how to start the divorce process. The therapist inquires if Linda feels the same. Although she agrees, she still wants to continue with the therapy, and cites her own need for support and help with stress management and parenting strategies. Luis suggests that Linda continue with the therapist individually. The therapist explores

> this possibility with the couple, explaining that she will close their couples' chart and open a new one for Linda, and explains that she will not be able to do couples' work with them in the future if anything changes, since she will now be Linda's individual therapist. Everyone agrees, and the therapist schedules a final termination session for the couples' work for the following week.

At this point, it appears that the therapist has acted ethically, professionally, and responsibly. However, might there be more here, lurking under the surface? Read what happens next:

> The final couples' session arrives, and Luis does not show. Linda texts her husband, and he quickly responds that he is sorry, that he forgot about the session, and that he doesn't need a termination session. The therapist decides to use the time with Linda alone as an intake session for her individual work. During the intake, Linda confesses to the therapist that she's a bit worried about Luis. Although they both were in total agreement about not wanting to stay together, they both felt relief, and their interactions were much better, she thinks Luis might be depressed, because he seems "lost" and distant. The therapist is a bit worried as well, since something seemed "off" about the unexpected way Luis had suddenly decided to end treatment. The therapist also recalls now that Luis had shared deep gratitude and an unexpectedly warm hug with her upon ending their last couples' session together. He appeared unusually tearful and sad.

Sticky: Now that Luis is no longer the therapist's couples' client, does she have the responsibility to check on him and ensure his emotional stability and wellness, given Linda's disclosure? Would it be in the best interests of the client/couple for the therapist to resume the couples' work to help support the dyad on discussions about this concern and ways to manage it within their home and relationship? In order for the therapist to contact Luis now, does she need a release of information from Linda to disclose the concerns she shared with the therapist to Luis?

Boil it Down: The couples' case was not closed, since the therapist had planned on having a final couples' session the day that Luis didn't show up. Therefore, she's able to reach out to him to assess his emotional stability. She also needs to offer Luis referrals for the continuation of care, perhaps individually now, with a new provider. After talking to Luis, if the therapist feels there might be a need for a higher level of care, she can help him access more immediate care.

Now, let's complicate this clinical situation further. After the therapist calls Luis to check in and offer referrals, she assesses him to be stable and without any ideation or intention of suicide. She closes the couples' case and opens a new case for Linda. She feels good about how she has managed the situation. However, the next day, she receives an email from Luis:

> Thank you again for all the help and support you have provided for Linda and me. I feel like I needed to tell you the truth about why I needed to end therapy with you. I owe you the truth. I have been having thoughts about you for a while now, and more recently, they've become overwhelming. It's just that you listen to me, you build me up, and you see me in ways that no one else does. I feel like a better person when I'm meeting with you. I think I might be falling in love with you. And I know that I can never have you. So, this is the right thing to do—I know you'd tell me that. Take care of Linda—I want that for her, and you're wonderful. You'll hear about me soon. So, I guess this is...goodbye.

Sticky: The case is now closed, but the therapist has received concerning information about Luis's well-being. Is it her responsibility to check on Luis? Is it appropriate for the therapist to contact Linda to check on him? Linda is currently the therapist's client, but is the sensitive and personal information Luis provided in the email to the therapist something she is at liberty to disclose to Linda? Is it appropriate for the therapist to call Luis to check on his well-being?

Boil it Down: Even though Linda is the therapist's client, the therapist cannot disclose information that Luis shared with her privately about his feelings for her. This is protected information that can only be disclosed if the therapist suspects that Luis is suicidal or homicidal. Since Luis is no longer the therapist's client, she is unable to assess his safety and emotional stability. However, the therapist feels strongly that she should check on Luis's well-being. One option is that the therapist could call Luis and explain that his email was concerning to her, and that although she appreciated his candor in sharing with her, she wanted to check on his safety (given the tenor of the letter) and be sure he has successfully connected with another provider for continuity of care and support.

In the case, this (above) is exactly what the therapist did, and Luis assured her that he was fine and safe, and apologized for the tone of the email. He explained his momentary hopelessness in writing it, and explained it to the therapist in a way that assuaged her fears and convinced her that he was in a stable place. He was scheduled to meet with a new therapist the following week. Once again, the therapist felt pretty good about the way she had ethically handled this additional layer of the situation.

Now, let's complicate it a bit more. For the next two days, the therapist continues to receive emails from Luis, that are turning increasingly desperate and angry. He writes:

> Oh. C'mon, who am I kidding anyway? You're like all the rest of the women in the world, why would I think you're any different. Fuck, you're not special. You'd just piss on me like all of the rest of them. I can't do this anymore. I need to let go of everything, everybody.

Sticky: The therapist's concerns for Luis's well-being and mental health and wellness have escalated now. But is she the one who should check in again on him, given the anger that seems to be directed at her in the last email? It is clear that Luis needs help, but the role of the therapist is not as clear.

Boil it Down: The therapist here recognized the sticky of the situation, and decided to call her supervisor to consult on the case. Together, they decided that the therapist had a responsibility to ensure Luis's safety, and that it wouldn't be appropriate to contact Linda, given their recent separation, the therapist's involvement with her, and that there was sensitive information she could not share with her. Given that it was impossible for the therapist to assess the seriousness or meaning of Luis's concerning email, they made the decision for the therapist to call the police to conduct a wellness check.

Now, let's add a final layer to this sticky ethical case. After the therapist calls for a wellness check on Luis to ensure his safety (her final obligation here), she receives a frantic voicemail from Linda:

> I just got a call from Luis. He told me you called the cops on him. Why did you call the police to go check on him? What's going on? Why did you call the police? Please call me back as soon as you get this!

Sticky: The therapist can call Linda back, but she can't share any of the specifics on Luis or why she called the police to do a wellness check. Linda now knows that something is going on, and since the therapist can't disclose any details, how will Linda feel towards the therapist? Is it appropriate for the therapist to continue to see Linda individually for therapy? What if Linda decides later she'd like to bring Luis and the kids into the session for family therapy or co-parenting work? How would the therapist explain that she cannot do that?

Boil it Down: The therapist, after connecting with her supervisor again, decided to call Linda back. The following dialogue demonstrates the course of action the therapist chose in order to remain ethically sound in navigating the situation:

THERAPIST: I'm so sorry for the confusion, Linda. But I really can't discuss anything about Luis with you. I hope you understand. I think you need to talk to Luis and ask him these questions, okay?

LINDA: I'm just so confused! He told me you called the police on him, and I just can't understand why you would do that! Is he okay?

THERAPIST: I understand how difficult and confusing this is, Linda. Please reach out to Luis on this, okay?

LINDA: I think we both need to meet with you right away. When can you fit us in for a session?

THERAPIST: Linda, we talked about me being unable to meet all together after we stopped doing the couples' work. I think we need to find a good referral for someone to continue work with you, and perhaps work with you and Luis on what's next.

LINDA: Why can't it be you? You know us already! I don't understand.

THERAPIST: I know it's hard to understand, and I'm so sorry that I can't say more. Please talk to Luis about this, and I will continue to support you until we can get you set up with another therapist. Can you trust me on this? Are you willing to see someone else?

LINDA: I guess so.

How do you feel about the choices the therapist made here? Would you have acted similarly with this case? Are there things you can think of that might have been other ethical options here? Although the therapist didn't feel great about how the case ended up, she did not feel like there were other options that were suitable.

Always Refer Out?

My graduate students always ask, "Can a therapist or counselor ever keep working with a client who has expressed suspected romantic or sexual attraction to them?" Great question! Read the following vignette:

> A female therapist enters her agency office one morning, remembering that it's Valentine's Day when she sees a gorgeous vase of two dozen red roses of the reception area counter. The therapist teases the front staff by asking, "Oooooohhhhhh, who got all the flowers?" The front staff laugh and point to the therapist and say, "YOU did! Read the card!" Knowing that her partner just wasn't the type to send two dozen roses to her office, she was confused about who would have sent them to her. She pulls the card from the tiny envelope and sees that it is from a recently divorced, male client (James) that she sees for therapy. The card says: "Happy Valentine's Day! On this special day that commemorates love and appreciation, you deserve these more than anyone I know. I wanted you to know how important you are to me and how much your caring presence in my life has meant to me. I don't know what my life would be like without you! Thank you from the bottom of my heart! With affection—James."

Sticky: The flowers, especially two dozen, red roses, on Valentine's Day, plus the content of the card, suggest that James might be overly dependent on the therapist, and may have a more emotional connection to her than might be appropriate.

Boil it Down: Clearly, the therapist needs to at least have a conversation about the situation with James and better assess the layers of it, and whether it might interfere with therapy. Should she continue to see James for therapy?

Read the following response from the therapist to James when they had a therapy session later that day:

> Hi James. I'm hoping we can start off today talking about something I want to share with you. First off, I received the beautiful flowers today from you, and want to thank you for the kind gesture. However, I did feel like we should talk about how you decided to send those to me. I want you to know that you never need to give me a gift—your progress and feeling better is all the gift I need, and it is my job to be present for you, to listen, to support. The flowers, although very beautiful and thoughtful, seemed a bit excessive, and it didn't go unnoticed that they were red, and given to me on Valentine's Day, a holiday that is kind of known for more romantic love. So, I wanted to let you know that either you can take the flowers with you, and give them to someone else you know who would love and deserve them, or I'm happy to leave them at the front desk for everybody who comes into the office to enjoy. But more importantly, I'd like to talk about whether it's possible that your positive thoughts about me might be stronger than they should be for a therapeutic relationship? I'm wondering if the divorce, and your disclosure of loneliness and frustration with dating, might be making you more dependent on our relationship to fill some of those voids?

How do you feel about what the therapist said? Do you like the therapist's management of the situation with her client? Do you consider the therapist's actions to be ethical?

In this case, the therapist's opening up of the possible layers behind the flowers resulted in a powerful conversation between her and James. They explored how he was overly focusing on the parts of her that made him feel good—how well she listened, validated him, never judged, and seemed to have unlimited patience and faith in him. James admitted that he had begun to see the therapist as "the perfect woman" from all the positive qualities and traits he saw in her. The therapist was able to reframe this into the notion that James had been able to figure out the things he was looking for in his next relationship, rather than hyper-focusing on his failed marriage and all the things that had traumatized him.

The therapist decided to continue with James, as she felt that the flowers, although an ethical issue that needed to be addressed, had opened up an important area for him to grow from. She told him that she would check in with him regularly, to be sure that the feelings that he had projected onto her were not interfering with them doing therapy.

How do you feel about this? Are you comfortable with the therapist still working with James? Why or why not?

Referrals

In many of the scenarios above, we can see that having solid referrals to other providers when needed is an important part of maintaining an ethical practice. Being able to provide referrals to clients who need them is the responsibility of the therapist or counselor. Creating a referral list benefits the therapist or counselor as well. In the process of reaching out to other providers and supports in the community, therapists or counselors make themselves known in whatever areas they practice. Coordination of services and care is an ethical way to create a web of support for clients.

There are various online advertising directories that offer information on a wide range of mental health providers. These are great resources for clients to quickly find not only lots of different providers, but also what their areas of expertise are, what ages they treat, what insurances they take, if they do in-person or teletherapy sessions, and whether they are open for new clients. This is a rich pool of data and a great starting point for client referrals.

The most common referral sources I have used in my practice are as follows:

- General Practitioner Doctors who are willing to prescribe psychotropic medications
- Psychiatrists
- Urologists
- OB/GYN Doctors
- Pediatricians
- Social Services
- Local Therapeutic Support Groups
- Local 12-Step Programs like AA or Al-Anon
- In-Patient Treatment Facilities
- Other community supports like LGBTQ-friendly places of worship, yoga and meditation programs, food banks, etc.

Therapists and counselors often confuse being active participants and guides in facilitating referrals for clients with being responsible for ensuring that clients follow up on referrals and have a successful transition. Within reason, therapists and counselors should try to ensure the continuation of care for clients that they must refer out. An example might be if a therapist or counselor gave a number of appropriate referrals for a client, and checked in a couple of times to see if the client had been able to connect and set up an appointment. If the client hadn't made any efforts or reported indifference on transitioning, has the therapist or counselor completed their ethical obligation here? If the client had difficulty in getting a new provider, are there additional resources the therapist or counselor can give to help the new connection happen more quickly?

Ending Treatment/Non-Abandonment

A normal and natural part of the therapeutic process is ending treatment when goals are met. Some clients may have a difficult time saying goodbye. There is a powerful quote by writer, Ellen Goodman (2010), that she penned in her final column. I have referred to it in my private practice many times when possible termination was discussed:

> There's a trick to the "graceful exit." It begins with the vision to recognize when [something] is over, and to be able to let it go. It means leaving what's over in the past, without denying its validity or its past importance to our lives. It involves a sense of future, a belief that every exit line is also an entry, that we are moving up, rather than moving out.

How does a therapist or counselor end treatment in an ethical manner, while adhering to the "non-abandonment" clause from the codes of ethics? The following are some helpful tips for ethical termination:

- Ensure that clients understand that the presentation of possible termination is not rejection.
- Explore any feelings that clients might have about termination, including the aforementioned rejection.
- If possible and feasible, offer clients the possibility of meeting less often as a scaling-back option before termination.
- If possible and feasible, remind clients that they can always return to therapy in the future if they encounter future issues that they are unable to navigate alone.
- Review things like progress, successes, strengths, and other resources with clients.

Perhaps most importantly, therapists and counselors need to remember that clients will sometimes continue therapy past their desire to do so, simply because they think they should, or feel the therapist should tell them when they are ready to end (Reynolds, 2019). Open communication throughout the course of therapy, including discussions on meeting goals, and if the therapy still feels important or necessary, is an important responsibility of the ethical therapist or counselor.

Sometimes, there are other reasons that treatment might need to be terminated—for example, if the therapy is "stuck," and the therapist or counselor wonders if a different provider might work better with the client. What if a therapist or counselor becomes sick and needs to take a medical leave, or moves away, or takes another job? Another reason might be if a therapist or counselor begins to feel abused or unsafe when a client has become angry or aggressive or abusive towards them. Regardless of the reason, therapists and counselors are still responsible for assisting in referrals or resources, and acting in ways that are in the best interests of the client. However, if a therapist or counselor feels abused, unsafe, or is threatened by a client, some codes allow simple termination (e.g., APA), while others require that termination be accompanied by assistance with offering appropriate referrals (e.g., AAMFT, ACA). Additionally, NASW requires that therapists and counselors take care to minimize adverse effects when a client is terminated quickly.

In many cases like these, it can be argued that the therapy is not beneficial to clients if they are angry, abusive, aggressive, or threatening towards a therapist or counselor. Separate codes on ineffective therapy or treatment that is not benefitting clients can also support the need for termination in these cases.

Battle of Structure vs. Battle of Initiative

In the famous book *The Family Crucible*, the authors describe the need for therapists to win the "battle for structure," while the clients must win the "battle of initiative" (Napier & Whitaker, 1978). Part of any ethical clinical practice is having the therapist or counselor in charge of maintaining the "battle of structure," while supporting the client to be in charge of the "battle of initiative." In simpler terms, the therapist or counselor needs to control things like "no secrets" policies, session fees, releases of information, duty to warn or protect, and enforce the "rules" in therapy, such as not having multiple or sexual relationships. The client is in control of their comfort with these things, their interest in efforts in therapy, like communication, behavioral change, agreement on rules, and follow-through on tasks.

The ethical pathway for therapists and counselors here is to ensure that the rules and set-up of the therapeutic experience are disclosed, explained, and discussed at the onset of therapy. A copy of a thorough informed consent document should be given to the client, which describes everything that the therapist or counselor wants the client to know. This should also be reviewed as appropriate, throughout the duration of therapy.

Likewise, if a therapist or counselor feels like the client is not fully engaging or on board with the rules and set-up of therapy, a discussion is ethically warranted. This is important to identify any miscommunications, perceptions, or constraints that might be in the way of more effective therapeutic relationship.

"Special Clients"

One of the best ways therapists or counselors can help ensure clarity and ethics in their therapeutic relationships is to be watchful for those who may feel like "special clients."

> A male therapist is seeing 14-year-old Mariska for therapy on a Friday late afternoon, just as the first flurries of a snow squall pick up. Mariska leaves the therapist's office to go down to meet her mother who was supposed to have picked her up about 20 minutes ago. The therapist gathers his things and exits the building. The therapist sees Mariska still waiting alone in the building parking lot. The therapist's car is the only one left in the lot, as everyone else has left for the day. The therapist has always felt really bad for Mariska—her single mother is cold and distant, and never prioritizes her daughter. He has felt protective of her, and finds himself so frustrated with the mom, who just does not seem to be able to show up better for her kid. The mother has allowed Mariska to be verbally abused by her stepbrother, and often berates Mariska herself. The therapist, hating to see Mariska nervously pacing and looking at her phone to see if her mother has texted, decides to drive Mariska home. He thinks, "It's ridiculous that any mother would leave her kid here without reaching out to let her know. This is not the first times she's done this—another example of mom not prioritizing her lonely kid."

In this scenario, the therapist has made decisions based on his "soft spot" for Mariska. This will happen sometimes—therapists or counselors may find themselves having certain clients that they feel especially connected to, worried about, or invested in. Perhaps a client reminds the therapist or counselor of a loved one, a friend, a family member. However, it is the responsibility of the therapist or counselor to recognize and explore these feelings, and ensure that they do not contribute to boundary crossing.

(Norris et al., 2003) describe these "special" folks as ones that the therapist or counselor may give extra session time to, overlooking unpaid balances, making extra allowances, or having meetings outside of the office or normal office hours if needed. They quote the following: "Therapists seeking consultation on such cases often begin the request with 'I don't usually do this with my patients, but in this case…'"

Could the therapist's special investment in Mariska, and the choices he made, lead to stickiness in the therapeutic relationship? The following are some things the therapist should have considered before making the decision to take Mariska home himself:

1 Had the therapist asked questions about whether Mariska had been able to reach her mother?
2 Is there another family member or trusted family friend who would be able to pick Mariska up?
3 Since Mariska is a minor, has the mother granted permission to have the therapist drive her home?
4 Will there be any suspicion about the therapist's motives here?

5. Has the therapist formulated premature opinions on the mother, since his sole source of information on the mother has come from a disgruntled Mariska?
6. Has the therapist explored the "why" behind his own soft spot and special care and interest in Mariska especially?
7. Considering the principle of Justice, would the therapist do the same thing for any other minor client he has?
8. Might Mariska feel "special" in this situation, and grow closer or more dependent on the therapist now in a different way? Might she expect special efforts in other areas as well? And might these possibilities contribute to a change in the therapeutic relationship?

Perhaps the best course of action for the therapist here might be to simply be supportive of Mariska by staying with her until another plan for pick-up could be arranged. The therapist might also reach out to Mariska's mother at a later date and share the importance of timely transportation arrangements, and discuss what the best course of action should be if the situation occurred again.

Contextual Therapy founder, Dr. Boszormenyi-Nagy (1987), constructed the therapeutic technique called "multidirectional partiality." This meant that therapists and counselors should be tasked with not favoring any one client in the room over another, and creating balance by helping out everybody at different times. A famous quote from him was "Everybody and nobody should feel special [in the therapy room]." This is an excellent reminder of the importance of keeping certain "special" clients in check and treating them equally.

Remember that being aware of special clients is an important part of a therapist's or counselor's ethical practice. Additionally, recognizing and being mindful of the interactions with a special client might help therapists and counselors avoid entering into multiple relationships or unintentional boundary crossing.

Chapter Takeaways for Therapists and Counselors

1. Remember the importance of *listening* to clients, in order to avoid making assumptions about them.
2. Remain aware of the cultural lens you are looking through when talking to clients.
3. Get comfortable being "wrong." Not always understanding clients is to be expected.
4. Avoid multiple relationships whenever possible. When a multiple relationship is unavoidable or expected to not infringe negatively on the client's well-being, be sure to communicate with the client about the circumstance, expectations, and navigation of it, and ensure that the therapeutic relationship is still in the best interests of the client (Beneficence).

5 Romantic and sexual relationships between therapists or counselors and current clients are *always* prohibited. Different professions have different codes on this for former clients.
6 When a client demonstrates a possible romantic or sexual interest in the therapist or counselor, it must be addressed and explored to see if a referral to another provider is warranted.
7 Therapists and counselors are responsible for being able to offer a reasonable range of referrals to other providers in the community if they are unable to meet clients' needs, or are unwilling to work with them for ethical reasons.
8 There are a variety of reasons that treatment may be terminated, and therapists or counselors are responsible for not abandoning clients, by working with them towards a continuation of care with another provider if appropriate.
9 The "battle of structure" (rules, fees, policies and enforcement, etc.) must be in the therapist's or counselor's hands, while the "battle of initiative" (accepting, sharing, making efforts, follow-sthrough, etc.) must be in the hands of the client.
10 Therapists and counselors are responsible for avoiding and assessing for situations that would constitute a conflict of interest for the client and the therapeutic relationship.
11 Therapists and counselors are prohibited from engaging in actions that exploit clients.
12 Be aware of clients who are "special," and remember that the therapist or counselor has the responsibility to ensure that boundary crossing does not occur with these clients.

3 Finances and Gifts

How do therapists and counselors "draw a line" about things such as what they will charge, how they will accept payment and manage overdue fees, etc.? Let's break some of these down, discuss the ethics of finances and gifts in clinical practice, and examine some clinical scenarios that center on these themes.

Fee Setting

When therapists or counselors are in-network with insurance, their fees are contracted by the insurance company. However, when therapists or counselors practice privately, they may set their own fee structures. How can they go about deciding this while adhering to an ethical framework?

The following is a good set of things for therapists and counselors to think about when deciding on their fee structures and payment policies:

- Research the rates of other therapists and counselors in your area to be sure you are considering the norms.
- Think about whether your fees will disallow certain sectors of your potential client pool to afford therapy with you.
- Consider if your fees are commiserate with your training, experience, area(s) of expertise, etc.
- What are the "costs" of your business versus what your income will be at this stated fee?
- Might your fees be exploitative to clients?
- What "message" might your fees send to clients and other providers in the community (e.g., you garner a higher fee because you are a "better" provider than others)? What are some ways you could ensure that this is not the message you send by charging a higher or lower rate than the norm in your area?
- Will you have a sliding scale in order to meet the needs of clients who cannot afford your rate?

Some codes (e.g., ACA, NASW) instruct therapists and counselors to give consideration to clients' ability to pay before setting fees, but do not make

DOI: 10.4324/9781003745136-4

specific requirements on the specifics of this. However, *all* the codes require that therapists and counselors are honest and upfront about costs and fees for services, and inform clients of any changes to this for the duration of the treatment.

In keeping with the foundational principles, it is important for therapists and counselors to be truthful about fees (Veracity), not doing harm to clients (Non-Maleficence) by putting undo financial stress on them, and assisting clients in finding more affordable options for services (e.g., community subsidy programs), sliding scales that they are more able to pay, or, if they prefer, referring to another provider who may be able to accommodate their financial constraints better (Autonomy).

After considering the aforementioned areas, and setting up a fee structure and financial policies that are ethically sound, therapists and counselors should then think about the types of situations they might find themselves in regarding financial set-ups. Read the following vignettes and discussions that follow each, and think about what you would do in these same situations:

1 Kaia (who the therapist does not charge for therapy, but instead has her in a "pro bono" slot) is a client of a therapist, Marguerita. Marguerita has been seeing this client for over three years now, and is beginning to wonder if she still requires therapy, as she seems to be doing really well. When Marguerita brings this up with Kaia during their next session, she reports that seeing Marguerita every week is very helpful. Should Marguerita continue to see Kaia for therapy as long as she wishes to come and reports it being helpful?

Sticky: Since Kaia does not pay for any sessions with Marguerita, she may not be invested in ending treatment with her. Even if Kaia is feeling better and doing really well, why end therapy with Marguerita when she enjoys meeting with her and it doesn't cost anything? Kaia might also feel anxious, or rejected by Marguerita, if she suggests ending treatment.

Boil it Down: Although Kaia *can* decide when she wants to end therapy (Autonomy), Marguerita is responsible for ensuring that the ongoing treatment is helpful to the client (Beneficence). Marguerita might also consider that by continuing to see Kaia in a pro bono spot, she will be unable to take on another client that might be in need of therapy, and unable to afford it. What if every pro bono client wanted to keep seeing Marguerita forever?

One ethical course of action for Marguerita to take might be for her to begin by having an honest conversation with Kaia, exploring therapy goals, progress, her thoughts on the client's progress, policies, etc. (Veracity). The transparency here, coupled with the leaning into the client to collaboratively make decisions, is ideal. This conversation will also give Marguerita the opportunity to be supportive, and assuage any fears or feelings of rejection that Kaia might encounter in thinking about Marguerita's suggested termination. Marguerita might consider moving Kaia to monthly sessions for a couple of months to gauge her ability to be able to function well on her own, without weekly sessions.

2 Henry, a prominent businessman, sees a therapist named Dr. Bonner, on a weekly basis. Henry is a full, self-pay client. Dr. Bonner charges Henry $200 per session. After one particular session that Henry felt was incredibly helpful, he overpays the invoice and instead submits $600 for the session. When Dr. Bonner inquires about the overpayment, Henry responds, "I've been in therapy with many different therapists over the years, and you helped me have an epiphany last session, and I saw things I'd never seen about myself before. You deserve the extra money—you helped me so much."

Sticky: Dr. Bonner is concerned about the "fallout" if he accepts the extra money from his client. Will Henry only pay $50 of the invoice next time if he feels the session wasn't very helpful? Is it ethical to take a "tip" for an especially good session? Is taking the extra money going to send any particular message to Henry? What if Henry tells someone else that he has done this—will Dr. Bonner be in trouble? Will it hurt his reputation?

Boil it Down: First, Dr. Bonner must "win" the Battle of Structure in his sessions, and so he must adhere to the payment amounts and policies he has put into place. Following his own payment rates and policies is also an example of doing what he said he would do (Fidelity). Although Dr. Bonner knows that Henry is financially secure and can afford the extra money, accepting it violates his own policies on fees for services. Taking extra money may reflect poorly on Dr. Bonner's reputation should Henry choose to tell anyone—perhaps others would view Dr. Bonner as taking advantage of his client. Perhaps most importantly, conducting a therapy session is a professional, paid service. There is a fee set for this service, just as there is in any professional medical setting.

One ethical way for Dr. Bonner to proceed is to have a conversation with Henry about the situation. Consider Dr. Bonner's response below, and think about how it resonates with you, and if you would choose a similar response:

> Henry, I appreciate your favorable feedback about how helpful our last session was. However, it is my job to conduct therapy with you, and there is a set rate for that, regardless of how you felt it went. Although I appreciate your generous effort to pay me more than the session fee, this is not necessary, nor can I accept overpayment. I can either initiate a refund of the overage for you, or apply it to your next two sessions.

"Sliding Scales"

Sliding scales are commonly part of therapists' and counselors' private practice fee structures. These scales are set up to allow for those who have more financial constraints to be able to attend therapy at a reduced rate. Since not every potential client who is in need of therapy is able to afford to pay for it out-of-pocket, many providers offer a sliding-scale option. Some collect financial data, like income statements, or completed financial worksheets, or tax returns in order to "qualify" clients for a reduced fee. Yet others do not do a formal "assessment"; rather, they just negotiate a reduced rate that the client feels they will be able to pay.

Sometimes, a therapist or counselor may decide to hold a couple of pro bono spots in their practice, for clients who simply cannot afford to pay for therapy. This can be a good way to create space in one's practice for people who might not otherwise be able to access therapy due to financial constraint. It is important to note that having pro bono clients, however, does not mean that therapists and counselors treat these clients any differently than those who are paying full fees. The same intake process, setting treatment plans, chart notetaking, and informed consent (including how long the sliding scale will remain the same, and what happens if a client on a sliding scale suddenly gains employment or is in a better financial position) are required. Not taking payment does not mean any less responsibility or paperwork!

Can you offer sliding-scale fees of different amounts to different clients? Consider your thoughts on this. Let's say a therapist offers to see client A for $50, and sees client B for $35, and client C for $70. Is this ethical? It certainly *could* be, but it could also open up sticky areas for the therapist. Consider the following possibilities:

1 Clients A and B and C all know each other and discuss their differing payment amounts outside of sessions. Client C confronts the therapist and asks why client A pays less, when client C knows that client A makes far less money than C does.
2 Client B refers a friend and a family member to the therapist. At intake, both of the referrals ask to be seen at the same sliding-scale cost as client B pays.
3 Client C starts spreading the word in the community about the therapist being so wonderful and "far more affordable than others in town." Soon, the therapist is inundated with requests for therapy from folks who can't afford to pay the full price and need a sliding scale.

Although there is not one singular way that therapists or counselors must navigate sliding-scale fees, it is best if their policies avoid the possibility of stickiness. Doing this will help decrease possible ethical concerns that can stem from these policies. Consider the following therapist's response to the request of explaining her sliding-scale policy:

> I hold two sliding-scale spots in my practice at all times. When someone reaches out for therapy and requests a reduced fee, I let them know that I have these two spots. If I do not currently have two sliding-scale

> clients, I will fill those vacated slots with the new clients who request them. I do not collect financial information, but do ask them to complete a short questionnaire that includes a section to describe what they think they can afford. If any client, sliding-scale or regular self-pay, ask me about varying fees, I state my policy. For example, I might say, "I'm sorry, but I can't discuss any one client's payment information with anyone else. However, I can share my payment policy from the informed consent—I always maintain two sliding-scale spots, and when those are filled, I only take regular self-pay clients. If there is a more imminent need for treatment at a reduced fee that I cannot immediately accommodate, I have several colleagues, and there is a local counseling center that can work with them. My sliding-scale spots range from $0 to whatever amount a client feels they can pay."

How do you feel about this therapist's policy? Does her policy seem ethical and as sticky-avoidant as possible? Does the policy adhere to the foundational principles of ethics? Can you think of other ethical ways that a therapist or counselor could structure their sliding-scale agreements and policies?

Managing Unpaid Balances

What if clients do not pay the contracted fees? Some examples might be clients who "forget" to bring a check or credit card to session, "missed" or "didn't get" the invoice or bill in their email, or set up payment with a credit card that gets declined. How can a therapist or counselor best manage situations like these, while adhering to an ethical framework?

First, it is imperative that therapists and counselors have written policies on their payment structures, collection procedures, and how they handle unpaid balances. These policies should be the guide for the therapist or counselor when encountering issues with non-payment. Similar to other topics in the book, having clearly written and detailed policies that are explained to clients is a great way to start with a strong ethical grounding. There should be no surprises for clients about how their therapist or counselor handles the collection process.

Next, therapists and counselors should communicate early on with clients who have a pattern of defaulting on payment. This way, they can gauge the possibilities for assisting these clients with payment and try to make a plan. Perhaps the client needs a subsidy service that some communities offer, or a sliding-scale set-up or payment plan. The therapist or counselor might set be able to create an alert for the client that an invoice has been sent, so that the client attends to it in a timely fashion. Some clients, depending on their progress and stability in treatment, may be able to move to biweekly or monthly sessions to reduce the cost to them.

If the aforementioned steps are not successful in alleviating the non-payment issue, and the therapist or counselor is unable or unwilling to see the client at a (further) reduced fee, they may decide that they cannot continue to see that client anymore. If this is the case, the therapist or counselor is responsible for working with clients to ensure an appropriate continuity of care, if necessary. This means helping them locate other providers or agencies that have financial supports, subsidy, reduced fee, or pro bono services. Most communities have an agency such as a social services office or community hotline to help identify the resources a client might require.

Therapists and counselors may designate an unpaid fee collection policy in their paperwork. Some of the codes (e.g., AAMFT) require therapists and counselors to give "reasonable notice" to clients before enforcing collections steps. "Reasonable" is another "gray area" term in some codes that can be confusing. Rather than telling therapists and counselors exact measurements for this term, it is left up to the therapist or counselor to show evidence of "reasonable." This might be demonstrated through a history of documentation of conversations with the client about remedying the unpaid balances, attempts to have the client follow through on seeking out referred resources, and documenting a timetable that is set up with the client for payment, or winding down sessions and referring to another provider.

In some cases, therapists or counselors may decide to keep seeing a client, despite the battle of non-payment, and just take the financial loss. Perhaps the therapist or counselor feels bad for the client, or feels uncomfortable broaching the topic of money and payment with the client. Remember, however, that this might not be in alignment with the foundational principle of Justice, if the therapist or counselor would not do the same thing for every client who did not/was not able to pay. Additionally, it is not sustainable for most therapists or clinicians to accept non-payment from numerous clients, and still be able to bring in an income that covers their own costs.

In the case of pursuing collections, therapists and counselors need to keep in mind that they *must* adhere to privacy and confidentiality standards, which in most cases (e.g., APA) means that no clinical information will be disclosed in an attempt to collect fees. The collection should simply be for unpaid fees where the therapist or counselor has completed (1) signed informed consent by the client for the practice's payment and non-payment protocols upon intake, (2) notifying the client of the intent to pursue collections, (3) reasonable attempts to work with the client to arrange payment, and (4) with no success in getting payment, or no response or follow-through from the client regarding payment.

In the case of pursuing termination for non-payment, therapists and counselors need to keep ethical principles (like Non-Maleficence), and other code standards (like referrals) in mind. Remember that clients who have unpaid balances may be experiencing anxiety, embarrassment, shame, or fear of judgment from the therapist or counselor about the situation. This can be distressing to clients who have anxiety or fear of judgment as one of their presenting issues. Can you think of ways to reduce the chances of these things occurring for clients in your practice?

In some cases, clients may avoid talking to the therapist, skirting around certain topics, or stop showing up for sessions, instead of addressing the payment issue. A string of no-shows from clients who are embarrassed about unpaid balances and their inability to bring them up to date opens another an entirely different problem for the provider!

Payment for "Late-Cancel" or "No-Show" Sessions

Many therapists and counselors have policies for when a client "late-cancels" or "no-shows" for a session. This can vary from a small fee to the client being responsible for paying the therapist's full session fee (which may be higher than the typical insurance contracted amount). In any case, the therapist or counselor is responsible for having these policies written out, clearly defined, and shared and discussed with clients at the onset of therapy. Again, there should be no surprises to the client for a late-cancel or no-show charge!

Many therapists and counselors create policies that allow for no financial penalties for first-time "offenses," or for unexpected events like a medical emergency or a death in the family. Again, these policies must be made overt to clients, and revisited as is necessary.

Perhaps most important here, after having clear policies for the situations described above, is focusing on preventing the *why* clients may late-cancel or no-show. Most therapists and counselors I know have found that the ability to provide teletherapy since the Pandemic in 2020 has decreased their general percentages of therapy no-shows. This is because teletherapy removes certain barriers like sickness and transportation or childcare issues that might prompt a client to otherwise need to cancel at the last minute. What are some other reasons you can think of for why a client might late-cancel or no-show? And what can therapists or counselors do in their practices that might alleviate some of these issues?

Cancellation fees remains controversial among professionals I know in the therapy fields, and there are some who argue that late cancellation fees might actually be a *contributor* to late cancellations. Caldwell (2025) writes about the cases made in the book *Blind Spots* (Bazerman & Tenbrunsel, 2011). He describes how the authors make the case that customers [clients] might actually view a cancellation fee as a simple business decision, and decide that the cost may be worth it. Caldwell (2025) suggests that therapists and counselors make some thoughtful consideration before deciding on a cancellation policy: Is the policy necessary for their practice? And will the policy actually do what they are intend?

Third-Party Payors

When therapists or counselors are in-network with insurance companies, their fees are contracted with them at the rate that the company advertises for each specific service code. Therapists and counselors cannot accept or charge more than those fixed amounts.

There are a few important things for the ethical therapist or counselor to remember here. First, when providers contract with insurance companies, they enter into agreements on several things, and are legally and ethically bound to do those things accordingly.

Second, it is important that therapists and counselors adhere to the principles of Veracity and Fidelity, where they are both truthful with clients and they do what they say they will do. In this case, this means that therapists and counselors must be truthful in their diagnosing, which is required by the insurance company, submitting accurate claims to them, and collecting correct co-payment amounts from clients.

Third, because many clients do not understand the complexities of how health insurance works, therapists and counselors should get written authorization from clients to bill their insurance, after offering detailed written and verbal information about the process. Clients should know that the therapist or counselor will send a diagnosis to the insurance company, as well as submit claims for the specific dates that sessions are held. Insurance companies may occasionally want to speak to the provider and ask questions about treatment in order to assess the client's functioning and to decide on authorizing more sessions. It is also a good idea to direct clients to their insurance companies to get more details on any questions they might have.

Now let's explore the ethics of payment of a client's therapy sessions by a third party *other* than a health insurance company. Consider the following clinical vignette:

> A therapist, Seema, has a private practice in an office space that houses other businesses in her same hallway. Due to the close proximity and shared bathrooms and entrances, Seema is friendly with other workers on her floor who are *not* therapists. One day, a woman who works in the office next to her tells Seema that she'd like to refer her sister-in-law to her for therapy. The sister-in-law has had a history of alcoholism, although she has been sober for five years now, and is depressed because she's going through a "nasty" divorce. Because her sister-in-law is struggling financially, Seema's colleague in the building tells her she'd like to pay for her sister-in-law's sessions.

Sticky: Is it ethical for Seema to accept this arrangement? Can Seema's colleague in the building act as the third-party payor for the new client's sessions, should Seema agree to see the sister-in-law for therapy? Does the sister-in-law even want therapy? Does the sister-in-law agree to this arrangement?

Boil it Down: Seema agrees to see her colleague's sister-in-law for therapy, as she does not assess the situation to be a conflict of interest. In order to arrange this ethically, Seema asks the colleague to have the sister-in-law reach out to her to set up treatment directly with Seema. Seema reminds her colleague that although she is happy to see her sister-in-law, she will not be able to disclose any information about the therapy. Additionally, Seema tells the colleague that to keep appropriate boundaries, she does not want the colleague to share information or try to discuss anything about her sister-in-law with the therapist. Seema asks the new client if she is comfortable with Seema's colleague paying for her sessions, and the client states that she is. Upon meeting with the client for the first time, Seema has the client sign a release of information that allows the therapist to send a simple invoice to her colleague with the day of the session and the amount charged ($100).

Has Seema acted ethically and "covered all the bases" of making an ethical arrangement? Now, let's complicate things further:

> Seema's colleague leaves a $100 bill in an envelope underneath Seema's door every Friday to cover her sister-in-law's weekly session. Everything is going well, until the sister-in-law does not show for her session one week. Seema tries to reach out to her several times, but the client does not respond. In the meantime, the $100 bill shows up under Seema's door on Friday, even though there was no session that week.

Sticky: Since Seema can't contact the colleague to discuss her client, what does she do? Seema can't accept payment for a session that didn't occur, so what does she do with the money?

Boil it Down: Therapists and counselors need to remember that, oftentimes, reaching out to the client to discuss can be the ethical answer to alleviating sticky. Seema leaves a message for her client saying that she is concerned about her, and if she doesn't contact her by the end of the day to let her know she's okay, she will reach out to the client's emergency contact. The client does reach out to assure the therapist she is fine, but confesses she has relapsed and has been drinking for the last few days and missed all her appointments. Seema helps the client get in touch with her old sponsor and gets her to back to AA. But what about the $100 Seema was paid for a session that did not occur? Seema tells the client that she will need to return the money to the client's sister-in-law, but Seema assures the client she will not give any other info except to tell her colleague, "You'll need to talk to your sister-in-law about the details." The client understands, and the two decide that going forward, Seema will bill the client directly, and the client can get the money from Seema's colleague. Perhaps this is what Seema should have done in the first place?

Remember, a good "rule of thumb" is to *avoid* sticky whenever possible!

Bartering

Bartering is the act of trading things or services, instead of money, for therapy sessions. The reason that most codes of ethics have statements on this practice is because bartering can create sticky situations or multiple relationships. However, especially in very rural or impoverished areas, clients may not have the financial resources to be able to pay for the services they need. Read the following vignette and think about how you might handle the situation:

> A female therapist, Jo, has a female client, Martine, that she sees for symptoms of anxiety and depression. After the therapist has some minor damage done to her car from a recent car accident, her car is towed to the nearest car repair shop (Rally Repairs). It's pretty much the only one nearby in the small town in which she lives and practices. When she calls up Rally Repairs to get some information on the status of the car, her client, Martine, answers the phone and says, "Hi, Jo! It's me—Martine, from therapy? I'm so sorry to hear about your accident, but no worries, we are going to take great care of your car and get you the best estimate!"

JO: Ohh…hello, Martine. I thought you worked at the middle school?

MARTINE: I do, but my husband and I own this place, and I work here sometimes after school and on Saturdays.

JO: Oh, well, I didn't know that! Thanks for your assurance that you'll be able to get the work done on it, Martine—I appreciate that!

MARTINE: I was talking to my husband, and he thinks it will only cost about $1500 with our "discount." And we also decided that instead of you paying us for the repairs, we can just call it even if I don't pay for my sessions for the next 15 appointments. We could use the extra money. It's a win-win!

The Sticky: Let's say that Jo decides to take Martine up on her offer of not having to pay for repairs to her car, in exchange for not paying for her therapy sessions. What happens if Martine doesn't need as many sessions as the car repairs cost equaled? Does Jo reimburse the client for the balance? What if Jo finds herself annoyed that the client didn't cut her a better deal? How might that impact the therapeutic relationship? What if Martine suggests that Jo get her tune-ups and oil changes at Rally Repairs going forward, and they can work out the same deal? What if Martine tells others that Jo will swap services in place of therapy payment?

Boil it Down: In this situation, it may be most prudent for Jo to avoid the possibility of all the stickiness above by simply saying no to the barter arrangement. Jo *does* decide to do the barter, so it is her responsibility to ensure the situation is not exploitative of the client in any way, and makes the arrangements overt and clear. For example, Jo writes up an agreement that specifies the one-time barter arrangement of $1500 of car repairs, equaling 15 therapy sessions, and she includes the specifics of how overage will be paid back, etc.

How do you feel about Jo's decision? Would you do the same? Did Jo act ethically according to your profession's code of ethics standard on bartering?

"Kickbacks" or Renumeration for Referrals

"Kickbacks" describe any payment that is made to a person who has participated in referring a client to a therapist or counselor, and these are prohibited in *all* the codes. To be clear, this refers to rewarding with money or gifts or discounts someone who has made a therapy referral to you. In the most basic unethical essence, therapists and counselors who pay someone who gives them clients violate the confidentiality of those clients. They do so by acknowledging that a client has indeed become a client, when offering the renumeration to the person who referred the client(s) to them.

Consider the following clinical vignette:

> A therapist, Malik, has heard that there is a new therapist in town who also has a nursing degree and specializes in microdosing psychedelics and medicinal marijuana for clients who are diagnosed with depression, anxiety, or post-traumatic stress syndrome (PTSD). Malik decides to tell several of his clients about this new therapist and suggests they try having a consultation with her. Malik has heard that many people have been able to get relief from their symptoms and get off their heavy doses of traditional medications for their symptoms.
>
> Malik has several clients who have done very well with the new therapist, so he begins regularly referring people to the new therapist for help. One day, Malik arrives to his private practice office and there is a small-canoe-sized basket full of wine, fresh fruit, packages of nuts, and other snacks. The note on the basket says, "Thank you so much for all the referrals! I look forward to continuing to work with you!" The signature is from the new therapist in town.

Sticky: The new therapist's gift basket and note make it clear that the intention is to continue to refer to one another. The new therapist gave Malik a very expensive "gift," seemingly in return for the referrals he made. Should Malik accept the gift? What is the implicit meaning to the new therapist if Malik accepts the gift? Is this "gift" the first of a series of implicit "kickbacks" that will be given to Malik for continued referrals? Does the gift influence how many clients Malik will send to the new therapist? What if Malik's clients see the card or the gift and feel used by him, and wonder if the referral was made in good faith or to get rewards from the new therapist?

Boil it Down: Although unspoken and perhaps covert, the gift to Malik could be seen as a kickback for referrals to the new therapist's practice. The following is how Malik handled the situation. First, he called up the new therapist and explained that he does not need anything in return for the referrals he makes. He tells the new therapist that the services offered have been a very helpful part of many of his client's journeys, and that he appreciates the coordination of care. Going forward, Malik shares that a kind email or sharing a cup of coffee out somewhere to learn more about each other's services would be preferred to any sort of gift or kickback for referrals. Malik also decides that he will remove the card and the wine, and leave the huge basket in the waiting room for clients to take items home with them.

How do you feel about Malik's choices here? Was this an ethical way to handle the situation?

Gift Giving and Receiving

Gift giving or receiving between therapist or counselor and clients can be one of the most difficult areas to navigate. There are many reasons that gift giving might occur, but without enough context or understanding of the gift's "social value," people will most likely determine the overall value of the gift based simply on its dollar amount (Zhang, 2019).

Within the therapeutic relationship, there are many more layers to consider when making decisions on giving or receiving gifts than the economic value of the gift itself. Most importantly, any gift that may cause bias, that is overstepping or too personal, that may create issues with clinical judgment or a conflict of interest, or are overly expensive should not be accepted. In these cases above, the gift itself is no longer the issue at hand; rather, the issues that may be created by the gift giving may negatively influence the therapy. The therapist or counselor should make *all* decisions about gifts in alignment with principles like Beneficence, Non-Maleficence, and Justice.

Let's start by looking at when, if ever, it is appropriate for a therapist or counselor to give a client a gift. One important thing to consider here is the ethical principle of ***Justice***. If a therapist or counselor chooses to give a gift to a client, would they do the same for *all* clients they see? Why or why not? If not, what is "special" about the client(s) the therapist or counselor wants to give a gift to? Furthermore, what is the *intention* of the gift? Is the therapist or counselor giving the gift to celebrate a client's achievement? Or because the therapist or counselor feels bad for a particular client? Is the gift an attempt to make the client feel better? Read the following examples of gifts that a therapist, Elsa, gave to her clients over a couple of years of practice. Which ones do you think are appropriate? Are there potential risks with any of her choices? What do you think Elsa's intention was with each gift?

- Elsa gave a client, who had just given birth to a baby, a beautiful board book entitled *Guess How Much I Love You?* The client was currently a single mother whose first child died at the hands of a violent ex-husband nearly a decade earlier. She had decided to use a sperm donor and IVF in order to have another child on her own, and leaned on the therapist to help her learn strategies for managing anxiety, working through her history of trauma, and creating healthy networks of support around herself.

- A couple who had worked through issues of depression and infidelity with Elsa had invited her to their wedding. Although Elsa declined the invite, she decided to send a beautiful card and a hand-crafted glass suncatcher that contained a word on it that had been an instrumental part of the couple's healing and growth.
- Elsa had been working with a couple who had thrived in her care, and they had recently ended therapy after reporting they were in a great place. A few months later, one half of the couple returned for individual therapy after finding out about his wife's terminal cancer diagnosis. They had given her three months to live, and her husband was devasted. When her client's wife finally passed, Elsa sent him a card and a small, inspirational book of healing quotes for unexpected loss and grief.

So how about when clients give gifts to their therapists or counselors? When clients (or *anyone* for that matter) feel supported and helped by their therapists or counselors, and want to express gratitude to them, they may want to give their providers a gift. Depending on the individual client, gifts may range from highly personal to small token items or much more extravagant ones.

One important consideration when looking at gift giving is the cultural relevance and meaning to the client. Some of the main mental health providers' codes include this important feature when considering gifts (e.g., ACA, AAMFT). However, the specifics or tips for navigating these situations are lacking. Most codes intend for them to be read this way, because they are clear on what therapists and counselors can and cannot do, yet there are often many ways to achieve these things.

An article by Stubbs et. al. (2024), highlights the cultural meaning of client gifts within the therapeutic relationship. Although they are clear that not every client from a particular background will carry the same experience and intentions, it is important for therapists and counselors to assess whether a gift might be influenced by a client's cultural norm or expectation.

The unique dynamics in each therapist or counselor and client relationship may require different approaches. For example, consider the two clinical scenarios of clients giving a gift to the therapist, and the differences in how the therapist or counselor might respond:

- Twelve-year-old client, Aiko, and her mother give the therapist a small basket of necessity items, like onesies and baby wipes, when they learn that the therapist will be going on maternity leave shortly. They also give her a candle, some special Japanese tea, and a mug emblazoned with the word "Aiko," on it, and explain that the word (and also the name of the therapist's client) means "love child" in their culture. Aiko and her mother tell the therapist that having a new baby is a very important milestone in a family's life, and that the rest, healing, and self-care of the mother is of the utmost importance in the first weeks, and they wanted her to have some items to help her do that.

- Forty-year-old client, Kate, brings a laundry basket of fancily wrapped gifts to the therapist, upon learning that she will be taking maternity leave shortly. Kate is a vegan raw foodist, an environmental advocate, and an eco-conscious, natural, and chemical-free mother of two. Many of the items are ones that Kate feels strongly about, like a book on attachment parenting, lead-free painted wooden toys, teas made with herbs from her organic garden, and bamboo clothing.

In most cases, a gift is generally meant to thank the provider, demonstrate gratitude, or offer good wishes or celebration. But sometimes the gift may come with a different "attachment." In some cases, the client's intention might be to set up a quid pro quo arrangement, where the therapist "owes" the client something in return for the gift. Consider the following email exchange between a therapist, Dr. Ramirez, and a client, Josh:

JOSH: Hi, Dr. Ramirez. My husband and I were looking forward to seeing you tonight for our couples' session, but unfortunately we need to cancel at the last minute. We're so sorry but we will need to reschedule.

DR. RAMIREZ: Hi, Josh, thanks for letting me know. I hope everything is okay. And since you never cancel on me, I will waive the late cancellation fee, and I'll send you some open appointments for next week. Sound good?

JOSH: Thank you for understanding! But of course I want to pay you for the missed session. It's only right, since you will lose out on that spot—it's probably too late to fill our time slot. So sorry again, for the late cancel. Please send me an invoice for the missed session and I will take care of it online immediately.

DR. RAMIREZ: Thank you for the offer to pay, but I cannot accept a full payment for a session that did not occur. There is no charge for the missed appointment tonight, and let's put something in the books for next week.

JOSH: I understand, Dr. Ramirez, but we *will* be paying you in full, as you kept up your end of the deal and were available for us, and it's only right that you get paid for your time. It's our fault that we scheduled with you without checking other commitments—that shouldn't be on you.

DR. RAMIREZ: Thank you again, but I will not be accepting the payment. No worries about the situation—no big deal. I'll see you next week.

JOSH: With respect, Dr. Ramirez, I request that you accept the money. We have discussed it and decided that you were available to us tonight, and we screwed up, and we would expect that you'd be there for us if we needed an emergency appointment or something, so we want to be fair and generous and respect your time, as we know you'd be there for us in our time of need. I'll just put a check in the mail then for the full amount if you don't send over an invoice. And we can do any night next week except Wednesday or Friday—let us know if you have any openings for those other evenings. Thank you!

In the above vignette, the therapist must "win" the Battle of Structure in abiding by his policies and enforcing them with his clients. More importantly, near the end of the dialogue, there is a "hint" of an expectation that Josh has of Dr. Ramirez. Although Josh claims the full payment for a session that didn't occur was about Dr. Ramirez's time and not being able to replace the income of their cancelled session in the short timeframe, might there be more here? Josh writes: "...and we would expect that you'd be there for us if we needed an emergency appointment or something, so we want to be fair and generous and respect your time, as we know you'd be there for us in our time of need." This statement might suggest that the extra pay will be "buying" flexibility or exception or special consideration in the future. The two—full payment for a late-cancel session, and making sure "emergency" appointments will be given—are very different things, and governed by different sets of rules or policies. Anything else would feel like the extra money would be a gift that has strings and expectations attached.

What would you do in the vignette above? In making your decision, would it matter if Josh and his husband could easily afford the money for the missed session? How do you feel about Dr. Ramirez's handling of the situation?

What other reasons can you think of that a client might want to give a therapist or counselor a gift? From these possibilities, therapists and counselors can discern that the importance of the gift is more about the *intention* behind the gift than the actual gift itself. Does the client feel obligated to gift the therapist or counselor? Does the client want to impress the therapist? Does the client think giving gifts to the therapist will make the therapist like them more? What if the client is seen as part of a family or one half of a romantic relationship that's "on the rocks"? Might a gift be intended to win the therapist over to the side of one of the clients? Will the therapist feel more warmly about a client who has given a gift, or look more favorably on the client? Might the therapist begin to expect the gifts, and perhaps even say or do things that prompt them?

Read the following examples of gifts that clients have attempted to give a therapist, Elsa. What are the messages and intentions behind each gift? Which ones should Elsa accept? Why or why not? How should she handle the ones she does not?

- **The Hermès bag:** It is Christmastime, and an affluent client, Diana, assumes that her therapist, Elsa, celebrates it. On their last meeting before the holiday, Diana brings Elsa an elaborately decorated gift bag and tells her it is "a little something to let you know how much I appreciate you!" Elsa opens the bag and finds a brand-new, expensive leather handbag inside. Diana says, "There is a huge waiting list to get your hands on one of these, but I know someone who was able to get me ten of these at cost. I chose the brown one because I thought it so nicely matched your hair and complexion, don't you think?" After thanking her for her thoughtfulness, Elsa explains to Diana that she cannot accept such a generous and expensive gift. She goes on to tell Diana that she does not need to gift her, but that just sharing her gratitude is all that Elsa needs and appreciates. However, Diana will not accept "no" for an answer and goes on to tell Elsa, "I bought them for all my supports in life right now, and you are definitely at the top of my list. You know I can afford this, and I'm not taking it back. It you don't want to keep it yourself, then you can give it to someone else, but I am definitely not taking it back. It's the least I can do to show you my appreciation."

Sticky: Diana is controlling the "rules" in the therapy room here, deciding for Elsa on what she will accept. If Elsa accepts the gift, she allows Diana to win the Battle of Structure—in what other areas might Diana think she can also make the rules for the structure of the therapy? The gift is obviously very expensive. If Elsa accepts this gift, she will likely receive more expensive gifts in the future.

Boil it Down: Elsa needs to have a conversation that highlights her policies on gifts and why she has them. At the same time, she needs to ensure that she expresses her gratitude for the gift, and that she makes sure Diana does not feel judged or rejected. One ethical course of action would be for Elsa to reiterate what her gift policy is, then thank Diana for her thoughtfulness, politely decline the gift, and suggest that Diana keep it for herself, since she had been working so hard in therapy.

- **The vase:** Gisele and Claude bring Elsa a hand-thrown and hand-painted vase to commemorate the new office space she has recently moved to. They share that they made the vase in their studio, and that the flowers were flown here from their extended family's French countryside gardens. The etchings were filled in with 24-karat gold, and the therapist's initials were threaded throughout the surface. It is clear to Elsa that this piece took a fair amount of energy, time, thought, and materials to create, even though it was through the couple's professional business.

Sticky: The gift is likely a bit expensive. If Elsa has a gift policy that doesn't allow her to accept this, then she should try to follow her rules. However, the vase is personalized with her initials, and this makes it hard to sell or give the gift to someone else. Since the couple has a well-known pottery business in town, what if Elsa's other clients recognize the style of the vase and ask if Elsa knows them?

Boil it Down: Elsa knows how important family and culture are to her clients. The vase is part of their business, and so the materials (like the flowers and clay and gold) are likely to be purchased wholesale or in bulk, thus reducing the cost. Rejecting the personalized gift might be hurtful both to the clients and to the therapeutic alliance, given the genuine intentions of the clients. One ethical course of action might be for Elsa to reiterate her gift policies, express gratitude for the kind gesture, and accept the gift with a firm message that no future gifts are necessary or will be accepted. Elsa should also have a conversation with the couple about navigating how the couple would like her to respond to any inquiries about the piece that will be displayed in her new office space.

- **Being left money in a client's will:** Elsa receives a voicemail from a local attorney, telling her that a prior client of hers has passed away and left her some money in his will. The attorney asks Elsa to return his call, so that they can arrange where the paperwork should be sent, in order to expedite disbursement when the estate is settled. The client whose name the attorney references was indeed a prior client of Elsa's. She saw him first for family therapy, and then later for individual work for depressive symptoms that cropped up after some medical issues he had tackled.

Sticky: First, Elsa must consider the laws and rules of the jurisdiction of her practice. Next, can she even call this attorney back to discuss, given that the client is dead and she cannot get permission to even acknowledge that he was a prior client of hers? Would it be appropriate and ethical for Elsa to accept the money the client left her in his will?

Boil it Down: Elsa decides to contact one of the prior client's family members, a brother who he had listed as his emergency contact in the intake paperwork. Elsa knew the brother, as he had attended some of the family sessions. He confirms that the prior client had died from a sudden heart attack. He also confirms that he had left Elsa money in his will. Unsure of what to do at this point, Elsa decides to tell the brother that she does not feel right taking the money and that she'd like the brother to pass that message on to the attorney. The brother responded vehemently, insisting that the whole family wants Elsa to have the money, because she was so helpful to the client when he was struggling most. "He wanted you to have that money, Elsa," the brother says. Elsa tries again to refuse the money, and after the brother's adamance, she decides that she will accept the money and donate it to a charity of the family's choice. They agree, and choose a cause to donate to that the client had been passionate about. The brother will inform the attorney, and the paperwork will be sent to Elsa to sign off on. How do you feel about Elsa's choices here? And lastly, are you wondering how much money the previous client left Elsa? Would the amount matter to you when deciding how to proceed? The amount was $10,000.

There is often no singular straightforward answer when navigating the ethics of gifts in a therapeutic practice. Perhaps most important when considering all the discussions above is that the therapist or counselor start from the most basic ethical stance. This means that whatever the fees and policies are surrounding payment and gifts, etc., the therapist or counselor needs to make the information clear and overt. Additionally, the therapist or counselor is responsible for making sure clients understand the information and policies. One way to do this is to be extremely detailed and thorough in the informed consent that is given to the client before therapy begins. Then clients should be given time to explore, discuss, and ask questions to be *sure* they understand all the policies and how they will be enforced.

It is always the therapist's or counselor's responsibility to consider all of the context and social meaning available when choosing on whether to give or accept gifts. However, when encountering a situation where declining a gift is ethically necessary, Stubbs et al. (2024) recommend that "the counselor needs to have an honest but careful conversation with that client so that the rejection does not reinforce conditions of the client's worth" (p. 71).

Remember the Battle of Structure from Chapter 2, and how the therapist or counselor must "win" this. Therapists and counselors must be in charge of the rules that are set for therapy, including fees, process for collection, policies for unpaid balances, gift giving, etc. They are also responsible for enforcing these rules appropriately and ethically. It is of the utmost importance that therapists and counselors think through their rules on a variety of financial and gift-giving matters, make them clear to clients at the onset of therapy, and review them as needed throughout the process. The following are some good questions for a therapist or counselor to ask before considering the giving or accepting of a gift within the therapeutic relationship:

- What is the intention or meaning behind the gift?
- Might there be an expectation on either side that the gift will become something that will occur more regularly?
- Is there a feeling of obligation behind the gift giving?
- What are the therapist's or counselor's policies on gift giving and receiving?
- How much is the gift worth monetarily?
- Would the therapist give a gift to *any* client in the same situation, or is the client the therapist or counselor is giving to "special?"
- Has the therapist or counselor considered the possible cultural norms of the client who gifts them?
- Is it possible the gift giving is meant to flatter, impress, or otherwise send a complimentary message?

Chapter Takeaways for Therapists and Counselors

1 There are many things to consider before setting up practice fees, payment and collection policies, etc.
2 "Kickbacks," or payments made for sending a therapist or counselor clients, are prohibited.
3 Gift giving and receiving in the therapeutic relationship can be tricky to navigate. The cost of the gift should be considered, but, more importantly,

the intention, cultural influence, and impact on the therapeutic relationship need to be included in the therapist's or counselor's decision-making process in this area.

4 It is imperative that therapists and counselors have clear policies on everything financial, including sliding scales, bartering, and how unpaid balances will be collected. This information must be disseminated to clients, and reviewed as necessary. There should be no surprises about these areas.

4 Privilege, Confidentiality, Privacy, and Record Keeping

Privacy for clients is not just a suggestion but absolutely necessary to create a safe and ethical environment for therapy. Ensuring privacy and confidentiality for clients gives them comfort, security, and calmness, knowing that whatever they share will be safeguarded.

Privilege

Like medical doctors and lawyers, mental health providers have special "privileged communication," which refers to all of the information shared between patients or clients and their health care providers that is related to their diagnoses, and any information exchanged within the treatment appointments. This "privilege" is a legal term and means that the provider may not be required by law (except in specific situation discussed later in the chapter) to disclose the information of their communications over the objection of the patient or client (State of Connecticut Judicial Branch, 2022).

Put more simply, therapists and counselors must abide by the special "privilege" that requires them to withhold sharing information about a client's diagnoses or anything that is shared in treatment in legal proceedings if the client does not wish for the information to be disclosed. The privilege belongs to the client, as a way for them to protect their own information.

One reason that privilege is important is that the release of personal and sensitive information that a client shares in therapy could be harmful to them. Therapists and counselors strive to maintain a non-maleficent ("do no harm") stance when treating clients. Privilege also supports the ethical principle of ***Autonomy***, allowing for clients to decide for themselves what personal information they wish to be disclosed. Another important reason that what clients' share is privileged information is ***trust***. Trust is a foundational part of therapy, and knowing that their information will not be disclosed is one way that clients can feel comfortable about being honest, vulnerable, and sharing sensitive things in treatment.

In short, therapy clients have privileged communication with their therapists or counselors, meaning that therapists and counselors are bound by

DOI: 10.4324/9781003745136-5

law to not disclose information about clients' treatment, except when mandated (as discussed below under "Limits to Confidentiality").

Confidentiality

Confidentiality has been defined as the expectation that information disclosed in a sensitive context (like therapy) will not be revealed to a third party without prior consent (Hiriscau et al., 2014). Kafka et. al. (2024) highlight that specific client populations, like children and adolescents, may be particularly concerned about confidentiality. This is because they are caught between wanting to talk privately with the therapist or counselor about sensitive matters and understanding that there are some things that their parents or guardians might need to know.

For *all* clients, and especially the child and teen ones, it is important that therapists and counselors ensure that they are always aware of the limits to confidentiality. It is difficult enough for therapists and counselors to understand and navigate, let alone their clients! It is imperative that ***Fidelity*** and ***Veracity*** are practiced by therapists and counselors, by ensuring that clients are informed and reminded regularly of their obligations regarding confidentiality. Research has echoed this sentiment: "Based on our findings, it is recommended to frequently discuss the boundaries of confidentiality while also emphasizing what information will be protected by it" (Kafka et al., 2024).

Consider the following clinical case for a therapist, her 15-year-old client, and the client's mother:

> A therapist, Kailani, sees a 15-year-old non-binary client, Trey, for therapy. Trey's mother emails Kailani, asking if Trey showed up for the session today, and if they told you about their breakup with their girlfriend, and if you have advice on how she can support Trey through the breakup. The mother shares that she is concerned about Trey. Kailani reads the email and is unsure if, and how, to respond. Trey had a session with Kailani today, but they never mentioned any breakup.

Sticky: Kailani doesn't want to respond to her client's mother, because if she did, she'd be put into a position where she would either need to lie to the mother or disclose confidential information. Not responding at all to her might raise red flags to the mother. Since the client is a minor, and the mother pays for the client's sessions, does the mother have the right to have information on the sessions? Should the mother's concern about Trey worry Kailani, or make her think about Trey's safety?

Boil it Down: Kailani has full authority to talk with her client, Trey, at any time. One ethical course of action might be for Kailani to decide *with* Trey how to navigate the conversation.

Consider the following conversation between Kailani and Trey, and then the follow-up message from Kailani to Trey's mother:

KAILANI: Hi, Trey. I wanted to reach out to you because I received an email from your mother today. Do you have a minute to talk about how we think I should respond?

TREY: I guess. What did she want?

KAILANI: Well, she wanted to know if we met for therapy today.

TREY: Well, we *did* meet.

KAILANI: Yes, we did—so you are okay with me confirming that to her? Remember that she gets an invoice to pay when we meet, so technically she knows when we meet or not.

TREY: Yeah, that's fine.

KAILANI: Then she asked if you had told me about the breakup with your girlfriend...

TREY: Oh, yeah, I guess I forgot to tell you that part.

KAILANI: Your mother seemed worried about you, and was asking if there was anything she could do to support you through the breakup. Is there a reason you didn't share the breakup with me when we met earlier, Trey?

TREY: (laughing): Um, not really. We broke up, but I started talking to some other girl at school the next day, and we are kind of into each other. I guess I kind of forgot about the breakup because we've both moved on. I think we both knew it wasn't going to work out with us together.

KAILANI: Oh! Okay, we can talk more about this when we meet next week, but how do you feel about talking to your mother tonight, telling her that we spoke, and sharing with her what you just told me?

TREY: I guess so.

KAILANI: Since you're a minor, Trey, there are times where it might be in your best interests, or required by law, that your mother and I communicate, or coordinate our efforts to best support you.

TREY: Like what?

KAILANI: Well, a good example would be if you had the breakup, and your mother saw you really upset and saying things that worried her, and she didn't know if you were safe or what she should do. If that ever happened, I'd want her to reach out to me, and I'd want to connect with you right away to be sure you were okay. If you were really upset, I might want to tell her that and ask her to do some things to ensure you were okay. Does that make sense?

TREY: Yeah.

KAILANI: And if it's okay with you, I will email her back and tell her we did meet, and that I encouraged you to talk to her tonight a bit to catch her up on the situation? And, Trey, is it okay if I ask her to join us at the next session for a few minutes so we can all review how the confidentiality works in our sessions together?

TREY: Yeah, that's okay.

Kailani's email to Trey's mother:

> Hi there, thanks for reaching out to me about Trey. They did meet with me today, and I spoke with them to encourage them to talk with you tonight to catch you up on the situation. I also asked Trey if it was okay to invite you into our next session for a few minutes, so we can review how best to collectively help and support Trey. In order for Trey to trust me and share things with me in session, I want to be sure to keep their information confidential. At the same time, as Trey's mother, I want to figure out how we can best work together to help Trey. Please let me know if you are able to join us for a few minutes at our next meeting!

How do you feel about the way Kailani handled the situation with Trey and their mother? Do you feel like this was a good situation to warrant a review of confidentiality? Would you do anything differently if this were your case?

Privacy

In the simplest terms, privacy describes the right of an individual to be protected against intrusion into their personal space (Hiriscau et al., 2014). The "personal space" here might be the client's presence in therapy.

When I'm teaching graduate therapy students, I ask them to consider themselves, and their own family members and loved ones. I ask them to think about how they'd feel if they were out in a public place and overheard a therapist talk about their mother in a gossipy way. What if they heard the therapist say:

> So, I have this client, and she's a real mess! She is going through a nasty divorce, and her wife cheated on her numerous times. The kids are all caught up in the middle of it, apparently, because they saw their mom all over some other woman at a concert. It's such a mess—and yet through all of this, the client still wants the marriage to work out! Can you believe that? I mean, these *people*—good riddance, and let the cheating ex go already!

How would it feel to hear information about a loved one disclosed in a disparaging and mocking way? Although the gossiping therapist did not disclose the client's name, there was private information shared about her, in a public forum, to an unauthorized person, that could lead others who know about the situation to figure out who the client is. Regardless of whether the person that the therapist is talking to has no idea who the client is, it is still an egregious breach of confidential information and privacy.

When considering the protection of clients' privacy, therapists and counselors are often asked to protect clients "within reason." "Within reason" likely reflects that it is impossible to completely guarantee a client's privacy.

For example, it's not a requirement of any therapist or counselor to provide an office space that is not within the visual range of other buildings. However, every effort should be made to shield a client's privacy whenever possible.

There are many things therapists and counselors can do to attend to the privacy of their clients. For example, they can be mindful when choosing the location of their office, trying to select a place that is tucked away and not visible from the main road. This decreases the likelihood that others will see a client entering the therapy space. One of my prior office spaces had two doors to the office, so that clients could enter through one door from the waiting room, and exit the office from a different door to the back stairs. This set-up also decreased clients crossing paths while entering and exiting the therapy space. White noise machines are a staple outside of therapy spaces, as they help protect the clients' confidential conversations from others outside of the office. Another important conversation for therapists and counselors to have with clients is how they would like the interaction to go if they see each other out in public. Most therapists and counselors adhere to the "rule" that they will not acknowledge a client, unless the client acknowledges them first.

Other ways for therapists and counselors to protect clients' privacy include not listing clients' names with their phone numbers in their cells, always opening and reading emails in a private space with no one looking over their shoulder, and trying not to book clients back-to-back that they suspect might work or go to school together. Therapists and counselors might avoid a certain store when they can, if they know it's a shift their client might be working. This is especially important if the client is someone who the therapist or counselor knows will feel uncomfortable or awkward about seeing the therapist out in public.

What happens when clients decide to disclose their own private information? Consider the following dialogue between a therapist, John, and his 13-year-old son, Jake:

JAKE: Oh my gosh, Dad! You never told me you see some kid in my class for therapy!

JOHN: You know I can't disclose who I see for therapy or anything about that, Jake.

JAKE: Yeah, I know, but this kid Tyler, from school, told me, "Hey! Dr. John is your dad? I see him for therapy and tell him all about my life and how much weed I smoke. Your dad is really cool!"

JOHN: Jake, I can't talk about any of this with you. I can't confirm whether I see this kid or not.

JAKE: Yeah, I know, but he said that he figured it out from some pictures of you and me that I put in a Happy Father's Day post on social media. That's how he figured it out. That's *crazy* that you talk about smoking weed with him!

Here, you can see how John is doing his best to respect the privacy of his client, Tyler. However, it is up to Tyler if he wants to tell others who he sees for therapy or what he talks about in those sessions. Regardless of Tyler's disclosure, John still must uphold his client's privacy. One possibility is for John to discuss in session with Tyler how and why and with whom he shares his therapy information. John might also explore the possible responses that others might have, and help Tyler decide if he wants to share his private information, and to what extent, with others.

Limits to Confidentiality

What happens when confidentiality needs to be broken? "Necessary breaches of confidentiality should be carefully considered, prepared for, and explained," (Chenneville et al., 2021). Confidentiality is not self-explanatory, especially not for minors—clear communication of confidentiality boundaries and respect for autonomy are crucial in mental health therapies for minors (Kafka et al., 2024).

There are four main reasons that confidentiality can/may need to be broken by the therapist or counselor:

1. In cases where the therapist or counselor believes that a client is an immediate danger to themselves (e.g., suicidality).
2. In cases where the therapist or counselor believes that a client is an immediate danger to others (e.g., homicidality).
3. In cases where there is suspected abuse or neglect of a minor or other protected population.
4. In legal situations where a specific, legally binding document is served to the therapist or counselor.

Also, remember that therapists and counselors are ***mandated reporters***, meaning that they are required by law to report when they reasonably suspect that a child has been abused or neglected. It can be a difficult duty for therapists and counselors to understand both that they need to maintain a safe, confidential, and supportive space for clients to disclose their most private struggles, and that they are bound by law to report the areas above. In making a required report, the therapeutic relationship may be negatively impacted. Clients might feel violated, betrayed, or angry. If this rupture is not able to be fixed, therapists and counselors may need to refer the client(s) to another provider, to continue the appropriate care they will need.

Is it possible to maintain trust and the quality of the therapeutic relationship when a therapist or counselor needs to break confidentiality? It may be. Research by Tufford and Lee (2020), offers several suggestions for areas that providers should attend to when attempting to repair a rupture in the therapeutic relationship after reporting child abuse or neglect. One thing to keep in mind, which is a thread that's stitched throughout this book, is that therapists' or counselors' clients may be their biggest asset when trying to navigate ethical situations. Consider the following dialogue between a therapist and his clients, a mom and her nine-year-old son, Matteus:

THERAPIST: Hey there! How's everybody doing today?

MATTEUS: (snarling): Bad! My daddy was mean again. *All* week. He was beating on me.

THERAPIST: (concerned): Can you tell me what you mean by "beating on me," Matteus?

MOM: He just means that he got in trouble and kept acting out this week and made his daddy mad. It wasn't no "beating"—that's exaggerating, Matteus!

THERAPIST: Thanks for adding that, Mom. And I need to hear a bit more about what happened, okay? Matteus, can you tell me more?

MATTEUS: Yeah, I was acting out, but Daddy was out of control—he gets like that sometimes. And when he's been drinking especially. But he kept hitting me and swearing at me. And he wouldn't take me to the hospital when my ear kept bleeding either—see? There's still a scab where his ring hit me. And I have this scab too on my arm and...

THERAPIST: (turning to Mom): Mom, I'd love for you and I to chat for a few minutes alone. Is it okay if we have Matteus play out in the waiting room for a few minutes while we talk?

MOM: Yeah. Here, Matteus—you can play that game on my phone in the waiting room for a few minutes while we talk, okay?

MATTEUS: Cool!

THERAPIST: So, Mom, I know you feel like what happened wasn't that serious, and maybe it makes you worried that Matteus shared it?

MOM: Well, I know we're gonna be in trouble now. Sometimes his daddy just goes a little too far.

THERAPIST: You're not going to be in trouble. But it is something I'm going to need to report to child services. In this state, hitting a child that leaves broken skin and scabs and bleeding is considered abuse. Not taking him for necessary medical treatment can be viewed as neglect. So I have no choice—I'm going to need to report this. But I want to let you know that I will tell them when I make the report how dedicated your family has been to coming to therapy, that there's been some real progress, and I'm going to make some recommendations for Matteus's daddy to get some individual help for himself. In fact, I'd like to make the call right here, now, in the office, so you can hear everything I say.

MOM: Oh, so I can be here?

THERAPIST: Yes, you can hear everything, and we will let them know that the most important thing here is to get the help you need so that the interactions with Matteus and his daddy go better.

MOM: Okay, yes, then let's do it now.

In this vignette, the therapist shows respect, support, and inclusion of the client and his mother, despite having to make the report of abuse and possible neglect. He also adheres to the principles of Beneficence, Fidelity, and Veracity. The therapist prepares the mom for how it will go and what he will say, and assures her that he will let the child protective services know how hard they have been working and how willing they have been to attend therapy. The turnout in this case is that the family decided to stay on with the therapist, and they worked with him through the investigation, in-home services, anger management and substance use interventions, as well as lots of eventual family therapy. How do you feel about the way the therapist handled the reporting?

Sometimes, deciding on when one must break confidentiality can be confusing for therapists and counselors. Consider the following clinical examples, and think about whether you think confidentiality needs to be broken and a report needs to be made:

1 A supervisor is meeting with a (student) therapy intern who is seeing a 15-year-old client for treatment. During the third session, the client reports she was using drugs and getting drunk on a regular basis. The supervisor decided the client needed to be evaluated for substance use, and told the therapy intern to talk to the client's parents about getting the client a substance use assessment. The therapist did not want to share this info with the parents for fear the teen would feel betrayed and end treatment.

Sticky: The client is a minor, so the therapist needs to be concerned both about the substance use and about the therapeutic relationship. If the therapist discloses the substance use to the parents, the client will likely feel angry and betrayed. However, if the therapist does not tell the parents, and something bad happens to the client while under the influence, the therapist will not have upheld the principles of Beneficence and Non-Maleficence. The parents would likely be very angry that the therapist did not inform them of the client's use, and might even have a case to sue the therapist for neglecting to report a minor being in danger.

Boil it Down: Sometimes it is difficult to make the judgment call of what things constitute a client "being at risk" in a way that warrants breaking confidentiality. The student therapist might just choose to follow the supervisor's directive (as the student is likely practicing "under" the supervisor's license anyway). Trust of one's supervisor is imperative. However, the student therapist is responsible for following laws and rules and codes, regardless of whether the supervisor does so. Remember that therapists and counselors must know the applicable laws and rules where they practice as it pertains to minors and reporting!

When you read the vignette, is there information missing that you'd like to know when making a decision in the situation? Are you curious to know what "getting drunk" entails? I know some 15-year-olds who "get drunk" off half of a lite beer. I have also had clients that brag or embellish in order to fit in or be cool. Where is the client getting the alcohol and drugs? From a parent's liquor cabinet? Or from a drug deal downtown after dark, or stealing it from a convenience store? There may be differences in the risk factor depending on these details. A thorough examination of the situation at hand, including important context is important.

So, what should the student therapist do here? The student therapist could have a discussion with the supervisor, expressing the concerns, and the two could work together to navigate the sensitive nature of the situation. Since the client is a minor, perhaps it is best for the student therapist to err on the side of caution and involve the parents, regardless of the potential for losing the client's trust.

There's one thing that's important to *not* forget here. The therapist has the 15-year-old client right there! In the vignette above, before deciding what to do, the therapist had an honest conversation with the client. The therapist said:

> I wanted to talk to you about something. I've been kind of feeling stuck here—you shared that you've been getting drunk lately, and doing drugs. I want you to have a safe space here to talk about those things, but I'm also required by law to report anything that I think might seriously endanger you. Not only that, but I care about you and your well-being, and I wouldn't feel right just letting you walk out the door today if I really felt concerned that something very bad might happen to you. And I know you think that nothing will happen, but I've seen lots of situations where that hasn't been the case.

In the discussion, the therapist showed up authentically to the client, and was practicing the principles of Beneficence, Non-Maleficence, Fidelity, and Veracity. The therapist "eased into" the more direct request for the client to understand and support the decision to contact the parents to discuss together in a family session. The therapist rehearsed the session and what they were going to say and *not* say. This helped the client feel more comfortable with the therapist's decision. This approach, to the best of their ability, preserved the possibility that the therapist could continue treatment with the client throughout the disclosure process and subsequent decisions. There is always the risk of "losing" clients and their trust by making legally or ethically required breaks of confidentiality. However, there is much that the therapist or counselor can do to try to avoid this by attending to the therapeutic alliance throughout.

2 A 12-year-old client tells his therapist that he has a "girlfriend" at school who he is worried about because she has lost weight and doesn't eat and told him she wants to die. The therapist tells the client that there will

need to be a report made on the girlfriend, because she is in danger. The client adamantly refuses and yells at the therapist, "No! You can't tell anyone. You told me what I say is private in these sessions! And my girlfriend would be *so* mad at me and probably never talk to me again if anybody knew about this. She would absolutely know it was me who told if anyone approached her about it! And I'm the only one she has..."

Sticky: The girlfriend is not the therapist's client. The therapist also does not have proof that her client is telling the truth, nor if his youthful and inexperienced assessment of his girlfriend is accurate. However, the therapist is a mandated reporter, and she has been given concerning information. The therapist considers the ***Autonomy*** of the client in what is shared outside of the session.

Boil it Down: Yes, all clients have some autonomy, but autonomy does not negate laws and rules on reporting risk of youths. First, the therapist needs to revisit the policies and rules on what is private and confidential in sessions, and what might not be. This is an important thing to do regularly, across the board with all clients, especially minors.

Next, the therapist needs to know the laws and regulations in the place of their practice, specific to reporting the endangerment or risk of a minor. If the therapist has a supervisor, it is a very good idea to consult with that person.

Like the vignette prior to this one, more details and context might be helpful when making a decision here. The therapist can ask more questions. For example, questions about the client's girlfriend's weight (e.g., How much has she lost, and in what timeframe?), if anyone else has noticed or said something to the girlfriend about her weight, what *exactly* the girlfriend said about wanting to die, or about other possible suicidal signs like depression, isolation, mood changes, or being bullied.

One ethical course of action is as follows. The client reported to the therapist that he thinks other kids have noticed his girlfriend's weight loss and have made comments to her about it. The therapist then reminds the client that it's possible that *any* kid could have told a teacher or guidance counselor about the girlfriend's weight loss or being teased. Then the therapist asks the client for permission to call the school guidance counselor and report the concern about the girlfriend. The therapist promises to ask the counselor to keep the concerns general, so as not to identify the client. The therapist also asks the client for permission to contact his parents and simply tell them that he had concerns about someone at school that might need help. With some coaxing, and validation for the importance of helping his girlfriend, the client agreed. The school counselor approached the girlfriend's parents and told them she had some concerns about what some teachers and kids had overheard about their child. The counselor asked the parents to seek out therapy for the girl, and set up twice-a-week check-ins with the girl at school.

Please note that the therapist did not need to do any of this prior to reporting. If the therapist believed in good faith that there was a child at real risk for suicidality, she could have just made the report. However, in trying to respect and support the client and the trust of their therapeutic relationship, the therapist attempted to include the client in the process. Fortunately, it worked in the best interests of all parties.

Record Keeping

Record keeping is a requirement in *all* mental health codes of ethics. The various codes include different specifics like keeping records that are necessary for professional practice (e.g., ACA), that accurately reflect clinical information (e.g., NASW), that are made in a timely manner (e.g., APA), and that document and record only information directly relevant to session (e.g., NASW). Regarding the recording of information that is directly relevant to the session, consider the following clinical example:

> A therapist, Aaliyah, had a client who was a 40-year-old single mother of four children. Aaliyah saw the client for six months. The client had presented with feeling overwhelmed, not having any support or help with the kids, financial instability, and a poor relationship with the father of her children. Aaliyah had been successful in helping the client get community support and financial assistance for childcare, and helped her develop better communication stances and boundaries to use in interactions with her ex-husband. When the client reported feeling much stronger and healthier, Aaliyah terminated therapy with the client. Five years later, Aaliya received a request for the entire clinical record from the client and her attorney. The client had hired an attorney to attempt to get two of her children back after the child protection agency in her state pulled the children out of her care for issues of neglect. After getting the appropriate release of information from the ex-client, Aaliyah pulled the client's chart and re-oriented herself with the information there, and prepared to send an encrypted email to the attorney's office for her ex-client. Aaliya saw some of her notes in the chart, and suddenly became uncomfortable. She reads her typed notes: "Client was overwhelmed and distressed with her kids and shared that she was about ready to give them away if she couldn't make them behave. Client admitted to locking herself in her room or going outside for a walk to get away from the kids. Client is struggling with parenting issues."

Sticky: Especially if taken out of context, one could read the notes as being the backdrop for eventual abuse or neglect. Aaliyah is worried about releasing the notes, as she is aware of the dire straits the client is currently in, and doesn't want to do her harm by giving them information that may be damning.

Boil it Down: Aaliyah must give the unaltered notes to the client if she has requested them, and if she has signed the appropriate releases. It is good that Aaliyah is thinking of the principle of Non-Maleficence in not wanting to harm the client by making her look bad. In fact, Aaliyah's perception of the client was that she was a good mother, and was anything but neglectful to the children. One ethical course of action would be for Aaliyah to contact her prior client and explain her concerns about some of the notes and how they might come off as reflecting negatively on the client. Aaliyah could then give the notes to the client, and offer to write a letter that speaks to the strengths and positives of her experience with the client. Of course, Aaliyah must be very careful to only speak to her past experience with the client, and make it clear that she cannot offer any insight into what has occurred with the client and her children since they ended treatment. ***Veracity*** is important here. Perhaps most importantly, Aaliyah has learned to pay more attention to her note taking. When asked in retrospect what she would have written for that day's note if she could do it over in a fashion that was more accurate, she responded with this:

> Client reported feeling overwhelmed and distressed with some of her kids' actions and how they treated each other. Client shared that she was "about ready to give them away," if she couldn't make them behave. Therapist explored what the client meant by these statements, and assessed that the client was joking. Therapist focused the remaining session on exploring what techniques the client was using for behavioral issues, and helping client implement more tools for this. Client shared that she locked herself in her room, and went outside for a walk to get away from the kids this week. Therapist assessed for safety of kids during this time, appropriateness of intervention, and helped client strategize for finding more support and time for self-care, and for exploring the roots of her frustration. Overall, client is making solid efforts, has a good parenting skill set, and is eager to continue working on parenting issues.

How do you feel about Aaliyah's chart note now? Would it be a more accurate reflection of her experiences with the client, and leave less openings for someone to misinterpret or inappropriately use the lack of detail in the first note against the client? Do you think Aaliyah offered too much, too little, or just the right amount of information here?

A good "rule of thumb" that I recommend to my graduate students is to write or type your notes while you pretend that your client, a "pitbull" attorney, or the general public was looking and reading over your shoulder. That can be a good self-check to be sure the notes are accurate, and written in a professional and appropriate format. If your session notes were displayed on a jumbotron in Times Square on New Year's Eve in New York City for everyone to see, would you feel comfortable with that?

Due to the variations of this code, and many of the other ethics' standards across the different mental health professional codes, it's imperative that therapists and counselors understand and abide by the specifics of their own code. The general themes are often similar, but the specifics most certainly vary between APA, NASW, ACA, and AAMFT.

One reason for documentation and record keeping is to retain an accurate "snapshot" of what the clinical treatment included, and the information surrounding that. Therapists and counselors cannot be expected to remember every client, and what happened in each session with them forever! Documentation creates a written record that can have many uses.

Another reason record keeping is important is that it helps to clearly draw the line between a professional, clinical relationship with formal recordings and a relationship that feels more casual, like a "friendship." Notes may ensure that a therapist or counselor is staying within appropriate therapeutic work with clients. Additionally, the notes add a layer of accountability if there are ever concerns about the work within the therapeutic relationship.

Records can help the therapist or counselor have (and give clients if requested) accurate documentation of things like session dates, payment, diagnoses, medication changes, interventions and feedback, etc. This information is vital when looking at the coordination of care with other providers (such as medical doctors, lawyers, psychiatrists) that may be involved in the client's treatment. Likewise, accurate record keeping allows any future providers of clients (who are no longer seen by a particular therapist or counselor) to receive a record of treatment to facilitate the continuation of care with the prior clients. To some clients, it may also be important for them to have records so they are able to track the specifics of their *own* history of care.

Not only does documentation have practical purposes, but it can also support and protect both clients *and* therapists and counselors. This is why it is a required part of "best practices" in conducting therapy.

There are a few additional notes on documentation in therapy that are important to consider. First, therapists and counselors may *not* withhold a client's records directly because of unpaid fees or balances according to *all* the mental health codes. How therapists and counselors manage unpaid fees, balances, and the collection of them is a separate policy that should be outlined in the informed consent and financial paperwork at the first meeting. A client's record may include information about financial discussions, but it is not a reason to withhold a client's clinical information.

Next is the importance of the storage and disposal of any documentation regarding a client and the clinical treatment. How long client files must be stored before destroying fluctuates greatly depending on where a therapist or counselor practices. Different states and provinces vary on other specific requirements here, so it is vital that therapists and counselors are up to date on the rules and regulations of the location in which they are licensed and/or practicing.

General ethical rules on the storage and disposal of clinical documentation hinges mainly on the standard of confidentiality. This means that charts need to be stored securely, in a manner that ensures that the protected health information (PHI) of a client is not accessible without the client's consent. This is true for both hard copy items and electronic files. There are many therapy platform choices that offer secure, encrypted ways of storage and communication with clients. It is also possible to "stitch" together the parts of a therapy practice in secure ways as well (e.g., teletherapy platform, end-to-end encrypted email, secure file storage).

What is a Business Associate Agreement, or BAA? When therapists and counselors are considering privacy and confidentiality, the BAA is an important part of this. Especially for those providers practicing solo, or in small group practices, it can be an arduous task to properly secure everything internally. When looking for what services to use in delivering one's practice, a BAA is an agreement between the therapist or counselor and a third-party vendor that they partner with for services (e.g., Zoom™ tele platform, or Square™ billing services) that ensures that the vendor understands the PHI regulations of clients' information. They have securities in place to protect clients' PHI. This BAA is legally binding and gives the therapist peace of mind that if they are giving confidential information (e.g., session dates, diagnoses, procedure codes) to a third party, that information will be secure and protected.

"In accordance with applicable law" is a common add-on to various code standards. This is because the codes cannot accurately reflect all of the laws that govern therapists and counselors in the various places that they practice. I cannot stress enough how important it is for therapists and counselors to know the rules and regulations in the location(s) in which they practice. Additionally, these regulations can change quickly, so regularly checking state or province websites or other documents is a *must*.

Chapter Takeaways for Therapists and Counselors

1. "Privilege" is a legal term, and means that the provider may not be required by law to disclose the information of their communications over the objection of the patient or client.
2. "Confidentiality" is the requirement that information disclosed in therapy won't be shared with anyone else without prior consent. There are several conditions when a therapist or counselor may need to break confidentiality. Those include in cases where the therapist or counselor believes that a client is an immediate danger to themselves (e.g., suicidality) or an immediate danger to others (e.g., homicidality), where there is suspected abuse or neglect of a minor or other protected population, and in legal situations where a subpoena is served to the therapist or counselor.
3. "Privacy" describes a client's right to be protected from others having knowledge about their personal choices (like going to therapy).

Although this is not a therapy mandate, it is an ethical standard that all therapists and counselors should try to maintain within reason.

4 *All* therapists and counselors must keep professional, clinical records.

5 Different states and provinces vary on specific requirements of record storage and disposal, so it is vital that therapists and counselors are up to date on the rules and regulations of the location in which they are licensed and/or practicing.

6 Therapists and counselors may *not* withhold a client's records directly because of unpaid fees or balances according to *all* the mental health codes.

7 A Business Associate Agreement (BAA) is an agreement between the therapist or counselor and a third-party vendor that they partner with for services that ensures that the vendor understands the PHI regulations of clients' information. This BAA is legally binding, and gives the therapist peace of mind that if they are giving confidential information (e.g., session dates, diagnoses, procedure codes) to a third party, that information will be secure and protected.

5 Professional Obligations

It can be easy for therapists and counselors to slip away from professional obligations, especially when there is a minimal chance there will be any negative outcome from doing so. Some examples might be "I'm getting behind on clinical notes—no big deal, I'll get to them in a couple of weeks when things slow down" or "I have to renew my license, but I haven't done the required continuing education (CE) trainings this year—no big deal, who is going to check to see if I did them anyway?"

An integral part of an ethical practice is prioritizing the professional obligations that therapists and counselors are required to fulfill. Things like maintaining competence, staying up to date with records, licenses, and CE trainings, accuracy in advertising, and seeking help when necessary are all requirements at the core of ethical and sound treatment.

Competence

The Oxford Dictionary defines the word competence as "the ability to do something successfully or efficiently." More specifically, psychotherapeutic competence includes a therapist's general and treatment-specific *knowledge* and *skills*, as well as his/her ***values*** or *attitudes* while implementing interventions (e.g., Muse et al., 2016).

When looking at the art of doing therapy, what things make up competence? Perhaps more importantly, how is competence measured? Castonguay and Hill (2012) write, "We know that psychotherapy works—research shows that a substantial number of people who come to see therapists will not only benefit from therapy but will also demonstrate clinically meaningful change."

Despite different theoretical and empirical contributions, relatively little is known about the beliefs of laypersons as to what characterizes a competent therapist (Kühne et al., 2020). This is what prompted this team of researchers to design a questionnaire that centered on two important questions: "In your opinion, what makes a good/competent psychotherapist?" and "How do you recognize that a psychotherapist is not competent?" From their study's resulting data, Kühne et al. (2020) found that there were many things that people who had or had never had therapy thought made for a

DOI: 10.4324/9781003745136-6

competent therapist, including things like effective and professional interpersonal interactions with therapists, unbiased, non-judgmental therapists, and good listening and empathy, while maintaining eye contact from therapists.

So, how do we know if a therapist or counselor is "competent"? Let's start by looking into a few main areas that help build up a therapist's or counselor's ability to perform competent therapy.

Educational Credentials

All mental health professions in the United States have detailed requirements for who may practice in their specific fields. They generally begin with an educational track that yields a degree. For example, Licensed Clinical Social Workers (LCSWs) must first complete a master's degree in Social Work. Following the successful completion of a degree, the next step is generally obtaining a license in the discipline that one has gone to school for. This may include passing a national licensing exam, getting endorsements, and/or completing post-degree clinical hours and supervision. Each field and each state or province may have distinct requirements for those seeking to practice within that jurisdiction.

Along with educational credentials, there is also the topic of "accreditation" at an educational institution. Accreditation means that an institution is held accountable by an accrediting body, by regular review and the submission of documentation. The accrediting body monitors institutions and makes sure that they are engaging in established standards and meeting required levels of excellence. This ensures the overall quality of the educational experience that an institution's students and trainees will have. We can see here how holding an institution to a high standard of excellence through the accreditation process can contribute to graduates who will have the best chances of developing as competent therapists and counselors.

Training/Experience

All mental health training programs that yield professional clinical therapists or counselors have a clinical hours requirement. The *quantity* varies between different professions. This means that the number of clinical hours that training therapists and counselors must conduct in order to graduate, and then for subsequent licensure, can be different for counselors, social workers, psychologists, and marriage and family therapists.

The *quality* of a therapy or counseling student's training may vary as well. Some programs have an in-house clinic, while others partner with outside hospitals, clinics, schools, and agencies. Things like presenting issues, severity of mental health diagnoses, socioeconomic backgrounds, culture, family makeup, and dual diagnosis can vary from site to site. For this reason, some therapists and counselors may have graduated with a range of experiences, and therefore some might be more skilled and competent in certain areas than others are.

The quality of supervision that therapists and counselors in training receive can also influence their skills and competence. Fortunately, many training programs expose their students to a variety of professors and supervisors over their time in the program, thus allowing for a broader range of experience to learn from.

Continuing Education

A graduate degree and clinical training are foundational, but they are not all that is needed to ensure competence in therapists and counselors throughout their career. Times and generations change, societal and political landscapes shift, and new research on therapy and best practices is churned out every year. It is for these reasons that therapists and counselors must ethically continue their education throughout their careers, in order to stay competent and relevant.

Many states and provinces now have requirements for license renewal that includes obtaining a certain number of Continuing Education Units (CEUs) or Continuing Education Credits (CECs). There may be state-specific types of training required, including a common one—*ethics*! Additionally, some states might have limits on how many hours can be self-paced learning (like reading an article and taking a quiz at the end for credits). Since the Pandemic, there are so many more remote opportunities to obtain continuing education; however, some states have a certain number or percent of units that *must* be taken in person. Likewise, states and provinces, and professional bodies differ in whether therapists and counselors can count CEUs/CECs from other related professions.

It is therapists' and counselors' responsibility to know their state and province standards and requirements for licensure, including CE. The requirement of CE helps to ensure the competence of therapists and counselors by making sure they are up to date on the latest models, theories, trends, and research in their profession. In addition, CE helps therapists and counselors brush up on skill sets they may already have, but don't use often. The units may also be an instrumental part of learning new skills, and updating others.

Seeking Assistance

As we've explored above, the educational and training components of becoming a therapist vary greatly. However, regardless of the quantity, quality, and type of training and education a therapist or counselor received, the various codes of ethics hold those individuals responsible for ensuring they have the ***competence*** to practice. Read the vignette below, and consider whether the therapist (Mo) that her client (Pauline) is reporting to the supervisor is competent to perform her duties as a therapist:

PAULINE: Thanks for making the time to meet with me. I finally stopped seeing my therapist, Mo, here at the agency last week and felt like I needed to report her to you. I don't think she should be a therapist.

SUPERVISOR: I'm happy to make the time, Pauline. I'm so sorry this was your experience with Mo, but I am eager to hear about your experience, since you sound very upset.

PAULINE: I have only seen a therapist once before, so maybe I'm not an expert here, but I don't think Mo should be doing the things she does.

SUPERVISOR: Can you give me some examples, Pauline?

PAULINE: Sure. She takes calls while she's in session with me, she's chronically late and sometimes doesn't show up at all, and I'm waiting on Zoom for like 20 minutes before she messages me that she needs to cancel. She talks a lot about herself—too much if you ask me. And then tells me what to do, even though I've said that's not what I'm interested in doing. And honestly, I think I bore her, because she looks zoned out in sessions, yawns, and says things I have no idea what she's trying to say. And she tells me things sometimes that I don't even think are correct.

SUPERVISOR: (taking notes): What sorts of things does Mo say that you think are not correct?

PAULINE: Well, like that my daughter's mood swings when she's manic could lead to her killing herself. Mo said bipolar people take their own lives often.

SUPERVISOR: I want to thank you for reaching out and letting me know about your experience with Mo. I apologize for the situations that have made you feel uncomfortable, and I assure you that I will meet with Mo to discuss these things and address some of your concerns. In the meantime, I'd love to offer for you to see another therapist at our agency, and I will make sure we can get you an appointment right away.

In the vignette, there are several concerning things that Pauline shared with Mo's supervisor. However, it's hard to tell from the basic dialogue how much is Mo's therapeutic incompetence and how much Mo has things going on that might be interfering with her ability to be present in an appropriate manner for her client. In this vignette, is it possible that the client could have shared these thoughts and experiences with Mo directly, and she would have been able to hear the client and respond in a way that would have salvaged the usefulness of the therapy? Or is Mo simply chaotic, irresponsible, uninformed, or unskilled at therapy? It's hard to know.

A requirement of clinical ethics is that Mo is responsible not only for her competence in doing therapy, but also for seeking assistance if she has issues or constraints that may be getting in the way of her being competent. For example, let's say that Mo is going through a difficult divorce, has calls coming in from her lawyer and her child's school, and is not sleeping well, all of which lead to distractibility and poor time management. Although understandable, it is not an excuse for incompetence. If Mo's personal experiences are causing her to forget clinical appointments, take calls and be distracted when doing therapy, and be short and insensitive (or inaccurate) in her responses to clients, it is her responsibility to both be aware of this and seek assistance.

What are some ways that therapists or counselors can get support or assistance when they feel they might be incompetent, or that their ability to perform competent therapy may be compromised? Utilizing supervision is a great start. Attending their own therapy, getting treatment and/or medication for substance use disorders or other mental health issues like depression, or taking a short leave from their practice are other good ideas for therapists and counselors who find themselves in these situations. But in *any* case, it is important to remember that codes of ethics require therapists and counselors to be responsible for recognizing their need for assistance. Self-awareness and accountability are *key* here.

Gatekeeping Roles

There are certain entities that have the gatekeeping role of ensuring competence. Graduate school instructors and supervisors have an important task in reasonably ensuring this. For this reason, instructors and supervisors must hold their students, interns, or employees accountable for both competence in the therapy setting and adherence to their profession's code of ethics.

In the educational setting, while still in training, instructors and supervisors are responsible for students and interns. Since they are not yet degreed or licensed, it is generally expected that the educational programs will be responsible for students' and interns' competence and performance through monitoring, measuring competencies, observation, etc.

Once graduated and/or licensed, therapists and counselors must serve as their own "gatekeepers" on competence and ethics, although their supervisors may have some governance over this. Some states and provinces have standards and regulations that require therapists or supervisors to report the unethical or incompetent behaviors of other therapists or counselors. The main mental health codes of ethics also require this.

In short, clients may not recognize a therapist's or counselor's incompetence; clients often do not know what therapists or counselors are supposed to know or do, especially if they have never been to another therapist before. In keeping with the ethical principle of Beneficence and protecting clients' best interests, it makes sense that there are gatekeepers to competence in the mental health professions.

Client Feedback, Outcomes, and Effective Treatment

Many times in this text, the idea of leaning into your clients for how to navigate tricky issues will be highlighted. Therapists and counselors often forget that their clients are right there in front of them, and they have full access to appropriately asking, discussing, and sharing with them. Working *with* clients is an excellent first step for receiving feedback on the efficacy of therapists' or counselors' treatment.

When thinking about a therapist's or counselor's competence, getting clients' feedback is important. The most simple and basic way for therapists and counselors to do this is by checking in with clients. Consider the following dialogue between a therapist, Pat, and his client, Jamie:

PAT: If it's okay with you, Jamie, I'd like to spend a few minutes to start our session by checking in with you.

JAMIE: Ummmm…sure? What did you want to check in on?

PAT: Well, we've been seeing other for a few months now, and I wanted to check in on how you think therapy is going.

JAMIE: Oh, okay. Well, it's going fine, I guess. I feel less depressed. And I definitely know how to deal with my boyfriend better.

PAT: Okay, that's good. I'm glad to hear that, Jamie. Are there any things you were hoping for in therapy that I haven't covered?

JAMIE: No, I don't think so.

PAT: Okay. I like to check in with my clients periodically to see if they feel like therapy is effective and meeting their needs. I like to be sure my skill set meets your expectations.

JAMIE: Yeah, I think you've been very helpful.

The therapist here checked in with his client on things that might point towards his competence. Questions like "Do you feel like therapy has been effective?" or "Are there things you had hoped I'd cover but haven't?" or "Do you feel like my style and skill sets meet your needs and expectations?" are useful prompts for clients that can help the therapist or counselor get important feedback. However, it is important to remember here that there is not a perfect overlap between effectiveness and competence. Sometimes, an effective therapist or counselor might be incompetent, and vice versa. Effectiveness is one possible data point to consider, but not the only one when it comes to looking at competence!

Another way for therapists and counselors to gauge their competency and effectiveness is to measure clients' outcomes. Some therapists or counselors use standardized measures to track things like the client's satisfaction with the therapy, changes in symptoms, or the improvement of a client's presenting issue. For example, the Better Outcomes Now website (https://betteroutcomesnow.com) offers outcome tools that

> involve a real-time collaborative comparison of client views of outcome with an expected treatment response that serves as a yardstick for gauging client progress and signaling when change is not occurring as predicted. With this alert, counselors, clients, and organizations have an opportunity to shift focus, revisit goals, or alter interventions before deterioration or dropout.

Using measurement tools to better track the efficacy of treatment and competence of the therapist or counselor is an important way to ensure that clients' experiences are considered and included when looking at competence.

The efficacy of treatment is one possible indicator of a therapist's or counselor's competence. When clients go to therapy, they are hopeful that the therapist or counselor has tools and strategies that will help them feel better. Indeed, well-trained, knowledgeable, experienced providers should have a multitude of ideas and interventions for helping the clients they see. Therapists and counselors should not only ask their clients, but also themselves on a regular basis, things like: *Are my clients improving? Are they feeling better? Are they navigating things well? Are they learning new strategies that have helped them function more effectively?*

"Expertise"

Therapists and counselors, in abiding by the ethical principle of Veracity, must strive to be truthful with clients about any areas that they tout as areas of expertise. The Oxford Dictionary defines "expertise" as "Expert knowledge or skill in a particular subject, activity, or job." The definition is not particularly helpful in deciphering *specifically* what is necessary to constitute having *expertise*! However, there are some general things that therapists and counselors should consider here.

First, if a therapist or counselor is touting their expertise in an area—let's say working with eating disorders—the following might add credence to that claim:

1 The therapist or counselor has had a prior internship or employment at a clinic that specializes in eating disorders.
2 The therapist or counselor is experienced with this population, having had many clients who suffer from eating disorders, and worked successfully with them.
3 The therapist or counselor has advanced training, certification, or coursework in the particulars of this treatment.

"Scope of practice" is a term that is often used when exploring areas like competence and expertise from a legal lens. Therapists and counselors need to be careful to *not* practice outside their scope of practice, meaning that they should not be doing things they are not competent to do with clients. This is where many codes of ethics will fall. For example, let's say that a newly licensed psychologist opens a private practice and decides to list "specializes in couples' treatment" on their webpage. Ethically, the psychologist should have been trained and supervised in at least some couples' work models, and worked effectively with many couples before.

"I want to work with [in my practice]" does not equate with the descriptors "specializes in" or "expertise in." Being honest about one's scope of practice is one way to ethically ensure that clients have accurate information from which to make decisions about their care (Autonomy).

Informed Consent

Informed consent is arguably one of the most important documents a therapist or counselor creates when it comes to the ethical principles of Fidelity and Veracity. This is the document that describes, in writing, everything the therapist or counselor wants clients to know. It explains the rules and policies, and specifically how everything will go in therapy, from billing or recording practices, to the limits of confidentiality and things like a "no secrets" policy.

It is the therapist's or counselor's responsibility not only to create a thorough document and share it with clients, but also to explore and discuss it with them to ensure they understand everything contained in it. This confirmation of understanding can be documented in the client's chart. Having a copy of the informed consent can be an invaluable tool for clients to refer back to as situations come up in therapy that may feel confusing to them. When the informed consent is first introduced, clients might *think* they understand it, but they may "forget" policies, practices, etc. when they are in times of distress. For this reason, it is also important for therapists and counselors to revisit the informed consent with clients, especially if issues come up in therapy that directly relate to those policies. For example, before a therapist or counselor agrees to have the spouse of a client join in sessions, it would be helpful to remind the client of any particular policies surrounding this. Some examples might be informing the client that:

1 The therapist will be billing a different service code to the client's insurance company—for example, couples' session code instead of individual psychotherapy code.
2 The therapist will create a separate chart for the couples' documentation, and should either party want those notes, *both* parties will have to agree and sign off on this (this may have slight variations by state or province).
3 The client's spouse must sign all the appropriate paperwork and intake documents, HIPAA, etc., before joining the therapy.

These are a few items from the informed consent that the client might have breezed by and forgotten since he or she initially came on as an individual therapy client. Now that the client has decided to transition to couples' work with the therapist, it is important to review some of the policies that pertain to treating couples, rather than individuals.

The informed consent, and subsequent documentation of a discussion with the client that yielded confirmation of understanding the contents, is a responsibility of the therapist or counselor that ensures the client is an accurately informed party in the therapy. Likewise, the informed consent can protect the therapist or counselor by ensuring they have done their own due diligence in making sure the client is informed and understands, thereby adhering to a framework that honors the foundational ethical principles.

As it pertains to competency, expertise, etc., the informed consent is the place where anything and everything that therapists or counselors want clients to know and understand resides. This is where therapists and counselors can share information about their training and areas of expertise, as well as the limitations they may have. They might also include here the possibility of referring to another provider with more experience in a certain area, if the therapist or counselor and the client feel that a different scope of practice or different specialty or training might be more beneficial to the client.

Advertising

Therapists and counselors, much like folks in other businesses, may choose to advertise their practices to get more "customers" or clients. Also like others, therapists' and counselors' practices generate income that is used for them to pay their bills and live on. Advertising their practices can be an important part of exposure and marketing for providers. However, an important part of many mental health codes of ethics includes mandating that therapists and counselors are mindful of *accurately* advertising their practices. The following are some common advertising mistakes that I've seen therapists and counselors make:

1 Inaccurate listing of a degree. For example, a new Masters in Social Work graduate lists herself as an "LCSW" on her practice website.

Sticky: Although she has the degree and has passed the national exam, she cannot obtain a license until she has completed other steps. States and provinces vary greatly in the specifics of what is required after graduation (such as 1,500 additional clinical hours), before full licensure is allowed. Additionally, different states and provinces may have different requirements for how these folks advertise themselves. For example, some states require the pre-licensed therapist to use the term "associate" or "pre-licensed intern" in their title until full licensure has been achieved.

Boil it Down: This therapist needs to check her state or province's website for licensing information, and for the requirements for accurate displays and advertising. It is the responsibility of *every* therapist or counselor to ensure this.

2 Inaccurate listing of areas of expertise. For example, a therapist lists "Expertise in sex therapy with individuals, couples, and other intimate relationships."

Sticky: "Expertise in Sex Therapy" needs some clarity here. What's the difference between this therapist's offerings and those of a *Certified Sex Therapist*? Although therapists and counselors know the difference here, clients likely will not. Clients might easily assume both offerings are the same thing.

Boil it Down: Ethically, the therapist could easily reword the listing to be more accurate, as well as to ensure more clarity on what the therapist *actually* specializes in. I doubt that therapists or counselors exploring sexual issues with a client would consider themselves as "expert" as a Certified Sex Therapist. A better, more accurate listing for the therapist might be "Experienced in working with individuals, couples, and other intimate relationships who present with sexual concerns, or wanting to enhance their sex lives."

3 Inaccurate use of another degree. For example, a therapist advertises himself as "John Smythe, LCSW, PhD."

Sticky: John is accurately displaying his degrees, however, only the LCSW degree is in a mental health field. His PhD is in Computer Science. Clients would have no way of knowing what his PhD was in, and would therefore assume it was in a mental health field.

Boil it Down: Although John is displaying degrees that he did, in fact, earn, it is John's responsibility to ensure he follows the ethical principle of Veracity, by ensuring that clients know what degrees he has, and which ones will be used in treatment. Including the PhD in a very unrelated field misleads clients and may "trick" them into thinking he has more advanced degrees and training as a therapist than he really does. It is best for John to omit the "PhD" from his advertising for his clinical practice. Conversely, if he really wants to display the "PhD," he needs to clarify that it is in Computer Science.

Another facet of ethical advertising that mental health codes of ethics require is the correction of any false information that a therapist or counselor becomes aware of. This has become increasingly more difficult with the advancements of the internet and the prevalence of artificial intelligence (AI). It can be difficult to keep up with any incorrect or misleading information that might pop up about a therapist's or counselor's training, degrees, or practice. Therefore, you will often hear language like "within reason" to describe the responsibility of the therapist or counselor to correct misinformation. In short, if a therapist or counselor uncovers information that lists the wrong degree, prior experience they did not have, a practice specialty they are not trained in, etc., they must immediately attempt to correct it.

Assumptions or lack of knowledge of clients can also contribute to misinformation. For example, consider the dialogue below between a therapist, Jake Calloway, LPC, and his client, Benny:

BENNY: Hey, Dr. Calloway! How was your weekend?

THERAPIST: Hi, Benny. My weekend was great—how about yours?

BENNY: It was pretty good! I told my boyfriend you helped me a lot, even though we only had one meeting last week. Even he says I'm in a better mood. He told me you are a shrink with a magic wand, haha.

THERAPIST: I'm really glad to hear that you have been feeling better, and that there was some stuff we talked about last week that seemed to be helpful to you and made you feel better. That's great.

BENNY: Sure is!

THERAPIST: And, Benny, there's something I'd like to clarify quickly if I could? First, you called me "Dr." Calloway when you came in, and I wanted to correct that for you—I'm not a doctor of any kind. I'm also a counselor, not a "shrink." A "shrink" is a casual name for a psychiatrist—and a psychiatrist *is* a doctor—a medical doctor actually—and they can prescribe medications, which is something I cannot.

BENNY: Oh! I thought all therapists were doctors and could prescribe medication! Thanks for clarifying that, MISTER Calloway! Is that okay, then?

THERAPIST: Sure, it's okay, Benny, but most clients just call me "Jake," if that works for you?

In this vignette, the therapist does a good job of correcting misinformation for his client, in a way that maintains his therapeutic relationship. This is an excellent example of the therapist maintaining both accuracy and understanding for the client, as well as maintaining the ethical principle of Veracity.

Accurate advertising and the timely correction of any errors ensure that clients have the full and correct understanding of a therapist's or counselor's background, training, skill sets, etc. It is also an important part of adhering to the ethical principles of Veracity and Fidelity in clinical practice.

Plans for Practice

All of the mental health codes have some reference to the responsibility of providers to ensure some sort of plan for the care and continuation of services for clients in the case of incapacitation or death. In keeping with the ethical principles of Beneficence and Non-Maleficence, therapists and counselors need to have a plan for the support and continuation of care of clients, should an expected or unexpected event occur that would influence the clinical practice.

Given that the welfare of clients is always paramount, the most important factors in the case of the therapist or counselor needing to temporarily step away, or in the case of incapacitation or death, may be:

1. Not leaving clients without treatment and support (non-abandonment).
2. Ensuring the confidential protection and handling of client records (confidentiality).
3. Ensuring minimal disruption in care (Beneficence).

For example, what happens if a therapist or counselor gets into a terrible car accident on the way to the office and is hospitalized and in a coma for the better part of week? Who will know to inform the clients and cancel their appointments, given the confidentiality of who sees the therapist or counselor? What if some of the clients were in crisis at the time of the therapist's or counselor's accident and need immediate attention? Some of these things might be mitigated if a therapist or counselor works in a group practice or agency, where others are aware of and regularly manage phone calls and emails from clients, and interact with their files.

However, in a private practice setting, there may not be a single other person that knows a client is in therapy. Furthermore, a therapist's or counselor's family members and friends will not know the names or any other identifying information about the clients their loved one had been seeing. So, what are some ethical ways that therapists and counselors can best prepare for situations like these?

First, death, incapacitation, injury, unexpected hospitalization, pregnancy, and medical leaves are a few of the situations that might leave clients unsupported. Although not always avoidable, reasonable plans should be in place, and discussions should be had, about what would happen in the case of a therapist or counselor experiencing one of these issues. Information can be included in the intake paperwork, and revisited in any situation in which the therapist or counselor becomes aware of a possible need for a lapse in treatment.

Next, therapists and counselors can provide a family member or colleague with instructions and a short script for a message to leave on the therapist's or counselor's business or cell voicemail in the case of a medical emergency. The message can contain local emergency resources, therapists, and other community hotlines and supports, and any other specific instructions on the situation. The family member can leave updates as needed. Additionally, the therapist's or counselor's website can be updated to include a message there as well.

Another idea that some therapists and counselors take on is to create a "professional" will that appoints someone to take care of the practice in the event of incapacitation or death. Very strict guidelines must be included here, ensuring the adherence to confidentiality and all state or province rules and regulations regarding the protection and disposal of records.

Role Reversal

When an accident, illness, pregnancy, or other emergency occurs that leaves a therapist or counselor needing to be away from clinical work, there can sometimes be a shift in the therapeutic relationship when the therapist or counselor returns to the office. Consider the following clinical description:

> Melanie is a therapist in private practice. During her final session one evening with a couple, Sam and Dani, the therapy is interrupted by a repeated series of Melanie's cell phone vibrating on the desk behind her.

MELANIE: I'm so sorry for the phone vibrating so much. I leave it on "do not disturb" during sessions, but my family knows how to call and ring through if it's an emergency. Would it be okay if I just picked this up quick? I'm so sorry.

SAM: Of course! Please, get the phone.

DANI: Yes, Melanie! Pick it up, it might be an emergency…

MELANIE: (after picking up the phone and listening for a minute to her mother who is talking frantically on the other end): I'm so sorry, but I'm going to need to end our session early and head out. My father has had a medical emergency, and I need to rush over to the hospital.

SAM: (standing up quickly and gathering his and Dani's jackets and personal items): Oh my gosh, we are so sorry Melanie. By all means, no worries, let's get you out of here. We'll keep you and your family in our thoughts and prayers tonight.

Melanie heads to the hospital, where she finds out that her father is being airlifted to the trauma center for a terrible brain bleed from a stroke, and she must drive her mother two hours away to the trauma facility. Melanie's father eventually pulls through, but she must cancel all her therapy sessions for nearly three weeks while she helps her aging mother navigate the critical situation and care facility placement, etc. that comes afterwards.

Melanie had emailed and checked in on all her clients to be sure they were able to be safe without meeting for a few weeks. She gave them all resources for emergencies in her absence, and documented all of it in each client's chart. Upon her return to the office a few weeks later, she found herself feeling a bit anxious and uncomfortable. Many of her clients had been emailing or leaving phone messages, telling her they were thinking of her and wondering how her dad was doing. On her first day back, and for many months afterwards, several of Melanie's clients started sessions by asking about her dad's health and how she was doing.

As explored and discussed previously in this chapter, therapists and counselors have a professional obligation to have reasonable plans for disruptions to their practice, and for the non-abandonment of clients. Melanie did a pretty good job of ensuring her clients were supported and given resources for emergencies during her absence. However, in doing so, she needed to self-disclose something about her family and the emergent situation. This allowed clients to see her a bit differently, and have empathy for her, which in turn prompted them to want to lend support and check in on Melanie.

There is nothing inappropriate or unethical or wrong about the very natural way that Melanie's clients have developed empathy and concern for her. After all, Melanie has been strong and supportive and helpful to them over and over again. Who *wouldn't* feel grateful and warmly about someone who has really shown up and been there for them?

The shift in Melanie's relationship with some of her clients, from *being* the support and helper for the clients, to being the one *getting* the support and feeling like the "helpee," is completely understandable and well meaning. The shift is also something that is important for Melanie to monitor ethically. For example, if Melanie continued to have worry and stress over her father's health, it would be easy for her to slip into spending more than a few seconds talking about herself and her parents in sessions where clients "opened the door" for her to talk about how she's doing. In sharing too much, therapists and counselors may inadvertently make the therapy about themselves, or let the sessions become too chummy and personal.

If Melanie were trying to ensure that the therapy stayed about the clients, and that she didn't lean too much on her clients for support during her own difficult times, how do you feel about the following interaction?

DANI: Oh, we're so glad you're back, Melanie! We've been worried sick about you.

SAM: Yes, we've been keeping you and your dad in our thoughts and prayers every day.

MELANIE: Thank you so much for your good thoughts and kind words. I appreciate that! We are all hanging in there. How have *you two* been?

DANI: Oh, please. We're fine. It's *you* who is having the hard time. We can only imagine...

MELANIE: Oh, Dani, that is very kind. And I appreciate you checking in, but I want you to know that everything is okay on my end, and that I'm looking forward to refocusing back on where you and I left off before my leave. I'd love to spend a few minutes getting caught up with what's been going on between you in the last few weeks that you think I should know about.

Kooperman (2013) succinctly describes the experience of therapists and counselors navigating situations like this: "It can feel overwhelming to balance one's own needs with the needs of clients, and it is especially difficult to listen to our clients' expressions of disappointment and anger when we are not always available to them."

This article also highlights the importance of having a practice plan for crisis, including appointing a trusted colleague with instructions, ensuring emergency access to clients' records, and seeking supervision to ensure the appropriate care for clients (Kooperman, 2013).

Chapter Takeaways for Therapists and Counselors

1 There are many things that contribute to a therapist's or counselor's competence, including their degrees, training, experience, and continuing education.

2. It is the therapist's or counselor's responsibility to seek assistance for any personal issue that might stand in the way of their competence in practicing therapy.
3. There are many "gatekeepers" to therapists' and counselors' competence, including instructors, supervisors, and employers.
4. When trying to determine competence in doing therapy, clients are an invaluable resource to get feedback from.
5. Informed cssonsent is arguably the most important document therapists and counselors create. This document should include all the information about the practice and policies so that clients are fully aware of the treatment protocols.
6. It is the responsibility of therapists and counselors to accurately advertise, as well as to make immediate attempts to correct any misinformation about themselves or their practice that they discover.
7. It is the responsibility of therapists and counselors to have plans in place for their practice in expected, or unexpected, situations like prolonged absence, illness, incapacitation, or death.

6 Technology, Teletherapy, and Social Media

As the advances in technology leap forward, faster than the speed of light, therapists and counselors can find themselves in a constant race to keep up. In order to maintain a competent and ethical clinical practice, it's important that therapists and counselors stay updated. How can they help ethics and science/technology "shake hands," and come together in a way that supports a competent clinical practice?

Although ongoing technological advances and teletherapy have been around for quite some time, the Pandemic thrust the majority of therapists and counselors into a world they were largely unfamiliar with, with very little preparation, support, or training. Utilizing these remote platforms and figuring out how to legally and ethically provide treatment, collect payment, etc., became a necessity. Having been a graduate therapy program director, the chair of the AAMFT Ethics Committee, and a private practitioner myself at that time, I can attest to the distressing and overwhelming nature of those early days.

Since then, many therapists and counselors have continued to use these platforms, and do so with far more knowledge, training, support, and competence. Since the Pandemic, there has been time for researchers to study the impact and efficacy of teletherapy, as well as the ethics and best practices of it. This chapter will focus specifically on the ethical components of competent teletherapy and the use of technology and social media. There are many books and resources and chapters dedicated solely to this topic area, but for this book, it is only one chapter. For this reason, readers should seek out far more than this chapter when preparing for all the technology involved in a teletherapy practice. There is simply not enough space and time to cover all the important nuances of these important topics here.

The following discussions, topics, and vignettes are meant to offer therapists and counselors some areas to think about, and clinical scenarios that demonstrate some dilemmas and possible solutions. Although the chapter is by no means all-encompassing, the hope is that there will be meaningful takeaways that will help enhance the readers' ethical and competent clinical practices.

DOI: 10.4324/9781003745136-7

Technology and Ethics

Unfortunately, technology is updating and changing faster than most therapists and counselors can keep up with it! However, it is still their responsibility to ensure that they use any technology in clinical practice competently and ethically. The following are some discussions on some of the main topic areas in technology.

Technology: Artificial Intelligence (AI)

The title of an American Psychological Association article (Abrams, 2026) best sums it up: "AI in the therapists' office: Uptake increases, caution persists." The article reports that almost one in three practitioners (29%) now use AI at least monthly in their practice. How do therapists and counselors use AI in their practices, and is it ethical?

Artificial intelligence (AI) is defined by the Oxford Dictionary as "The study and development of computer systems that can copy intelligent human behavior." These systems can be "trained" to emulate human abilities, and thus enabled to do things like thinking, creating, and decision-making that normally only actual humans can do. These systems increase productivity and make tasks happen more quickly and effortlessly. These are all things that can be of great assistance to humans in certain tasks, but are they ethical to use in the therapeutic setting?

There are many ways that therapists and counselors already use AI in their practices. Some of my friends and colleagues in the field use AI to create checklists, worksheets for clients, outlines for their professional presentations, or quizzes and tests. Others use AI to find information quickly, or for information on topics they may not know a lot about. But perhaps where the line of AI use gets "fuzzy" from an ethics point of view is when it is used in ways that may omit the essential layer of therapist or counselor assessment and judgment.

Consider the following areas that therapists or counselors might consider using AI for, and consider whether you think they are ethical to use in clinical practice:

1. Letting AI create ideas for possible treatment of clients presenting with certain diagnoses, e.g., major depression.
2. Letting AI handle note taking during therapy sessions so that the therapist or counselor can stay more present with the client.

In both scenarios above, there is the potential for stickiness that might include both illegal and/or unethical activity. The use of AI here may be more sensitive and risky, as it edges closer to things like clients' privacy and confidentiality. Since these things are mandated both legally and ethically, the use needs to be carefully vetted for compliance with laws and rules within the therapist's or counselor's jurisdiction.

In scenario #1, what if the client discovers that the therapist created treatment choices via AI? In an article in *Family Therapy Magazine* (Rastogi, 2025), the author describes a client who discovered that her therapist was using AI to partially conduct their sessions together. The article describes the client as feeling "shock and anguish," and terrified that her protected health information (PHI) and feelings were "out on the internet." Moreover, the client reported that she felt "completely misled and blindsided" by her therapist, and wondered why her therapist wasn't competent enough to conduct therapy with her without consulting AI. The client quickly terminated the therapy.

In scenario #2, there is the concern of where and how the notes are stored, who has access, if they are accurate, etc. An article by Psychology.org (Hudgens, 2025) highlighted a poignant example of how AI, and specifically the Large Language Model (LLM) "chatbots" that have become popular as coaches for clients, can be detrimental:

> When LLMs go rogue, they could give users false information or even harmful advice," McMahon said. She pointed to the National Eating Disorders Association's AI chatbot, Tessa, which was shut down after it began offering dieting tips to users struggling with eating disorders. "Trained human providers would know to avoid giving advice like that, but an AI chatbot might respond without following clinical judgment.

Perhaps the most prudent action by therapists and counselors is to consider the use of any sort of AI in their practice only *after* consulting with their clients. If the AI system will be used in a manner that touches on anything to do with the clients' PHI, therapists and counselors need to be certain they can ensure full compliance with all laws and rules.

Rastogi (2025) so wisely notes that:

> When therapists disclose client information with supervisors or for billing purposes, they obtain prior written consent for this. When supervisors use AI to help their trainees improve therapeutic interactions via the use of specialized software or generic AI programs, this too needs to be clearly explained to clients, or the information encrypted/deleted to protect PHI.

The article by Psychology.org (Hudgens, 2025) referred to above offers some suggested safeguards that therapists and counselors can put into place to help ensure the appropriate and ethical use of AI in clinical practice:

- Research all AI tools before using.
- Understand AI limitations.
- Prioritize safety and data privacy.
- Provide transparency and informed consent to all clients.

Gaddy summarized, "The therapeutic relationship is built on trust, empathy, and presence, key factors no algorithm can replicate" (Hudgens, 2025).

Technology: Email, Texting

In 2023, around 1.4 million mobile phones were stolen across the United States (Vincent & Sattar, 2024). In addition, although wonderfully small and portable, mobile phones are also very easy to lose, forget, or misplace. For these reasons, it is imperative that therapists and counselors do not keep sensitive information on their mobile devices. Doing so puts both the therapist or counselor and the client(s) at risk.

For the therapist or counselor, keeping sensitive, identifying, or HIPAA-protected client information on their phone leaves them potentially in violation of the standards of several codes of ethics. For the client(s), the risk is that their private and protected information may be unintentionally shared without their permission.

Some teletherapy options have their own secure messaging and texting capacity included within their system or device. For others, especially those who do not use an "all-in-one" platform, but rather piece together the parts of their practice, this may be a bit more difficult.

Regular cell phones do not have secure or encrypted texting. As per the Cybersecurity and Infrastructure Security Agency (CISA, n.d.), "cellular protocols do not provide end-to-end encryption for text messages and voice calls, and you can't guarantee that your phone is using the most secure protocol." According to this site, one can use apps with end-to-end encryption or Voice over Internet Protocol (VoIP), or add encrypted files to emails in order to maintain security. But what does the average therapist or counselor do when they just have a simple personal cell phone to use for their clinical practice? The following are some ideas for therapists and counselors to consider when thinking about having a competent and ethical practice:

- Does the therapist or counselor have written policies (that have been shared with clients via informed consent) on cell phone use? For example, do they give out their cell phone number? And is the number only to be used in emergencies?
- Has the therapist or counselor discussed what information is acceptable to send by text or not with clients?
- Does the therapist or counselor use a separate mobile phone and number solely for their clinical practice? Or do they use their own cell phone, but purchase one of the separate phone numbers from a service that forwards those calls or texts to the therapist's or counselor's primary phone?
- Is the therapist or counselor completely familiar with settings and other workings of their mobile device? For example, do they know how to

turn on a "Do Not Disturb" mode so that any calls or texts won't make sounds that interrupt a therapy session?

- Is the therapist or counselor careful to not "code" clients' numbers in their mobile phones with their full names or any other identifying information?

One really important thing for therapists and counselors to remember is that clients being able to contact them through a mobile device that they have with them at all times, and interact with regularly, increases their clinical responsibilities after hours. For example, what if a therapist sees several calls in a row come through from a client's number? Are they required to check the messages and make sure the client is not experiencing an emergency? What if they are in bed one night at midnight, unable to sleep, and are playing a game on their phone when they see a client's urgent text flash across the screen? Are they required to read it or respond to it?

There are a few issues to think about in the aforementioned scenario. First, did the therapist have clear policies around when clients should contact them via cell phone? Did the therapist provide the clients with information on when they would check their phone and when they would not (e. g., weekends or vacation)? Even so, do the policies the therapist provided negate the legal or ethical requirement the therapist has for things like ensuring a client's safety, or assessing for suicidal ideation, or reporting child abuse? Read the following clinical scenario and consider the options that the therapist, Katie, has in this situation:

> Katie is away on a two-week vacation in Europe with her husband, Tim, spreading the ashes of Tim's recently deceased father. Katie has her cell phone with her, of course, checking in on their teenaged kids at home, taking beautiful pictures, and occasionally playing a game on her phone before bed. One night, after a very long day of hiking and exploring, Katie is in bed, reviewing her camera roll of all the gorgeous nature shots she got that day. She sees a text flash across her phone, with the initials, "L. H.," which is how she has coded one of her client's names in her address book. She can only see the first few words of the text before it disappears, but it's enough to grab Katie's attention: "Help! I don't know what to do but I'm on the side of the road..." Katie is very anxious, because she knows that this client has been struggling with serious mental health issues lately, and has reported pretty serious emotional dysregulation.

Sticky: Although Katie is away on vacation, and her clients know this, she has still inadvertently seen a bit of concerning text from a client who has not been in a stable place lately. Katie is torn between looking at the text and not looking. If she looks, and it's something bad, she knows she will feel like she needs to take care of it to make sure the client is okay. If she *doesn't* look at the text, she won't *technically* know if there is anything serious going on with the client, and therefore doesn't have to take any action. No one would know that she even saw the text at all that night. Maybe she should take care of it tomorrow? But Katie can't get the thoughts out of her mind—she can't sleep, wondering if the bit of text she saw meant that the client was in a bad car accident. What if the client was alone and injured, her car rolled down an embankment, and no one else was answering her? She can't kick the worry about what the rest of the text says...

Boil it Down: Katie has a very clear and detailed policy on not responding to calls or emails or texts while she is away. She revisited this policy with all of her clients before she left for vacation. She also provided every client with local after-hours crisis numbers and other resources to use in an emergency while she is away.

Katie knows she doesn't have to look at the text message that came across her phone. But she also knows that because she uses her personal phone for work sometimes, she may carry a bit more responsibility than another therapist who does not use the cell phone at all in clinical practice. She saw a bit of a message that was concerning, from a client she has been concerned about.

She decides that it is the ethical thing to do to check the entire message, in order to ensure that the client is safe. When she reads the message, she discovers that the client texted to say that she had a very bad panic attack, felt like she couldn't breathe or stop crying, and that she had to pull over on the side of the road and didn't know what to do, and her mother and best friend hadn't answered her yet.

Is the client here in imminent danger? Perhaps, if her car is in a bad place, around a bend, where another car might slam into her. Or if the client has had a history of suicidal ideation during panic attacks. Or if by chance this wasn't a panic attack, but rather some other (potentially severe) medical emergency that the client wasn't aware of, like an allergic reaction to a new medication? Or is this just a "run-of-the-mill" panic attack that is stressful and difficult for the client to be having, but is not going to put her life at risk or cause her imminent harm?

Katie decides that, ethically, she needs to check in with the client, since she cannot assess the client's safety from the text itself. She doesn't feel right about turning away and ignoring the text. She knows that texting detailed info isn't secure, but since the client has already breached that by initiating the text to the therapist, is it okay for the therapist to reply by text?

Katie decides that it is better to call. So she tells Tim that she needs to make a quick emergency call, and locks herself in the hotel room bathroom to call the client and protect her privacy. The client answers right away, breathing heavily, crying hysterically. The client isn't able to speak enough information to assure Katie of what exactly is going on, or that she is safe.

Katie asks the client for her location, and tells the client she will call for ambulance to come out and take her to the hospital. They will be able to assess her, and give her some Ativan™ to help her calm down until they can reach her mom or friend. Katie also asks for verbal permission to make that call, and the client agrees. Katie will document this later in the client's chart.

Katie calls the emergency number and makes the report, being careful to only offer the least information she can, without disclosing anything more than what they would need to send an ambulance out. Then she crawls back into bed with her husband, and enjoys the rest of her vacation.

Do you feel like Katie acted appropriately in the "Boil it Down" description above? Did you feel any of your own self-of-the-therapist (SOTT) parts getting in the way of being able to easily figure out what a solid course of action here would be? Did Katie's choices demonstrate competence and adherence to laws and codes of ethics that were required in this scenario? Again, the tricky reminder that codes of ethics will tell you *what* to do, but not specifically *how* to do it!

In addition to the therapist's or counselor's use of a mobile device, it's important for them to consider how the *client's* use of a cell phone in therapy might impact the therapy. Mulqueen (2019) explores a myriad of issues regarding the use of cell phones in therapy. In the article description, the author so aptly begs her fellow therapists to consider "the good, bad, and ugly of client cell phone use in session." Here are a few of the important themes the author highlights for therapist and counselors to consider:

- Is the client tempted or distracted by the phone (e.g., needing to check when a chime signals a text has come in) in a way that their attention is not on the therapy?
- Is the presence of the phone simply routine or habit?
- Are clients accustomed to being readily available to others by phone or text?
- Are clients accustomed to needing to be available in the case of an emergency?

The author also highlights a few positive and helpful features with clients' phone use in session:

- Some clients might feel less anxious, calmed, or more comfortable in session when they have their phone handy.
- Some clients may be able to use the phone as a way to divert their eyes if they're feeling uncomfortable, or as a way to change the subject.
- Some clients may want to record things from the week and read the notes from their phone to the therapist in session.
- Some clients may want to share texts with the therapist so that the therapist can help them decipher the meaning of them, or any confusion about them.
- Some clients may want to show the therapist a picture of something from the camera roll on their phone.
- The therapist can get first-hand insight into clients' relationship with their phones.

In addition to the author's ideas above, there are a few more things that therapists and counselors can keep in mind when thinking about clients' cell phone use in therapy:

- Might the cell phone serve as a quick and handy way for clients to take notes on things in session?
- Might the cell phone serve as a helpful tool to quickly look up things in session?
- Is the client experiencing any guilt or shame about sneaking peeks at their phone during session?
- What if a client secretly uses their phone to record things that the therapist or counselor says in session?

In short, there are many uses for cell phones in sessions, with some being potentially beneficial and some being potentially harmful. So how is the therapist or counselor supposed to best navigate this with clients? Perhaps the most ethical stance here is for the therapist or counselor to use the cell phone as a way to check in, and open up a dialogue, with a client about it. Instead of assuming an "all-knowing" stance, could it be better for the therapist or clinician to co-create the meaning and utility of the cell phone use in therapy *with* the client? Read the following vignette and consider the way that the therapist explores cell phone use with a new client (Noah):

THERAPIST: Hey, Noah. Thanks for bearing with me, and for your patience in answering all the intake questions. Now, we start talking about what we want to work on here, okay? But first, is it okay if I ask you one more question?

NOAH: (laughing): Why not! You've already asked about a million!

THERAPIST: So, I notice that you have your cell phone on your lap, and I was wondering if I can ask you a bit about your relationship with it?

NOAH: (laughing): Ummm…my *relationship* with my phone?

THERAPIST: (laughing): Yeah, exactly!

NOAH: Okay, what do you want to know?

THERAPIST: Well, some of my clients like to have their phones right there with them in session just out of habit. But some of my clients actually feel uncomfortable when they don't know exactly where their phone is, and need it right there with them to feel less anxious. And I have some other clients who tell me they think they're "addicted" to their phones and *need* to be looking at it.

NOAH: Well, some of those are true for me too—I do just always hold onto it out of habit. And also so I don't forget it and leave it here when I leave or something.

THERAPIST: Okay, fair enough.

NOAH: But I also want to leave it out because I'm waiting for my girlfriend to text me back about whether I'm driving her to the game tonight at school or not.

THERAPIST: Ahhhh…well, that's pretty understandable. Anything else you want to tell me about your phone?

NOAH: Well, my mom thinks I'm addicted to it, but I tell her I just really need it for stuff.

THERAPIST: Do you think you're addicted to your phone? Or does just your mom think that?

NOAH: I don't think I'm addicted at all.

THERAPIST: Hmmm…you don't *think* you're addicted? Have you ever tested yourself on that?

NOAH: "Tested"? I don't think I know what you mean.

THERAPIST: Well, how about we try a little experiment? What if we write "Remember cell phone" on a sticky note and put it on the door knob so there's no way you can leave here without it? And then what if we put it in this basket over here and we can start chatting, and we can see if you are thinking about it and wanting it, or if it's not a big deal?

NOAH: I guess that would be a good test. But what if my girlfriend texts?

THERAPIST: How about if I set my fitness watch for 25 minutes from now and when it goes off, you can check texts?

NOAH: But there's other stuff I needed my phone to show you.

THERAPIST: Like what?

NOAH: I have some effed-up texts I wanted to show you from my mom so you can help me figure out how to respond to her without it blowing up.

THERAPIST: Okay, we can do that first.

NOAH: And then I wanted to open a browser and show you the side effects I'm worried about on this new medication my psychiatrist put me on and see what you think.

THERAPIST: Okay, let's have a look at the texts from mom, and the list of medication side effects so we have some stuff to work on, and then are you good with the "Am I actually addicted to my cell phone" test?

NOAH: Yeah, okay. But I bet I'm not gonna be addicted to it! (He laughs.)

THERAPIST: Okay, great! So we can put it to the test, and maybe mom will feel a little better about her worries if we can make this an easy-peasy part of our therapy sessions that you have no problem doing?

In this vignette, the therapist attempted to explore how, and to what extent, the client wanted to use his device in therapy. The therapist tried to refrain from control or judgment, but rather explored and suggested, all while monitoring the client to see if he was on board. This resulted in a balance of autonomy for the client, but also some explorative challenges from the therapist as he was getting to know the client better and help him figure out goals for treatment.

How do you feel about the way the therapist handled the case? Do you think it was therapeutically appropriate for the therapist to explore this area and to ask these questions? Was the therapist able to appropriately ask about, and understand, the ways in which the client's phone use might be helpful or not helpful to the therapy process? Do you feel the therapist was sufficiently collaborative with the client and respected his autonomy?

Just as there are many styles to approaching therapy, and different theories and models to lean on, there are also many ways that therapists and counselors can explore and decide on if/how clients' cell phone use will fit in therapy if applicable. Perhaps most importantly, laws and codes of ethics don't generally ever state that "A therapist or counselor may never use a personal mobile device for contact or interactions with therapy clients." But what they *do* specifically mandate are things such as therapists and counselors needing to ensure the protection of clients' PHI, or never sharing clients' personal or identifying information without the appropriate client permissions. For this reason, whenever therapists or counselors choose to use any technology, cell phones, teletherapy, or social media, they are the ones responsible for ensuring that their use is done competently, legally, and ethically.

Teletherapy and Ethics

Since the Pandemic, countless books, articles, research on best practices, and various other guides have surfaced. This section will not attempt to compete with those far broader-reaching resources, but rather will touch on areas of teletherapy that may make therapists and counselors be more likely to encounter *sticky*.

State/Province Laws and Rules

Perhaps the most important consideration for therapists and counselors providing teletherapy is the adherence to their state or province laws on practicing therapy across borders. During the Pandemic, these laws were eased in many places in order to allow easier support and access for the many clients who desperately needed it. Most of these emergency declarations expired a few years after the onset of the Pandemic. Since then, mental health providers have been required to follow their state or province-specific licensing laws. This requires that practice can only occur when a therapist or counselor is licensed in the state where the client is physically located. More recently, there have been even more changes and nuances to many state laws on license requirements and the ability to practice over borders. Therefore, it is an absolute *must* that therapists and counselors know the laws and rules of the states or provinces in which they are licensed, and follow them fully in order to maintain an ethical therapy practice.

There are many things to consider when providing teletherapy that are imperative when it comes to ethical practice. As stated above, the most important one is staying updated on and abiding by state and province laws and rules on the practice of teletherapy. Professional Ethics Boards do *not* consider "I didn't know" or "I wasn't aware" as acceptable excuses for violating state or province mandates. It is the legal and ethical requirement of therapists and counselors to know their state or province laws, rules, and regulations, and to follow them, in order to stay in compliance, as well as to maintain an ethical therapy practice.

Security of Teletherapy and Platforms

There are both laws and state/province regulations, as well as ethical considerations, that go hand in hand with the security of the specific platforms, and other components, of teletherapy. There are several ways for therapists and counselors to stay on top of ethics and security issues when engaging in teletherapy. In addition to the ones discussed below, one easy and important step is for them to attend training on telehealth and data security. There are countless workshops and certificate trainings on this, and it is one way to ensure that therapists and counselors have the appropriate knowledge, information, and training to engage in ethical teletherapy practice.

There are many resources that will guide therapists and counselors through setting up secure teletherapy practices, but the following are a few of the important ethical reminders:

1. HIPAA-compliant platforms for teletherapy are an absolute *must*. These will include things like data privacy and network protection, both of which are vital for maintaining confidentiality and the security of PHI. For example, a public computer in a library is not a secure platform, and not appropriate for seeing a client for therapy.
2. Contact with client(s) should be, especially if there is anything more than a simple schedule change or appointment cancellation, via a secure pathway. For example, using end-to-end encrypted email adds a layer of security.
3. Billing for teletherapy sessions should also be done through a secure network. Venmo™ or Paypal™, for example, are not appropriate platforms to receive payment from for teletherapy sessions.
4. The "Business Associate Agreement" or "BAA" is an important part of a clinical teletherapy practice. Unlike an in-person practice where the therapists or counselors themselves can collect signed paperwork or payment, remote therapy requires the trust of a third party to do these things. In fact, ethical therapists and counselors should maintain BAAs with every third-party vendor, processor, or collector that they share any PHI with.

Discussing Teletherapy with Clients

The following are some helpful areas for therapists and counselors to consider when they begin providing teletherapy.

Before the First Session

Even before the very first meeting, there are some important things for therapists and counselors to think about when striving to ensure ethical treatment of clients they see via this modality.

1. Be sure to give the client a thorough overview of how all the parts of your specific teletherapy will work, even if they've done it elsewhere with a different medical or mental health provider. Signed informed consent here is imperative as well.
2. You should center on the especially important part of *confidentiality* when first making contact with a new client. This includes things like using a secure teletherapy platform, conducting therapy in a secure and private space where no one else has access during sessions, and using "white noise" machines for sound masking.
3. Consider putting an FAQ page on your practice website or other advertising platform. Directing clients to this information can help them prepare, and ensure that they understand the teletherapy platform and that it is the right fit for them. This page serves as an easily accessible reminder of important questions clients might have, or for information they may need in order to gauge fit.
4. Assess for the appropriateness and fit of this modality for the specific presentation of each client. Some of the most important considerations here are things like age (a five-year-old may not be able to sit in front of a computer screen for 50 minutes, or might be distracted by not having toys and other manipulatives to play with during the session), lack of privacy (a teenager who lives in an apartment with her five family members, and who shares her bedroom with two siblings), or a client with limited technological ability, poor Wi-Fi, or unreliable access to a computer or tablet. Additionally, how will safety be assessed if a client is doing teletherapy from their home, and their partner (with whom they have a history of intimate partner violence) overhears them saying something and confronts them after the session? Is teletherapy from home the best modality for the client in this case?
5. Explain all parts of the teletherapy and give instructions to help the client to get set up for their first session. Things like ensuring the exchange of phone contacts and email addresses, and having downloaded the necessary apps or operating systems are imperative. This may include helpful hints such as how to face the light source in order to get the best video, or how to mute.

6 After ensuring the client fully understands the information they are given regarding teletherapy, having appropriate consent for treatment and other applicable forms signed by all parties that will attend sessions.

During Teletherapy Sessions

During the course of teletherapy, there are other responsibilities that therapists and counselors have to ensure appropriate and ethical treatment for clients. The following are some helpful hints for therapists and counselors to remember when conducting teletherapy that have important ethical implications:

1 Having a clear plan for disruption of services, like a power outage or dropped connection. How will connection be reestablished? How will the therapist or counselor contact the client?
2 What is the plan for emergencies? For example, if a client drops off of a meeting unexpectedly, and there was a serious concern of depression or suicidal ideation with the client, what will the therapist or counselor do? For in-person sessions, the client doesn't just drop off unexpectedly, so there is time to assess or talk through any concerns with the client. Remotely, it is impossible to know what happened to the client. Does the therapist or client act prudently here and immediately call the emergency contact for the client?
3 How can the therapist or counselor ensure that the client is in a private space, with no one else present? Since the therapist or counselor would need to have signed paperwork, etc., in order to have additional folks in the session, how will they know if a client's girlfriend, for example, is sitting in the room off camera?

Therapists and counselors should remember that, when offering teletherapy services, they still must ensure that all ethical standards are considered and will be met. Policies and discussions need to occur before *and* after the onset of teletherapy, and may need additional attention depending on the occurrence of certain events or situations that may crop up during treatment.

Clinical Application

Now, let's look at some ethical issues that might crop up for therapists and counselors providing teletherapy, and ideas for how to navigate them ethically.

Consider the following case vignette, and think about what specifically teletherapy-related ethical considerations might be important here:

> Mol is a 15-year-old transgender male client. Mol's mother came in to the first intake session with him, but has supported individual sessions thereafter with Mol and the therapist. The therapist has never met Mol

or their mother in person. Six months into the teletherapy with Mol, the therapist holds a session where Mol presents with an unusual amount of tearfulness and distress. While the therapist is working through the unique presentation with the client, Mol suddenly collapses and disappears from the screen, and is unresponsive to the therapist trying to engage him.

Sticky: The client is a minor, and the therapist is concerned about what appears to be some sort of emergency. The therapist knows there is a responsibility to ensure the welfare of the client, especially given that he is a minor, but is unsure how to go about it.

Boil it Down: Indeed, therapists and counselors are responsible for ensuring the safety of a client in their care if an emergency should occur. In this case, the therapist had Mol's mother listed as the emergency contact for the client, and was therefore able to call the mother to enlist her services in checking on the client. The therapist had decided that if Mol's mother was not immediately available, and was not at home with Mol at the time, a 911 call would be warranted. However, in talking to the client's mom, the therapist discovered that there was an important part to Mol's treatment that had been neglected. The mother shared that Mol had been struggling with an eating disorder, something that the therapist had neglected to focus on in sessions with the client, because Mol had denied it actually being a problem after intake. Unfortunately, the teletherapy platform did not enable the therapist to see the client's weight loss over the months, because Mol had attended the sessions in a bulky hoodie sweatshirt, and the therapist could only see from the client's neck up. It turns out that Mol had collapsed on camera from severe dehydration and malnutrition from a hidden, severe eating disorder. The therapist had not been able to note the weight loss week to week, nor had they been able to see the downy hair that was growing on Mol's arms, a common sign of an eating disorder, Anorexia Nervosa.

This vignette is an example of one of the limitations of teletherapy when working with certain clients. For example, weight loss from serious depression or an eating disorder may not be able to be appropriately tracked without the therapist's full-body, in-person visual capacity. What are some of the ways this therapist could have potentially prevented the situation with Mol from happening while using teletherapy as the treatment modality?

Quick Checklist for an Ethical Teletherapy Practice

- **Teletherapy platform:** Is the therapist or counselor using a teletherapy platform that is secure? Does it have a BAA?
- **Email:** How is the therapist or counselor corresponding with the client(s) or getting billing alerts? Does the email have end-to-end encryption? Does the client share an email address or computer with anyone else in the family?
- **Online billing:** Are clients alerted to billing invoices or directed to payment portals that are secure? Do they have BAAs?

- **Electronic medical records:** If the therapist or counselor is not using a HIPAA-compliant electronic medical system, how are they keeping client files, forms, or other paperwork? Are those methods compliant with things like being able to transmit e-records to clients if requested?
- **Voicemail:** Does a therapist's or counselor's voicemail notify callers if it is secure? Does it offer return contact policies and timetables, and does it direct clients to emergency contacts in the interim?

The following are a few clinical situations to consider when embarking on offering teletherapy sessions in practice:

- How will the therapist or counselor handle a teen client's mom listening at the door while they were in a teletherapy session?
- Is it appropriate to see a couple in their bedroom/on their bed for a couple's teletherapy session because it's the only private space they have away from the kids in the home?
- Is it appropriate to see a teletherapy clients outside—in their backyard, for example? How will the therapist or counselor ensure confidentiality when there could be a neighbor or delivery person that shows up while the client is on camera?
- Will the therapist or counselor require clients to wear headphones when doing teletherapy, to protect the therapist or counselor from others who might inadvertently hear what they are saying?
- How will the therapist or counselor ensure that clients will not record sessions (out of view of the camera)? For the safety and confidentiality of both the client *and* the provider, how will the therapist or counselor ensure that there are no Ring™ cameras, or other devices that might capture the teletherapy session?
- How does the therapist or counselor feel about clients that come on camera drinking an alcoholic beverage during the teletherapy session, as this is their usual practice when they get home from work each night?

The aforementioned scenarios are things that would generally *not* occur in therapeutic in-person settings. Keeping in mind that the therapist or counselor is responsible for maintaining an ethical practice, as well as ensuring they win the Battle of Structure, it is important to consider how unexpected events like the ones above can be navigated with clients.

Social Media and Ethics

Social media is a prevalent part of many peoples' lives, and this may include therapists, counselors, and their clients. It is important for therapists and counselors to think about the boundaries and rules and regulations they will have for how to navigate social media issues if they show up in their practice.

Setting Boundaries Around Social Media

It is an important part of ethical practice to set up boundaries around social media use with clients before the start of therapy. Not only should these rules be listed and explained in the detailed informed consent document, but they should also be discussed with the clients at the first meeting, and revisited as needed.

There are many questions for therapists and counselors to consider here. First and foremost, they need to follow the rules of their professional code of ethics if they contain standards on social media. The following are a few things to think about, and some common suggestions for its use:

1 Always follow your agency's or institution's social media policies if they have them.
2 Consider having a social media account for professional use, separate from any personal ones a therapist or counselor might have. This way, you are providing appropriate, professional information on the account that clients and others can follow, but maintaining personal privacy for friends and family.
3 Make sure to include social media policies in the informed consent document that clients sign, and revisit the policy as appropriate.
4 Consider having a personal policy of only accepting friends or followers from people you have confirmed that you know (clients may disguise themselves as other people or have several accounts with different names).
5 Always be mindful of what you share or post on social media. Even if settings are private, things can "leak" or be screenshotted, reposted, or shared. Would you feel comfortable and proud about the things you posted if you knew that clients or their families could see them?
6 Have a policy for how to handle clients that you take on that are already connected to you on social media. For example, will you temporarily unfollow or defriend during the time of treatment?
7 Since therapists and counselors generally don't want to share their personal pictures and posts with their clients, they should have the same respect for the clients and not "creep" on their social media accounts.
8 Be mindful that what you post may be perceived as a reflection of your personal values or causes or experiences. Consider how thinking this might influence people's thoughts about you, and if that might negatively impact your practice.
9 Be sure you fully understand how social media works, and all the specific rules and settings that it contains. Make sure you know how to silence or block people, make your accounts private, or set up approval for all attempts at others' tagging you or photos you are in.

No matter how well therapists or counselors plan and prepare for securing their social media platforms, there can always be unexpected situations.

Consider how the therapist handled the following situation with her client, Patrice:

THERAPIST: So, Patrice, I wanted to base with you on something to start today if that's okay?

PATRICE: Sure. What's up?

THERAPIST: I noticed that you friend requested me on Facebook™ last week, and I just wanted to remind you of the policy I have about social media. It's been a while since our intake session, so you may have forgotten about that policy.

PATRICE: Oops, yeah, I didn't remember that. I didn't think it was a big deal.

THERAPIST: It isn't a big deal. I figured you had forgotten, so no worries. However, I just wanted to remind you that I try really hard to keep my professional and private lives separate. My Facebook™ page is for close friends and family to see holiday and baby and dog pics—stuff like that. So I just wanted you to understand, and not take it personally that I will decline the request. It's just a policy that I made for myself years ago that I think is an important part of me keeping those clear boundaries for myself between professional and personal.

PATRICE: Totally! I get it, not taking it personally at all!

THERAPIST: Great, thanks for giving me these couple of minutes to go over that again, and for your understanding of it.In the vignette, the therapist did a pretty good job of revisiting a policy as appropriate, was empathic and non-judgmental in her dialogue, and was able to "win" the Battle of Structure. The therapist felt pretty good about how she handled the situation, competently and ethically. Until two weeks later, when there was a second unexpected event with her client, Patrice:

PATRICE: Oh my gosh, I just need to say that your four boys are just SO stinking CUTE! I didn't know that you had four little ones so close together, but honestly, they are the cutest kids I've ever seen, I think. With that red hair and freckles and the little button noses…they look just like their daddy! And, oh yeah, what an amazing vacation you guys had this year—what island were you on that the water was that color, and how did you get those gorgeous sunset shots out on the water?

THERAPIST: (Silence.)

PATRICE: I'm sorry! Am I asking too many questions? I know this is supposed to be my session, but I just have so many questions about all the cool places you've been and how you get your kids to travel so well…

Sticky: In this vignette, the therapist finds herself very uncomfortable with Patrice's unexpected information and questions. The therapist scrambles to figure out how the client saw all of her personal photos. The therapist knows she did not accept the Facebook™ friend request, and she doesn't have any other social media accounts. In addition, she finds herself feeling violated (she did not consent to the client accessing such intimate details of her personal life), defensive, protective, and a bit angry. In her agitated and stunned emotional state, the therapist is unsure of how she wants to address this with the client, as well as not being sure she will be able to express her message to the client without inappropriate emotionality.

Boil it Down: In this vignette, the therapist has to do some SOTT work to figure out what's going on with her, as well as to remain competent and ethical in the session. She needs to address the situation with the client, but isn't sure how to approach it. The client hasn't done anything "wrong," per se, so the responsibility is on the therapist to work through this with the client. The following is the way that the therapist decided to approach the situation:

THERAPIST: I have to be honest, Patrice—I'm feeling a bit overwhelmed by all of this, and, frankly, very confused about how you accessed all my family photos?

PATRICE: Oh, sorry, I should've started with that, silly me! I was at my brother's wedding this weekend, and his best man's wife was a girl I used to room with in college—Kaia Wilcox. So, I guess Kaia was scrolling through some stuff on Facebook™ and showing a few of us some stuff from some other college friends we used to hang out with, and then I saw a picture of you on her feed! I was like, "Oh my God, is that my therapist?" And Kaia was like, "Oh my God, you see her for therapy?" So then she told me that you two were friends and neighbors, and one of her kids went to school with one of yours, and they had playdates together. So we laughed about it, and she told me how cute your kids are, and how your husband is a marathon runner and such a good father, and how you guys travel to the coolest places. I thought you'd find that so funny—it's a small world, isn't it?

THERAPIST: Patrice, can I be honest with you for a minute?

PATRICE: Of course…is there something wrong?

THERAPIST: It's not that anything is wrong; it's just that I need to tell you about how I'm feeling. Remember a couple of weeks ago when I shared with you how important it was that I keep my professional and personal lives separate? Well, this is kind of what I was talking about. Our relationship and our time together is about *you*. It's why therapists don't go out as friends or on romantic dates with clients they are seeing for therapy. Sharing personal experiences and conversations together can blur the lines of what's supposed to happen in therapy, the goals we have.

PATRICE: Oh my gosh, I'm so sorry! I figured that since I didn't friend-request you, and I didn't ask Kaia to show me your stuff—she volunteered it to me—that it'd be okay if I looked at it.

THERAPIST: Listen, it's fine, Patrice. It's fine that you looked—you didn't do anything wrong!

PATRICE: Are you sure? You're not mad at me? I've made two mistakes in the last couple of weeks.

THERAPIST: I'm definitely not mad at you. Again, you did *nothing* wrong here. You didn't know. It's my job to set up and point out the policies that protect our time together, and that keep us focused on you. It's also my job to figure out what boundaries I need for me, and that's why I'm sharing them with you.

PATRICE: No, I'm really glad we talked. I feel bad that I didn't think about it that way, but I totally get it now. Thanks for being honest.

THERAPIST: And I want you to know how much I appreciate your willingness to be so open and understanding of this conversation with me.

PATRICE: Okay, so are we cool now?

THERAPIST: (laughing): We were *always* "cool," Patrice! But before we move on, can we talk about how we both think you should handle the situation if it comes up again with Kaia?

PATRICE: Oh, I think I know how to handle it—I'm actually just going to tell Kaia that it's cool you guys are friends and everything, but that it feels weird creeping on my therapist's family and vacation photos, and I don't want to make you uncomfortable, or things to be weird between us, so I don't want to see your stuff. How does that sound to you?

How did you feel about the way the therapist approached the situation with Patrice? Do you think the therapist attended appropriately to her SOTT reactivity? Was she able to maintain control of the Battle of Structure in the therapy? Did she act competently and ethically in the session? Do you think there was a rupture in their relationship, or do you feel like a healthy therapeutic alliance was maintained?

The protection of a therapist's or counselor's social media content, the usage of it, clinical policies on it, and strategies for navigating any issues related to clients with it are important legal and ethical areas for consideration.

Chapter Takeaways for Therapists and Counselors

1. It is the responsibility of therapists and counselors to ensure that any technology they are using in clinical practice is done so competently and ethically.
2. AI is an emerging field that can be complicated for therapists and counselors when looking at its use in clinical practice.
3. Regular cell phones do not have secure or encrypted texting.
4. Therapists and counselors should have very clear and detailed policies that describe and explain all technological components of the clinical practice.
5. Just as there are many styles to approaching therapy, and different theories and models to lean on, there are also many ways that therapists and counselors can explore and decide on if/how clients' cell phone use will fit in therapy if applicable.

6 Perhaps the most important consideration for therapists and counselors providing teletherapy, is the adherence to their state or province laws on practicing therapy across borders.
7 Professional Ethics Boards do *not* consider "I didn't know" or "I wasn't aware" as acceptable excuses for violating state or province mandates.
8 Therapists and counselors should have ample time to cover possible issues with teletherapy both *before* the treatment begins and *while* it is going on.
9 HIPAA-compliant platforms for teletherapy are an absolute *must*.
10 Contact with client(s) should be via a secure pathway, especially if there is anything more than a simple schedule change or appointment cancellation. For example, using end-to-end encrypted email adds a layer of security.
11 Billing for teletherapy sessions should also be done through a secure network. Venmo™ or Paypal™, for example, are not appropriate platforms to receive payment from for teletherapy sessions.
12 The "Business Associate Agreement," or "BAA" is an important part of a clinical teletherapy practice. Unlike an in-person practice where the therapists or counselors themselves can collect signed paperwork or payment, remote therapy requires the trust of a third party to do these things. In fact, ethical therapists and counselors should maintain BAAs with every third-party vendor, processor, or collector that they share any PHI with.
13 It is an important part of ethical practice to set up boundaries around social media use with clients before the start of therapy, and navigate any issues with this *promptly* throughout the course of treatment.

7 Self-of-the-Therapist (SOT or SOTT)

Perhaps one of the most important things a therapist or counselor can do to minimize the personal toll that this work can take on them is to focus on self as a regular practice. Remaining emotionally grounded, being clinically sound, and addressing one's own unresolved issues are an important cornerstone of being an ethical provider.

The term "self-of-the-therapist" (SOT) was coined by the famed family therapist Virginia Satir. Lum (2002) explains how Satir advocated strongly for therapists to look inward and work on their own unresolved issues in order to be effective clinicians. Self-of-the-therapist (also known as person-of-the-therapist or POTT) training is an essential component in various therapeutic programs across disciplines (Scott & Wendt, 2018). For clarification purposes, some programs will use the acronym "SOT" for the self-of-the-therapist, while some will use "SOTT." For simplicity and matching, SOTT and POTT will be used in this chapter.

Harry Aponte and his colleagues created a person-of-the-therapist (POTT) training model with the main focus of the model on the use of self that emanates from the personal depths of the individual who is conducting the therapy (Aponte & Kissil, 2017). In short, understanding oneself and showing up fully and authentically in session are an important part of good therapy.

If we view SOTT and POTT from an ethical lens, we can see a common theme. As the great philosopher Socrates was famous for saying, "Know thyself." Likewise, an important part of being an ethical therapist or counselor is understanding oneself. Let's explore a bit about the "why" SOTT work is such a necessary part of ethical practice.

SOTT work is vital because it helps highlight the power of family, cultural, and religious influences in therapists' and counselors' lived experiences. The importance of self-awareness for therapists and counselors cannot be understated. Understanding the parts of self that are deeply wired or unresolved *before* going into the therapy room can help therapists and counselors be more prepared. This awareness can assist them in figuring out strategies beforehand that will hopefully help them avoid reactivity and discomfort in sessions. Consider the following vignette between a therapist and his client, José:

DOI: 10.4324/9781003745136-8

THERAPIST: So tell me about how the visit with the psychiatrist went last week.

JOSÉ: It was okay. She diagnosed me with major depression and gave me a prescription for a couple of antidepressants.

THERAPIST: Okay, how do you feel about that? Are you feeling good about the medication?

JOSÉ: I guess. I just have to accept that I'm going to need it the rest of my life. Bad depression runs in my family. My father and my grandfather both took their own lives after being depressed for pretty much their entire lives. My mother was on meds for depression, my brother...

THERAPIST: Yes, that's a lot of stuff there for you to carry and worry about. But you're doing the right things to try to feel better and have a different experience with depression than they did, right?

JOSÉ: I guess so. But this deep depression—it's in my blood. It's just so hard to accept I'm going to live with this my entire life.

THERAPIST: Maybe we shouldn't jump to that judgment right now? You are *not* your grandfather or your father or your mother or your brother. You're doing this differently than they did. You're getting help. You're working hard to get on top of it, José.

JOSÉ: I know. It's just hard to look forward to anything. What good is life if there's no joy? No pleasure?

THERAPIST: José, you've told me *lots* of things that have made you happy. The bonus you got at work, when your son started to crawl, the family party you had at your house over the holidays.

JOSÉ: That's as good as it gets, I guess...

THERAPIST: There's so much joyful stuff out there, José! Life is a *gift*, and unlike your dad and grandfather, you chose to stay and enjoy that gift.

JOSÉ: (Silence.)

THERAPIST: I notice that you're pretty quiet—is everything okay, José?

JOSÉ: Sorry. Yes, I'm okay. I'm just having a hard time with something you said.

THERAPIST: What did I say?

JOSÉ: You said, "Life is a gift."

THERAPIST: Yes...?

JOSÉ: I don't buy that. At all. Life is not a gift to me. Life is very, very *hard*. Every day. Life is a burden, not a gift.

Sticky: In this vignette, the therapist intended to be supportive and helpful to José, and help him understand that he is different from his father and grandfather. The therapist then tries to offer guiding principles, like "Life is a gift," to help the client remain positive and hopeful. However, in approaching the client in this way, the therapist didn't think about the possibility that José might not share the same worldview or perspective on life. Although these are noble and well-intentioned efforts, the therapist is only looking through his own lens. This results in the client's silence and subsequent disagreement with the therapist's message.

Boil it Down: To the therapist, who did not have a family history of depression and suicide, and who had never struggled with depression himself, the belief that "Life is a gift" was simply the only view he had ever considered. Although unfortunate that the therapist wasn't aware of his biased point of view in the discussion, it happens! The therapist is lucky here, in that José is direct and forthcoming about his disagreement. Furthermore, he is quick to offer up the rationale he has for feeling that life is *not* a gift. Perhaps what matters most now is how the therapist takes the client's feedback and opening into his perceptions on life. The therapist must adjust his approach and further statements to better align with the client's personal experience and views. *Please note: The therapist did a thorough assessment on José for suicidal ideation or intent before engaging in the dialogue provided above.*

Upon subsequent reflection of this situation in supervision, the therapist was able to understand this personal "lens" with which he viewed "life," and that others may not share that same perception. He worked with the supervisor to create a less personally biased way to support José. The supervisor helped the therapist create two different approaches. Read the following ways the therapist might respond to José and consider how you feel about each one, and which you would choose to use:

1 Some people choose to think about life in different ways that might help inspire them, or at least keep them on track to work towards a better experience in their daily existence. How do you feel about the statement "Life is a gift"? Does that resonate with you or make you feel hopeful?"
2 Sometimes people use the phrase "Life is a gift" to describe their existence. But perhaps not everyone feels that way about life. Tell me about how you feel about life…

Both responses allow the therapist to share a personal, and possibly helpful, point of view with the client. However, the phrasing of them invites José to respond and share in ways that will help the therapist understand the *client's* worldview on life, rather than operating solely from the therapist's.

Before Entering the Field

The ideal place to start SOTT work is *before* entering a therapy or counseling training program. The motivation to become therapists or counselors has historically been associated with the concept of the ***wounded healer***. This suggests that those who enter the field of mental health often do so as a result of their own personal struggles and challenges (Cruciani et al., 2024). In my experience over many years of reading applications from people wanting to enter a training program, I agree. Most folks are looking to do so because of their own personal history. These histories may include things like having been a child in the middle of an acrimonious divorce, or experiencing trauma or abuse, domestic or intimate partner violence, or a complicated loss.

In the case of the wounded healer, it is especially important that therapists and counselors ensure they have dealt with their own personal struggles and challenges before attempting to jump into the arena to accompany clients in their work. Ongoing attention to the therapist's or counselor's "self" is so important. For example, if a therapist, John, grew up in an abusive household, where beatings, alcoholism, and neglect were prominent, the following are important questions for John to explore:

1. Does John feel ready to lead a session with a family where there is a history of similar abuse?
2. Does John feel able to remain neutral when working with the abusive parent(s)?
3. Does John feel confident he will be able refrain from overcompensating for the parent(s) towards the child(ren)?
4. Does John feel able to leave the therapy at the office, and not take home the emotional distress from it into his personal life?
5. Is John maintaining an ethical, professional, and clinically sound presence in the sessions?
6. Does John have a good relationship with a supervisor, so he can process this case on a regular basis, and receive feedback on his work with the family?

Another popular reason for applicants wanting to enter the field is having been in therapy with a good therapist or counselor who made a positive impact in their lives. The inspirational bond these applicants experience with prior therapists or counselors can serve as a wonderful model of how to do therapy. Applicants may carry their therapists' or counselors' style, models for treatment, communication stances, or even specific, targeted interventions that they found very helpful, into their own clinical work. However, in this case as well, it will be important for therapists and counselors to be mindful of their own experiences in therapy, however positive they may have been. What stylistically works for and is preferable to one person may not be the same for another person.

Personal Value System

Wilcoxon et al. (2013) quote Rokeach's (1973) definition of a ***value***: "an enduring belief that a specific mode of contact or end-state of existence is personally or socially preferable to the opposite or converse mode of conduct or end-state of existence" (p. 286). In short, what do you believe in? What are the strong feelings about certain things that you will be carrying into the therapy room with you? And what are some of the ways those beliefs might show up when interacting with a client who has an opposing belief? Read the following narrative from a therapist who describes how she discovered how her personal values were getting in the way of being a good therapist for a particular client:

> I had this client, Bryan. He was a 40-something-year-old divorced man, who was seeking out therapy for depression and frustration with the online dating experience. Over the first weeks that I was seeing him, I found myself feeling increasingly more annoyed with him and just had a general sense overall that I didn't like him. This hadn't really happened to me before, so I was a bit concerned about why I began dreading the weekly sessions with this client. After talking to my supervisor a few times about it, she asked me a kind of weird question. She said, "What are some of your personal values? What things in life matter most to you?" I was confused about why she was asking me those questions, but I answered her anyway, telling her that the first thing I thought of was that we should all strive to be kind and thoughtful to others and strive to make the world a better place every day. I told her I try to live my life in a way that touches on other people only in positive ways. She laughed, not surprised with my answer coming from a therapist. And then she asked me, "And does this client you are struggling to like have a similar worldview, do you think?" I thought about it for a minute. Bryan was always late for sessions and pushed his sessions over every time, making me late for my next person. He spoke meanly about the women he met online, and seemed to lack self-awareness about his own obvious flaws. He would bring food into my office and eat it messily during session, talking with his mouth full. He said disparaging things about everyone—from waiters at his favorite restaurants, to the checkout people in the grocery store. And then it struck me—Bryan did *not* share my worldview about how to regard people and touch their lives. After further reflection with my supervisor, I was able to create both an important reality for myself (I was responding negatively to the client because he was not a person who embodied similar values about how to treat people) and a framework for being able to do better work with him. I reminded myself each session that he was *not* a person I chose to be in my personal world. I didn't have to like him or ever be friends with him. I had the skills to help him navigate depression, and realized that my newfound information might enable me to gently challenge him on ways that he might be more successful with the women he met on dating apps.

In this narrative, the therapist did some great SOTT work. This enabled her to both improve her experience with the client and to create new pathways to help him. The following are some helpful prompts to think about your personal value system:

1. What breaks your heart?
2. What rules do you live by for yourself?
3. What makes you angry?
4. What adjectives would you use to describe the people you like and admire most?

5 What drains your energy?
6 What makes you defensive?

The answer to these questions may highlight some important themes that both make you *feel* something and show areas that are important to you. Clients who do not fit well with your responses here might be the ones that bring something up inside of you during sessions.

For example, let's say a therapist or counselor identifies being accused of being wrong when they absolutely know their information is correct as the answer for question #6 above. Think about what might be happening inside the therapist or counselor when a client, 42-year-old Mona, is speaking about her recently arrested 13-year-old son, Darius, in the following statement:

- **Mona:** I'm sorry, but you were way off base here. You said Darius was a "normal" kid and that how he was feeling was "developmentally appropriate." You went on and on about how the label of "problem child" wasn't really accurate or helpful. Where did you get your degree? Because I don't know where you learned what you did, but you clearly do not know anything about kids. You were so wrong! Darius *is* a problem child—look at him, arrested at 13 years old for God's sake! And *that's* not a "problem child"?!

In this example, the therapist or counselor may be feeling a lot of different things. Defensive? Frustrated? Angry? Attacked? Blamed? Challenged? There is a difference between the therapist or counselor who can quickly identify a personal value they have previously reflected upon, that feels misunderstood, activated, or violated by a client, and one that cannot. The following are two examples of how that difference might show up in the therapist's or counselor's response to Mona:

- **Therapist #1** (*has not* done SOTT work on personal values): Mona, everything I said to you is accurate and developmentally sound for a 13-year-old. Yes, sometimes 13-year-olds get arrested. They can act out as a way of dealing with conflict and issues at home or when they are bullied at school. This does not make Darius a "problem child." It will not be helpful for him to keep hearing this label from you.

In Therapist #1's response, the focus is on defending the developmental frameworks for adolescents, and the realities of how they sometimes make choices and act. In this response, the therapist may be "accurate" in some of the statements; however, there is a risk that Mona will feel alienated because the therapist is neglecting to be present for her in *her* feelings and experience.

- **Therapist #2** (*has* done SOTT work on personal values): Mona, I totally understand that you have rules and expectations for Darius, just like many other parents do. And I also know that this has been a terribly upsetting and disappointing experience for you. You probably want to lash out and blame someone or something. Things like this happen with teens sometimes, and I want to be able to support you both as you move through this. I want to help you to both understand how adolescents sometimes "work," while also giving you a place to express how awful this feels. Darius has been dealing with a lot lately, and he has not figured out a better way to cope with those things than to act out. He's going to get some help in doing that now, and I hope you're willing to work with me on the things that might help or hinder us getting him to a better place.

Therapist #2's response attempts to validate the mom's experience, while "gently" adding some plugs for a developmental explanation. The response is more focused on Mona and Darius, and invites the client to work together, highlighting *two* sets of perspectives and areas of expertise (Mona's and the therapist's) that might be helpful in the common goal of helping Darius be in a better place.

Cultural Awareness and Responsiveness

Another important area of SOTT work is understanding the cultural influences that flavor therapists' and counselors' views, words, and actions, as well as those of their clients. Also important is thinking about how these things can show up in sessions, and how to navigate them when they do. Cultural misunderstandings can sometimes serve as constraints to otherwise solid clinical work.

Consider the following dialogue between a therapist and her clients, a mother (Zainab) and her 16-year-old daughter (Khadija):

THERAPIST: How have things been at home?

KHADIJA: Nothing is better! I still hate him! He is so mean to me! And he grabbed my arm so hard and spit in my face and threatened to kill me!

ZAINAB: Khadija! That's enough. We are not going to talk about this.

KHADIJA: Oh, yes, we are, Mama. I'm not covering for him. We don't live in Pakistan anymore. We live in the United States and fathers here aren't allowed to do these things to their daughters. He abuses us, Mama!

THERAPIST: Khadija, did your father leave those bruises on your arm?

KHADIJA: Yes! And it's not the first time.

THERAPIST: Khadija, can I ask you to give your mom and me a few minutes alone? If you don't mind, can you sit in the waiting room while I talk to your mom?

KHADIJA: Sure. Talk some sense into her please. (Leaves.)

THERAPIST: Zainab, I need to talk to you about this. I've asked your husband to come to therapy, and he has refused. I've asked you to intervene when these altercations crop up between Khadija and her father. You must tell him that it's not okay to grab her in ways that leave marks on her body, and he cannot threaten to kill her. You need to step in and stop him from doing those things. It's so important that you protect your daughter, Zainab. Your husband is being abusive towards her, and I'm going to need to make a child services report today, okay? Do you want me to explain how that works and what will happen next?

ZAINAB: (crying): You don't understand.

THERAPIST: What don't I understand?

ZAINAB: I cannot intervene with my husband. It doesn't work that way in our culture. The childrearing is up to me, but the father makes the rules to protect the daughters. And he will enforce them however he must. I cannot tell him to stop.

THERAPIST: I understand, but if you can't stand up to him and protect Khadija, then the state will make sure that she is safe. They may choose to take her from the home for a while if they feel she isn't safe there.

ZAINAB: (crying): That will never happen.

THERAPIST: Unfortunately, that is what must happen sometimes. It's what they need to do sometimes to keep a minor safe.

ZAINAB: He will never let them take her away. He will kill all three of us first before he'd let that happen.

In the vignette, the therapist either lacks awareness of or is not incorporating the client's culture into the way she is approaching the situation. Although the rules and regulations of mandated reporting are very clear and necessary for child safety, the *way* that the therapist goes about navigating them with the client is very important. Consider a different approach that the therapist could take with Zainab below:

THERAPIST: Zainab, tell me about how communication with your husband has been going about how to parent Khadija?

ZAINAB: We don't really communicate. It doesn't work like that.

THERAPIST: Tell me if I'm missing something here. Are you feeling like you are *not* able to work together on decisions of how to approach Khadija?

ZAINAB: I don't think you understand Pakistani marriages. The wife is more restricted. Co-parenting doesn't look the same as it does in the U.S.

THERAPIST: I understand that I'm missing how the Pakistani culture contributes here. Please, Zainab, tell me more about how things look in your marriage and your family…

ZAINAB: The wife is the manager of the home and the children. But the father will not allow disrespect. He won't allow Khadija to do certain things. And I cannot stand up to him.

THERAPIST: What would happen if you did?

ZAINAB: (shaking head): (Silence.)

THERAPIST: Okay, so I want to understand and respect the way it is in your household. But I'm also responsible for reporting things that are considered abuse in the state. Can you see my dilemma here? We have a lot of information on the impact of situations like this on kids' mental health and wellness. I want to help you and your husband work on things like disrespect with Khadija, but we can't have things like grabbing that leaves bruises, or threats to kill your daughter.

ZAINAB: He won't agree to that. He doesn't believe in therapy. He will never attend.

THERAPIST: Okay, I understand. I'm still going to have to make a child protective services report today, and I want you to figure out how I can best support you and Khadija through this. Do you think there is a chance that your husband would actually hurt or kill Khadija when he finds out about the report today?

ZAINAB: I don't know.

THERAPIST: Okay, so we need to make sure that you and Khadija are safe. Do you have somewhere you can go tonight and stay with someone?

ZAINAB: Yes. But he will find us.

THERAPIST: Okay, I'm going to ask Khadija to come back in and I will explain this to her. Then we are going to make the child protective services call together right now, and they may choose to involve the police to make sure you two will be safe.

ZAINAB: I'm scared.

THERAPIST: I know this a new way of doing things for you, Zainab. I can hear your fear. I know it must be difficult to honor your husband and adhere to his expectations, and also protect your daughter. I'm going to be here the whole time to support you, okay? I know how hard this is for you…

ZAINAB: I'm not scared of doing this. I know this is the only way to make sure my daughter is safe. But I am scared…of *him*.

In this response, the therapist still attends to the necessary reporting mandates and necessary efforts to create safety for Zainab and Khadija. However, she also remains culturally sensitive and curious about Zainab's experience, and the way that it impacts the situation. The therapist attempts to understand and honor the way the client's family runs, and at the same time is straightforward about her dilemma, and how she must make choices that ensure safety. This allows the therapist to maintain the therapeutic alliance with Zainab (which will be an important part of the therapy progressing), while strengthening her understanding of how cultural differences contribute to how Zainab navigates the situation.

Research supports that there is increased disengagement from therapy among Black, Indigenous, and people of color (BIPOC) clients (e.g., Aggarwal et al., 2022). Aggarwal et al. (2022) also propose that this might be due in part to BIPOC clients' perceptions that their therapists or counselors misunderstand their experiences because of differences in cultural background that are not discussed in therapy. On average, clients who identified as BIPOC were 3.56 times more likely than White clients to discuss cultural identities at some point during treatment (Kuo et al., 2025). How can therapists and counselors be sure to attend to these important themes in sessions? The following are some starting points for therapists and counselors to include in their clinical work:

1 Get comfortable talking about cultural identity and influences, privilege, and oppression. Normalize the inclusion of these in sessions, as appropriate. Therapists' and counselors' own comfort and readiness is imperative to ethically helping clients explore these areas.
2 To highlight the importance of cultural identity inclusion in therapy, include questions about these topics at the very first intake meeting. This will give the immediate message to clients that exploring cultural influences, experiences, and differences can be part of therapeutic discussions.
3 Remember that some clients may want or need to express and process heavy or angry or fearful feelings around current events, even if they don't directly impact the therapist or counselor. Ethical therapists and counselors take the responsibility for making a comfortable space for these discussions as part of therapy when appropriate.
4 Stay knowledgeable about social, systemic, and political issues, and strive to understand how these can impact different groups.

Remember that it is the therapist's or counselor's responsibility to attend to *all* parts of a client, and everything that might help them understand their client's experience. This includes asking about things that might be impacting them, like current affairs, difficult political environments, lack of safety, discrimination, or oppression.

Let's think about privilege for a minute. Privilege is defined as a special right or advantage that a particular person or group of people has (Oxford Dictionary). There are many types of privilege; some we are born into, and some we acquire. As therapists and counselors, advanced training and education render us with privilege that many of our clients may not have. Being aware of this, and other privilege, is a foundational piece of SOTT work. Perhaps more important than acknowledgment of privilege is what therapists and counselors *do* with it.

For some therapists and counselors, they've rarely had to think about their privilege, because they've never had to experience the oppressive side of things. For therapists and counselors to *understand* privilege, they must make efforts, actively, to understand events as they are experienced from the perspective of less privileged people. For therapists and counselors with privilege, it's impossible to just shrug it off. They can't get rid of it, but they can *acknowledge* it. When therapists and counselors bring discussions of privilege into sessions and explore with clients, they are striving for a sort of solidarity with those clients who may not have the same privileges. This contributes to a stronger therapeutic alliance, and helps make the divide between experiences smaller.

Read the following dialogue between an able-bodied therapist and her wheelchair-bound client, Bambi. Consider where you think the therapist could acknowledge and incorporate privilege and the differing cultural experiences the therapist and client have had. Do you think that the way that the therapist contributed to the session resulted in a more equitable therapeutic relationship? Or do you think it put more divide between the therapist and the client?

THERAPIST: Hi, Bambi. It's good to see you again—I know it's been a few weeks since we last had a session.

BAMBI: Yeah, I've been in court a lot the last couple of weeks, trying to fight this domestic thing my mother is trying to pin on me.

THERAPIST: Well, hopefully you have a good lawyer!

BAMBI: *I* don't have money for a lawyer! I get a public defender sometimes. Or I just represent myself.

THERAPIST: Are you sure that's a good idea?

BAMBI: I don't have a choice. I don't have money to pay a lawyer, even a bad one, haha.

THERAPIST: Oh Bambi, that's terrible. I'm so sorry you're in this situation.

BAMBI: This is the story of my life, I guess.

THERAPIST: Don't say that, Bambi! This will *not* be the story of your life. There's a better life out there for you; we just need to start taking steps towards that, okay? How do you think we could start taking those steps?

BAMBI: I don't think you understand.

THERAPIST: Of course I don't understand completely, but I get it, Bambi, really I do. I have an autoimmune disorder that flares up sometimes and I can barely get out of bed on those days. Even walking hurts when I have an episode. It sucks.

BAMBI: Yeah, it sucks for you, but you are able-bodied. You're not stuck in a chair the rest of your life. You have bad days, painful days, but at least you can still walk. And when you don't have a flare-up, you're fine. It's not the same.

THERAPIST: I know, you're right, I don't have it as bad as you do, for sure, but I was trying to join with your experience and share that I sometimes know physical struggles…

BAMBI: Did you have a mother who beat you your whole life? And when you finally got old enough to stand up to her, she pushed you down the stairs and you broke your neck and lost the use of your legs for the rest of your life?

THERAPIST: Bambi, I don't know what to say. No, those things didn't happen to me. But even though those awful things happened to you, it doesn't mean you can't have a better life.

BAMBI: That's easy for you to say—rich, White, able-bodied, educated, came from an intact and loving home, I bet? People like me, we don't get to have what you have.

THERAPIST: And what is it that *you* want, Bambi? I want to help you get that...

The therapist in the vignette was well intentioned in what she said to the client, and obviously felt empathy and sadness for Bambi. However, the therapist lacked the awareness of how her privilege was showing up in the room, and she failed to recognize and acknowledge it. For this reason, the dialogue seemed to get stuck on the differences between the two, rather than on more useful things like helping Bambi navigate the situation she is dealing with.

Think of the junctures in the dialogue where the therapist could have owned the differences in privilege and highlighted culturally different experiences. Consider the impact if the therapist had said:

> I'm sure it is hard for you to buy into my hopefulness for you having a better life, coming from someone who has no idea what it's like to not be able-bodied and having the privilege of having grown up in a supportive household. Thanks for calling me out on that—there are gonna be times where I'm looking through my own lens over here, and I might miss the mark on yours.

Checking Vision

Wilcoxon et al. (2013) describe "checking vision" for therapists and counselors as activities that help therapists and counselors consistently be aware of and check in with their own values and perspective. They suggest things like taking continuing education (CE) classes, engaging in supervision or consultation with other professionals, and seeking out one's own therapy when appropriate. Additionally, I share the following ideas with my graduate students for keeping "checking vision" prominent in their clinical presence:

1 Read. Make a regular practice of reading what others have written. This exposes therapists and counselors to other points of view, or to the experiences that others have had as therapists. There are countless scholarly journals in our field, as well as books and other online resources.

2 Continue to engage with and discuss issues within one's own family of origin or other family relationships. This ongoing dialogue may help to keep a continued focus on addressing unresolved issues in the therapist's or counselor's personal relationships.

3 Consult with other professionals. Learning from other professionals about areas we may not have as much exposure to can aid in broadening our understanding of clients and their experiences. For example, talking to a family law attorney might lend information about the process of divorce or litigation.

Assumptions

A therapist's or counselor's personal *assumptions* about clients or their situations might be accurate or not, but they are not *facts*. It is important for therapists and counselors to remember that what they "see" in clients or therapy is always going to be filtered through their own unique lens. This unique lens is what makes all of us vulnerable to making assumptions.

A good way for therapists and counselors to add an important reminder that what they see may be biased, flawed, assuming, or "missing" something is to add one of the following phrases to the thinking about or processing of a clinical case:

1 "...or at least that's my theory of what might be happening here."
2 "...or at least that's the story I'm putting together in my mind."
3 "...and this is solely based on my own, unique lens."

Each of these "add-ons" reminds the therapist or counselor that they may not have a singular "truth" of the situation. In turn, it begs them to remember that the best view of the client or family is created collectively between the two "experts" in the room—the client and the therapist or counselor. I like to say that clients are experts on *themselves*—what they think and feel, what resonates most with them, what they agree with or not, etc.—and therapists and counselors are experts on *not* being the client(s)—looking at situations outside of the client and their complicated thoughts and experiences with it, and not having emotional ties or reactivity to issues.

Consider the following vignette with a therapist and his 37-year-old client, Kyle:

THERAPIST: Well, I'm glad that you found the office okay, and glad you could make it in. I know you shared in our initial phone call that you have some physically difficult days...

KYLE: Thankfully, it's a good day today. And I'm so glad I found you—your office has an elevator and a ramp, and easy access for my walker.

THERAPIST: Of course. So tell me a bit more about why we are meeting today.

KYLE: Well, like I told you on the phone, about a year ago, I was in a bad car accident. I had terrible burns over 60 percent of my body and lost part of my leg, and had a traumatic brain injury. It's been a rough ride this last year, and recently my wife told me she can't do this anymore and wants a divorce.

THERAPIST: What can't she do anymore?

KYLE: She can't deal with the changes to our sex life. We've tried to figure things out together, but she just says I can't give her what she needs anymore and it's just too hard.

THERAPIST: And what about you, Kyle? What do *you* want?

KYLE: I love my wife. Yes, things have changed, and it's my fault they changed. I own that. But I don't want the divorce.

THERAPIST: I'm so sorry, Kyle. Your story saddens me. So, have you and your wife tried to find ways to create a new sex life around the changes or limitations?

KYLE: She doesn't want to try. She can only accept things the way they were before the accident.

THERAPIST: Has your sex drive or abilities changed since the accident, Kyle?

KYLE: No, not at all. I have the same sex drive. I just can't ejaculate anymore, but I've been able to achieve sexual pleasure without that part.

THERAPIST: Would your wife be willing to come in to these sessions with you? I'm wondering if we might be able to help her see a new pathway to a fulfilling sex life. What do you think?

KYLE: Probably not. I'm pretty sure she's done. But I can try to ask her if she'd be willing.

How do you feel about the way the therapist explored things with Kyle in the vignette above? He clearly attempted to understand Kyle's experience, and asked clarifying questions. He showed empathy and attempt at solutions. The therapist felt bad for the client—not even a year after the traumatic incident, Kyle's wife wanted a divorce. He likely felt rejected sexually. The therapist was certain that the "right" pathway was to help Kyle's wife buy into the prospect of a new sex life that met both of their needs.

But here's what the therapist *didn't* know. As the session continued, Kyle shared a vital piece of information with the therapist. He added:

> The thing is, the accident has taken all of my "manhood." I can't golf anymore with the guys, I can't drive a car, I can't sit normally like other people. My face is disfigured. And my dick doesn't work like it used to. But my sex drive is still there. And I found that the one way I can still feel like a man is sexually. And my wife just can't keep up. And it's not fair for me to ask her to. So I started to find other women to have my modified version of sex with—I don't care about any of them, but they make me feel alive and like a man. My wife isn't okay with it—even though I've told her it's only sex, and a lot of it, and she is the one I love.

The therapist had made an incorrect *assumption* that it was Kyle who was not able to please his wife sexually. He *assumed* (correctly) that Kyle's accident and subsequent injuries were the cause of the change in their sex life. However, the therapist never considered what Kyle shared with him about needing to have multiple sexual partners.

The important thing for therapists and counselors to remember here is that *we can't know what we don't know*. That will always be a possibility, no matter how long someone has been doing therapy. Yet our brains will attempt to figure things out, draw connections with the data we have received. *And we will not always be correct*.

More importantly, therapists and counselors need to keep this awareness present in every session, knowing that they can make an assumption at any time. One way to help avoid this, is to adopt the rule of "Ask, don't tell." This means that when a therapist or counselor thinks they "know" something, they can always "check it out" with the client before taking that "truth" any further. Read the following two examples of how therapists or counselors might "tell" a client what they think is going on:

Scenario #1

THERAPIST: Wow—that's a powerful statement your mom made to you.

CLIENT: I know. I can't believe she said that. It's *so* mean.

THERAPIST: Your mother probably didn't mean it. I'm sure she said it out of frustration or anger.

CLIENT: Probably. But it doesn't matter. She still said it. And it was out of line.

THERAPIST: You need to talk to her and tell her how that made you feel. You two need to agree on some sort of a time out *before* hurtful things are said.

Scenario #2

THERAPIST: Wow—that's a powerful statement your mom made to you.

CLIENT: I know. I can't believe she said that. It's *so* mean.

THERAPIST: Do you think your mom may have said that out of frustration or anger?

CLIENT: Probably. But it doesn't matter. She still said it. And it was out of line.

THERAPIST: Okay, so how would you feel about maybe talking to her and telling her how that statement made you feel? Maybe the two of you can agree on some sort of a time out or something that either of you can take *before* something hurtful is said?

In scenario #1, the therapist *tells* the client how it is and what needs to be done. This method does not leave space for the possibility that the therapist isn't completely correct in her assessment. Additionally, it doesn't consider the client's or the mother's perspectives or intent, but rather is directive. Lastly, although the therapist might be accurate in her assessment of what happened with the mom, the way she states it could be interpreted as "siding" with the client.

In scenario #2, the therapist check in or *asks* the client how it is and what might be done. This method leaves space for other perspectives or intent, thus opening up the possibility that the therapist doesn't have it completely right. Again, although the therapist might be completely correct in her assessment of what happened with the mom, there is no suggestion of "siding" here.

"Siding" with Clients

Therapists or counselors, based on their own histories, interactions, and lived experiences, might sometimes feel more aligned with one client than another. This could become problematic if there are multiple people or family members in the same therapy session, and the therapist or counselor identifies with or supports one client more than the others.

It can be a normal thing for therapists and counselors to identify with some clients more than others, but it is important that they recognize this. Additionally, they need to be able to navigate the therapeutic relationship with *all* clients in the session in fair and equitable ways (Justice).

One of the pioneers in family therapy, Ivan Boszormenyi-Nagy (2014), touted that ***multidirectional partiality*** was an important part of doing effective therapy. This means that at the very same time, *everyone* and *no one* feels special in the therapy room. Everyone is regarded and "seen" by the therapist or counselor, yet no one feels more special than another.

Consider the following dialogue between a therapist, Dr. Melvin, and his clients, a couple, Hannah and Lynn:

DR. MELVIN: So how was the week, you two? Were you able to practice the "I statements" we talked about trying last week?

HANNAH: No, we didn't even try. It was a rough week...

LYNN: Yeah, it was a rough week because of you, Hannah! You were an asshole all week. Your crappy attitude sucked, and the way you talked to me...

HANNAH: I hate you, Lynn—I really do. I'm done, I'm totally done. This relationship with you is totally toxic and the way you gaslight me... It's freaking over, Hannah—I truly can't stand you. I'm literally crawling out of my skin having to sit here and look at you.

LYNN: You see what I have to deal with, Dr. Melvin? The way she treats me? "I hate you"? I mean, is that an appropriate thing to say to your wife? Tell her how messed-up that is, right, Dr. Melvin?

DR. MELVIN: Well, I can understand where you're coming from, Lynn. Hannah, can you understand how Lynn feels having you tell her you hate her? That's a pretty strong statement to make to your wife.

HANNAH: (angrily): Are you kidding me? The two of you ganging up on me now? Did you miss the first things out of Lynn's mouth today were that the week sucked because of me, and that I had a crappy attitude and I was an *asshole*? And *I'm* the one being told that what I said is hurtful? Wow.

Sticky: Dr. Melvin attempted to arrest the escalating anger and frustration in the room by focusing on one of Hannah's statements—"I hate you." Unfortunately, Hannah's perception of Dr. Melvin's comments is that he is siding with her wife, Lynn. Hannah reports feeling that the two of them are ganging up on her. Although Dr. Melvin's intention was to simply encourage Hannah to see how her words landed on her wife, it resulted in a rupture with Hannah, and a divide in the therapy session.

Boil it Down: Whether or not you think that Dr. Melvin handled the situation appropriately, the result of the intervention yielded a negative outcome in the room, and Dr. Melvin will need to attempt to repair the rupture. Consider the following comments that Dr. Melvin makes in attempting to salvage the session and the therapeutic relationship with Hannah:

DR. MELVIN: I'm so sorry that my statements came out in a way that made you feel that Lynn and I were ganging up on you. Let me try this again, okay? It sounds like the two of you had a rough week. You both have different thoughts about why that was, and you both are carrying frustration and hurt about how you feel your partner acted towards you. Help me figure out where we should begin today. Maybe we all take a deep breath, and you can take turns sharing what you need from each other today in order to have the session be productive?

How do you feel about Dr. Melvin's attempt at repairing the rupture in the room with Hannah? Was Dr. Melvin successful at showing up in a neutral way here that made both Hannah and Lynn feel supported and heard by him?

Consider the following dialogue with yet another couple that Dr. Melvin saw that day, Bill and Carrie:

DR. MELVIN: How was the week for you both? How are things going?

CARRIE: I don't know anymore. I just don't think Bill can give me the emotional support and presence that I need from him. He just sits there and shuts down whenever I'm struggling.

DR. MELVIN: I see. Okay, so, Bill, do you understand what she's talking about here? And do you agree with her?

BILL: (shrugs): (Silence.)

CARRIE: See what I mean? I mean, how would you feel, Dr. Melvin? Could you even fathom having a partner who can't even talk to you when you're hurting? I'm sure you'd tire really quickly of it too!

DR. MELVIN: It doesn't really matter what I would personally feel about being in your shoes, does it? What's matters most here, Carrie, is that you are saying that Bill's emotional presence and support is what you need from him, right? This is clearly upsetting to you. So let's bring Bill into this conversation a bit, okay?

BILL: (Still silent.)

DR. MELVIN: So, Bill, do you know what Carrie means by "emotional presence"? What does that look like?

BILL: I don't even know. I don't know what Carrie needs from me anymore. I try to talk to her. But I just never seem to say or do the right things that help her. I think I've kind of given up. I don't think I'll ever be who she needs me to be.

DR. MELVIN: Well, how about we give it a try? Let's ask Carrie to try to be very clear and explain, with solid examples, how she would like you to show up for her, okay? (Turns to Carrie.) Carrie, can you think of any times that Bill said or did something that was really helpful to you when you were struggling?

This time, Dr. Melvin avoided siding with either Carrie or Bill and was able to keep the focus on their interactions and clarifying their needs. I call this the "Teflon™ Technique." Teflon™ is a non-stick substance that coats some pots and pans. When food hits the surface, it makes contact, but doesn't stick. Likewise, when something is "lobbed" at the therapist or counselor that may "stick," and thereby make them side with one person in the room, they need to know how to shrug it off.

If one client throws out a hook to reel the therapist or counselor onto their "side" (e.g., "Right? I know you agree, Dr. Melvin, that saying you hate your partner is not a respectful way to talk to them"), the therapist or counselor must know how to slip off it. In the case with Bill and Carrie above, Dr. Melvin was able to quickly take Carrie's "hook" (in attempting to get him to validate her by agreeing that he would *personally* be unhappy with a partner like Bill) and turn into a therapeutic conversation between them.

An important thing to remember is that it is *totally* okay to feel the various things that come up for us—we are human first, before we become therapists or counselors! We are all regular, flawed people, capable of being activated and having visceral reactions to things that don't "sit right" with us. Common and expected, but awareness and management is *key*. As Wilcoxon, et al. (2013) so simply and fittingly state: "Such self-awareness must entail a clear understanding of the values we invoke in professional decisions. Failing to intentionally examine our value structure may significantly impede our ability to assist clients" (p. 12).

Chapter Takeaways for Therapists and Counselors

1 Self-of-the-therapist (SOTT) work is an important cornerstone of being an ethical provider.
2 The motivation to become a therapist or counselor has historically been associated with the concept of the ***wounded healer***.
3 SOTT work includes therapists and counselors exploring their own personal value system and privilege. Incorporating discussion on these into therapy can create a more equitable therapeutic alliance.

4 SOTT work includes understanding the cultural influences of therapists and counselors and their clients, and how to navigate those in session.
5 *Checking vision* is a term that describes the activities that can help the therapist or counselor to check in with their own values and perceptions. These activities include attending workshops, reading articles and research, and getting supervision on clinical cases.
6 SOTT work includes understanding *assumptions*, how therapists and counselors can make them, and how they can negatively impact the therapy.
7 Nagy's term "multidirectional partiality" means that, at the very same time, *everyone* and *no one* feels special in the therapy room.

8 Best Practices for Being an Ethical Therapist or Counselor Collaboration

Famed Narrative therapist and Reflecting Team creator, Tom Andersen, believed that when more than one [therapist's] perspective is considered on the same situation or issue, this will most likely create new possibilities (Friedman, 1995). Hence, collaborating with other therapists or counselors can help expand one's understanding or ideas on the case.

One way to encourage ethical practice is to be intentional about collaborating with others on clinical cases. If therapists or counselors practice in an agency, hospital, or other institution with additional practicing folks, this can be much easier. Many of these institutions offer things like case consultation groups, group supervision, or "grand rounds." These are spaces where presenting cases, asking for feedback, and listening to others' professional opinions and ideas can keep any one therapist or counselor well rounded in their view of the case. It can also illuminate assumptions or self-of-the-therapist (SOTT) constraints that may be present for a therapist or counselor. Additionally, collaboration can help generate new pathways or treatment strategies that are in the best interests of the client.

If a therapist or counselor is in a solo practice, it is still important to collaborate with other professionals in the same field, or involved in some capacity with the same case. Sometimes this is called "coordination of care," where a prescribing medical doctor and the weekly therapy support professional communicate and collaborate about the best course of treatment. Always remember that appropriate releases of information (ROIs) from clients are always required in order to collaborate about any specific clinical case.

Another important reason that therapists and counselors should utilize collaboration is that being in clinical practice, especially in *private* practice, can be isolating and lonely. The work that therapists and counselors do can be heavy or draining at times, with very few places to talk about or process their experiences and feelings.

Unfortunately, talking with friends or family about clinical work is not an option. Sharing clinical work can easily border on the very fine line of violations of clients' privacy and confidentiality, even if accidental. It is safer and more ethical for therapists and counselors to share how they are feeling

DOI: 10.4324/9781003745136-9

with their loved ones or other supports, rather than any specific situations from the client situations.

Consider the following two ways that a therapist, Nicole, shares her stress from clinical work with her wife.

Scenario #1

> **Nicole:** I have this client who is totally stressing me out. She is going through a divorce, and is just making every mistake in the book to damage those kids. It's so frustrating, and I see what it's doing to the kids, and she just will not listen to anyone. Her husband travels a lot, and she just uses him and trash talks him to the kids and she wonders why the kids are acting out! I just can't get through to her. And it's triggering me because I'm a child of divorce who was put in the middle, and if she just listened to me, her kids wouldn't have to go through the same thing...

In this first scenario, Nicole gives specifics of the case that are not really necessary for her wife to understand the stress Nicole is feeling from it. The details Nicole offers here open the door to the possibility that her wife might know the client. Perhaps Nicole's wife works with someone or chats with someone at the gym who has disclosed her difficult divorce. Nicole is potentially revealing confidential and protected information in this scenario.

Scenario #2

> **Nicole:** I've been feeling a lot of stress with clients lately. And I know a lot of it is me—I'm letting my own thoughts and personal experiences bleed into someone else's experiences. But I just feel so frustrated. It's hard when I can see the possible disaster down the road, but they won't listen to me. And I guess I get so focused on trying to prevent the disaster that I have a hard time staying in the present. I've just been carrying this particular case pretty heavily lately...

In the second scenario, Nicole refrains from sharing any potentially identifying details, yet is still able to have her wife understand the emotional toll that the case is causing for her. In Nicole's disclosure here, the focus is entirely on *her*, rather than on the client. The specifics she shares about her own feelings here are *not* confidential or protected information.

Another way for therapists and counselors to avoid isolation in clinical practice is to attend conferences, or other workshops or trainings where other like-minded professionals will be in attendance. Not only does this give therapists or counselors helpful information and shared experiences from the presenter(s), but it allows the opportunity for group discussion or questions. Some presentations and workshops allow for small, breakout room conversations and activities, which offers the chance for collaboration.

"The Twin Pillars": Consultation and Documentation

One best practice for therapists and counselors is to adhere to the "twin pillars of liability protection" (Appelbaum & Gutheil, 1991). These "twin pillars" consist of ***consultation*** and ***documentation***. When encountering a sticky situation in practice, consulting with a supervisor, colleague, attorney, or other expert involved is a wise and ethical step. However, it is important that in doing so, therapists and counselors ensure they stay within ethical parameters of privacy, confidentiality, and ROIs if necessary.

Ethical therapists should always make clinical documentation of any precautionary steps, consultations, discussions with and responses of clients, and the rationale for any decisions the therapist or counselor makes. This is another important step in keeping an ethical practice. Not only does documentation show good faith in record keeping, but it can aid in the accurate recollection of information and action in ethical and legal situations that come after treatment has ended.

Print Out Code of Ethics

Every mental health field has their own specific code of ethics. Unless a therapist or counselor is serving on an ethics board on a regular basis, or teaching an ethics class in graduate school, they may not experience or interact with many of the ethical standards contained in the code in their own practice.

The information in the codes may be easily forgotten when a therapist or counselor is not experiencing certain issues in their practices. Brushing up on codes, or code revisions and updates, can get easily delayed or pushed aside for many busy professionals. If the recollection of ethical standards and codes has gotten "rusty," it may be easier to slip up and make an error.

One way to interact more regularly with ethical codes is to print out a hard copy of your particular field's code of ethics and leave it on your desk, or another place you will see it often. Another idea is to laminate the pages, or put them in a clear, plastic binder to keep them sturdy. If the codes are printed out and instantly accessible, it is more likely that therapists and counselors will scan through them.

Remember that as licensed professionals with membership in professional organizations, it is the responsibility of therapists and counselors *to know* their profession's code of ethics, and the standards contained within it. In addition, therapists and counselors are required *to practice in accordance with* their profession's ethical standards.

A Regular "Date" With Your State

Different state and province websites vary in their ease of navigation, and in the clarity of information found there. Regardless of this, therapists and counselors are responsible for knowing their state or provincial laws, rules, and regulations.

One way to stay on top of these important things is to make a "date" with your state or province on a regular basis. Changes to state and province laws and rules can happen quickly, and it is easy to miss seeing an email or alert on these new policies. Regular interaction with state or province websites regarding changes in regulations is an important part of staying updated, compliant, and ethical in clinical practice.

Another important thing for therapists and counselors to do is to keep handy the names and contact information for the folks who manage their specific professions. If there are ever questions, concerns, or lack of clarity or understanding of rules and regulations, therapists or counselors can reach out to the state- or province-level people who can answer those questions.

Check In With Clients

A great way to create an additional level of assurance that therapists and counselors are competent and effective is to check in with their clients on a regular basis. It is easy to forget that *clients* are often the best "experts" on the quality and efficacy of the therapy.

Clients are the ones who experience the therapy, and they are solid judges of that experience. This privilege of lived experience over positional expertise allows for dialogue without rank (Bakhtin, 1984). Therapists and counselors can ask clients questions like "Are you still feeling like we are on the same page with goals for therapy?" or "I wanted to check in to see if you still feel that therapy is helping you?" or "Am I doing okay in tracking with you, or is there anything you'd like me to do more or less of, or differently?"

The benefit of eliciting clients' feedback is threefold. First, it allows the therapist or counselor to get feedback on the clients' view of the therapy. Next, it sends the message to clients that there are *two* "experts" in the room. Lastly, it forges another layer of collaboration and connection in the therapeutic alliance. These things assist therapists and counselors in ethically exploring if the work they are doing is truly benefitting the client(s) (Beneficence).

Work–Life Balance

It can be easy for therapists and counselors to experience the blurring of lines between work and their personal life. Research studies describe the maintenance of work–life balance as important for the mental health of therapists and counselors, and may help protect them from burnout (e.g., A. Rapp et al., 2021). D.J. Rapp et al. (2021) echo the important link between burnout and work–nonwork boundaries.

It can be difficult for therapists and counselors to recognize the possible lack of a healthy work–life balance until negative effects crop up that highlight the need for better balance. The following are some ways that therapists and counselors can strive to maintain a healthy work–life balance:

1. Saying "No"

Saying "no" can be difficult for some people. When therapists and counselors are in practice, only *they* know when they are at their maximum capacity. A supervisee I had years ago kept saying "yes" to taking on more and more relational clients at her site in order to complete her required hours for licensure. During the process, she started to struggle, feeling irritation towards her clients, experiencing exhausted, "snapping" at her family members at home, crying easily, and beginning to question whether she even wanted to be a therapist.

After working through this in supervision, she discovered what was at the core of this for her. Since her site had become used to her saying "yes" to every case that came through the door, she was worried that her site supervisor would be disappointed or judge her for not being able to handle the caseload.

The supervisee was able to talk to her supervisor and agree to not take on any more clients; also, there were a couple of clients that would be appropriate to transfer to a new intern. Soon after, the supervisee's mood began to improve, she presented far more emotionally grounded in supervision, and many of her symptoms had been alleviated. The supervisee was once again sure of her career path as a therapist!

When a therapist or counselor recognizes that they feel overwhelmed with their clinical load, they should talk to their supervisor right away. There is no shame in knowing one's limits, and being able to say "no" when at maximum capacity; in fact, this is exactly what codes of ethics expect from ethical therapists and counselors.

2. Managing Priorities

Another area that can be hard for some people is managing priorities. Focusing too much on clinical work, helping others, or making more money can sometimes come at the expense of the partners, children, or families of therapists and counselors. Many years ago, a colleague said to me, "My husband told me that I show more care and tolerance and support and patience to my clients than I do to him and the kids." This was something that stuck with me throughout my career and was a big part of my continual focus on prioritizing myself as a wife, mother, family member, and friend, above being a therapist.

More practical ways to ensure appropriate prioritization include scheduling client sessions around personal doctor or dentist appointments and important child or family events whenever possible. Another idea is to talk to a supervisor about personal obligations and get support surrounding these things. Remember to bring those therapeutic "skills" home with you;

things like good listening and communication skills, patience, and calmness should be a priority in therapists' and counselors' outside relationships.

3. Time Management

Time management is easier for some folks than it is for others. If therapists or counselors recognize that their work–life balance is off, managing time better might help out. Things like making sure to start and end sessions on time, and doing clinical recording between sessions can help therapists and counselors to stay on track and manage their work obligations in a timely fashion.

Leaving the office on time, creating schedules and timetables for the completion of work tasks, and utilizing cancellation spots to catch up on work are other ways to help therapists and counselors manage time better. The increase of working from home and using telehealth platforms in recent years has made time management more difficult for some therapists and counselors. Békés et al. (2021) looked into the impact of working from home on therapists and counselors, and found the following conditions that may contribute to difficulty in work–life balance and time management for them:

1 The lack of needing to commute in to see clients may leave ambiguous and flexible timelines.
2 Not having empty time spent waiting between client sessions may leave open time to do things in the home.
3 Not having a therapy space that is physically separated from the rest of their home and life may leave them with no transitional space like a car ride home.
4 Not being able to adjust one's mindset between therapy and other aspects of life, such as doing chores at home, answering emails, etc., when both are being done in the same space throughout the day.

These findings further stress the need for therapists and counselors who provide telehealth from home to make efforts to create healthy work–life balance and better time management.

4. Maintaining Healthy Boundaries

Therapists and counselors know the importance of "boundaries" for their clients, and incorporate it often in their work with them. It is equally important for therapists and counselors to maintain healthy boundaries for themselves in order to remain competent and ethical therapists.

Having solid policies on certain areas of clinical practice can help reduce the stress on therapists and counselors, as well encouraging decreased bleeding of clinical stress into their personal lives. The discussions about and the enforcement of these policies may sometimes feel awkward, uncomfortable, or stressful for therapists and counselors, but in the long run, they serve as important protective factors for them. A few of the areas in clinical practice that are important for therapists and counselors to create boundaries on include:

1 **Payment/collection protocols:** When will clients be expected to pay for sessions? Will special arrangements be made for payment plans for balances? Can clients pay monthly instead of weekly? What happens if a client misses a payment or their credit card is declined? What is the policy for unpaid fee collection if the client no longer attends therapy?
2 **Beginning and ending sessions:** How will the therapist or counselor ensure that sessions end on time? What is the policy for when clients show up late for a session? At what rate will the late-start session be billed at? *Note that it may be considered insurance fraud for a therapist or counselor to bill insurance for a session that was not the length that it is contracted to be paid at.*
3 **Late cancellation policies:** Will there be a limit to how many late cancellations a client can have? What is considered "late" for a cancellation? Does it matter what the reason is for the late cancellation (e.g., a medical emergency, a car accident)? Is there a fee for late cancellations?
4 **After-hours contact policies:** How are clients allowed to contact therapists and counselors after hours? What will the time frame of "after hours" include (e.g., weekends, vacation or parental leave, after 5 p.m.)? Will exceptions be made for clients contacting the therapist or counselor after hours if it is an emergency?

These sorts of policies are important for creating healthy boundaries for both the therapist or counselor and the client. These policies should be both stated clearly in the informed consent document, as well as discussed as appropriate with clients.

Perhaps most importantly, what will happen when clients do *not* abide by the policies that the therapist or counselor has set forth? Will clients continue to be seen for therapy or referred out? Remember that the foundational principle of ***Fidelity*** means that ethical therapists and counselors should follow through on what they say they will do. One of the easiest ways to adhere to this ethical principle is to create policies that are enforced. This avoids leaving ambiguity around how the therapy will be organized and run; remember that the therapist or counselor must "win" the ***Battle of Structure***, or be in charge of the competent and ethical way that treatment is conducted.

Healthy boundaries between *home* and home *office* is an important thing that therapists and counselors who are providing teletherapy need to consider. When therapists and counselors share their work space with their home space (as in doing teletherapy from one's residence), it is easy for boundaries to be blurred. The World Health Organization (2019) found that working from home can create job-related stressors that cannot be "left" at the "office," and are thereby not being effectively managed by the normal "rests" that might be found in work breaks, going home, weekend escapes, and time off from work.

For some providers, their teletherapy "office" may double as their bedroom. They may alternate a home office space with their partner or spouse on different days. And during the Pandemic, when all clinicians were forced to work from their homes, some had only the choice to retreat to the floor in the back of their closets for a private and secure space.

The following are some ideas to consider when providing teletherapy from home that can help foster a healthier boundary for therapists and counselors:

1 If at all possible, try to keep the teletherapy "office" space a separate room that is not used for other things such as sleeping or socializing.
2 Create very strict guidelines for family members to never interrupt or enter that space.
3 Always lock the door, and have a "white noise" sound machine on outside the space where teletherapy is being conducted. This should be done not only when you know a family member or roommate is at home, but also when someone who has access to the home *might* show up.
4 Consider closing the "office" door when done for the day, as a symbolic way of "leaving" work.
5 Consider scheduling breaks throughout the work day, as you might at an away-from-home job, like running out to buy a coffee, or sitting down at the kitchen table to eat lunch.
6 Be mindful of not scheduling more sessions than you would do at an eight-hour-a-day office job, just because you can.
7 Set reasonable work hours that leave a clear divide between time to work and time to live life.

Having healthy boundaries that support a reasonable work–life balance is essential for therapists and counselors in creating a competent and ethical practice.

Self-Care

The previous section explored the importance of maintaining healthy boundaries in order to create an ethical clinical practice. Adequate *self-care* is another important contributor to this. In fact, for clinicians, healthy boundaries are a *form* of self-care that can reduce the risk of workplace burnout, defined by the World Health Organization (2019) as the result of chronic workplace stress that isn't managed.

Another important consideration here is how the importance of self-care can hinge on the suggestion that therapists and counselors are personally responsible for systemic problems. Caldwell (personal communication, March 10, 2026) so poignantly writes:

> Becoming a therapist is stressful, emotionally and financially; some workplaces and even some larger mental health systems are set up in ways that are neglectful of clinicians' well-being at best, and actively exploitive at worst. Sometimes what you need isn't a day off, it's a colleague who can look you in the eye and say, "You're not crazy, I get frustrated with that part of our work too."

So if we can agree on the importance and need for self-care for therapists and counselors, where do we start in doing it? First, think about where examples of self-care already exist. Does a therapist or counselor have regular lunch dates out with their significant other? Do they sleep in late on weekends? Do they avoid scheduling late clients on Fridays so that they can begin the weekend earlier with dinner and downtime with their family? Do they work out or go for a run at night?

If therapists or counselors already have examples of where they include self-care, they need to be protective of those things when having a clinical practice. For example, let's say that a therapist, Melinda, has a favorite yoga class on Wednesday nights. She's been going to this class for several years and has developed some great friendships there. On some nights, a small group of them go out to a smoothie place after yoga. Melinda has greatly enjoyed these weekly outings. When she has a request from a couple she sees for therapy to switch their regular therapy time to Wednesday nights due to one of their children's sports schedules, what should she do?

Therapists and counselors are often giving and compassionate people. It might be easy for them to say yes to the couple, in order to accommodate their need and make life simpler for them. But does it always need to be the therapist or counselor who gives up their convenience in order to accommodate that of the client? Melinda has two possible ethical responses here:

1 She can tell the couple that she is not available on Wednesday nights, and work with them to find an alternate time or referral or temporary break from therapy if appropriate.
2 She can agree to the change permanently, temporarily, or every other week, in order to accommodate both of their schedules.

Option #1 clearly centers on maintaining Melinda's work–life boundaries and self-care. There should be no pressure or reservation or shame for therapists or counselors who make this choice.

Option #2 is also a possible choice for Melinda. However, with this option, Melinda must first do some SOTT work to explore the "why" she is making this choice. One valid reason might be that there is another yoga class on a different night that works for her new friends' schedules and is therefore not a big deal to switch. It is a good idea for Melinda to check her motivations for the willingness to change session times, and be sure it is not from common SOTT reasons like feeling obligated, pressured, or guilty, or not prioritizing self and self-care.

In her article on assessing self-care in therapists (Reynolds, 2018), the author stresses that "Doing therapy is clearly not like many other jobs. It requires mental energy, clear thinking, patience, and the ability to temporarily exit one's own life" (p. 39). These mental, psychological, and emotional "parts" that must be put into the art of doing therapy, must also be refilled somewhere, since therapy is not expected to be reciprocal.

The following are some reflection questions that may be helpful for therapists and counselors when looking at their own self-care:

1 Do I feel relaxed and happy when I'm working with clients?
2 Do I have things that I enjoy regularly outside of work (e.g., time with friends or family, exercise, hobbies, reading, or watching movies or TV shows)?
3 Do I feel healthy (e.g., do I cook for myself and eat healthily, do I get enough sleep, do I have time to get outside and move my body)?
4 Do my friends and family ever tell me that I'm often stressed out, snippy, irritable, angry, or sad?
5 Do I have any downtime, with no obligations, to look forward to?
6 Do my friends or family often complain I'm distracted or never available?

Answering "yes" to any of the above suggests that at least a SOTT exploration is a good idea. Although particular life stressors (e.g., single parenthood, financial strain, limited resources or support, food insecurity, family-of-origin stress, caretaking for aging parents, behavioral or medical issues with a family member) might make the possibility of increasing self-care seem impossible, oftentimes there are still small ways to increase it so that it makes a difference. Ideas might include going to bed a bit earlier, or getting up a bit earlier to have a cup of tea and some peace and solitude before beginning a hectic day. Other possibilities are asking a friend or family member to help out with transportation home from a school event, or using a last-minute client cancellation as an excuse to go for a walk outside, read a few chapters of a pleasure book, or get caught up on a task that will free up time later.

Remember that mental health professional codes of ethics range from describing self-care as an expectation or obligation, to a more general understanding that balance and SOTT work that keeps the therapist competent and ethical is necessary. However, regardless of the code, it is the ethical responsibility of therapists and counselors to monitor their own balance and needs that are necessary for them to remain competence and ethics in clinical practice. The "ethical imperative of self-care" isn't a luxury for mental health professionals (Abramson, 2021).

Get Help

It's an important task to stay on top of monitoring the clinical work of therapists or counselors who are having difficulties personally that appear to be overwhelming for them (Reynolds, 2018). This duty often falls to supervisors. Norris, Gutheil, and Strasburger (2003) write about the detriments that might happen when a therapist or counselor is stressed out—namely, the possibility of boundary crossings and other violations.

In an article about assessing the need for increased self-care in therapists (Reynolds, 2018), the author shares the case of "Caroline," who is in her last year of graduate school in Marriage and Family Therapy. While in supervision, Caroline breaks down and says that she is feeling "triggered" by many of her clients, and that it's affecting her ability to be fully present is her sessions. She admits that she is struggling with poor time management, is distracted, and even cried at a session with a client. However, she insists that she is still an effective therapist, and that doing therapy helps her feel better, gives her purpose, and helps her escape her own "difficult life" (p. 38).

Although it is the responsibility of the therapist or counselor to seek help when personal issues get in the way of competence in the therapy room, Caroline now has a supervisor who is aware of her struggles. Supervisors have several parts to their "job description" that enable them to help therapists, counselors, or trainees navigate these sorts of personal struggles, while remaining competent.

All mental health fields stress the importance of supervision for ensuring that therapists and counselors maintain an ethical and competent presence in clinical practice (Bradley & Becker, 2021). Supervisors can provide support, guidance, strategies, and important reminders for self-care and the necessity of managing personal issues so that they don't get in the way of competent clinical work. In extreme cases, the supervisor may have to make difficult choices, such as temporarily removing a therapist or counselor from clinical work, or reporting as per mandates at their agencies or practices, or by their professional codes of ethics.

If Caroline is not able to get on top of her situation and stressors in a way that maintains ethics and competence, the clinical work she is doing may become compromised. It is also very possible that Caroline was experience burnout. Burnout and other indicators of provider well-being are associated with negative client outcomes (e.g., Bradley & Becker, 2021; Salyers et al., 2015).

Therapists and counselors will need a strong relationship with their supervisors in order to feel comfortable sharing personal struggles and concerns over well-being with them and to seek out support as needed (Knox, 2015). The maintenance of the relationship between supervisor and supervisee is paramount in most effectively supporting therapists and counselors.

Never Stop Learning

The iconic writer and philosopher Ralph Waldo Emerson famously wrote: "Unless you try to do something beyond what you have already mastered, you will never grow." Growing, developing, and keeping current are important "ethics" for maintaining competence in clinical practice.

Even for the most experienced therapists and counselors, continuing to learn and update is an essential part of being a good clinician. Things change, society and people's experiences evolve, and new research is available. The following are some of the ways that continued learning supports therapists and counselors in their ethical and competent practice:

1 Learning new things may help ward off boredom, and may spark new/more passion for or excitement about clinical work.
2 Learning new things can help generate new ideas or techniques or strategies for treating clients.
3 Learning often results in the exchange of new ideas, where all parties involved benefit. The presenter of a workshop, for example, might be challenged by participants' questions, which generate new lines of conversation that enhance the conversation for everyone.
4 Learning new things helps therapists and counselors stay current on things like new research, models, or interventions.

I try to remain open to learning in all my educational and clinical settings. I have takeaways from teaching and the student questions I receive there, or from other therapists' clinical challenges when I provide supervision. In my clinical work, I am always growing. Every client that I see teaches me something. Couples demonstrate their particular ways of communicating and problem solving, which may help me in working with other couples who have similar problem. All of these serve as ways for therapists and counselors to be open to the availability of learning new things.

Reading journal articles and professional books is another way to generate new ideas and insights for therapists and counselors. Continuing education (CE) workshops and trainings can offer cutting-edge information and research in clinical practice. Several years ago, I attended a workshop on the experience of being transgender in a military setting. As a seasoned therapist, with experience with a broad range of client populations (including military folks), I realized that I had very little knowledge about the experience of this specific population. In the workshop, they were talking about the pros and cons of asking about clients' pronouns. At that time, I was trained to always ask for pronouns, in an attempt to be inclusive, respectful, and sensitive to how our clients self-identified.

I learned from another person who I was paired off with that she was transgender and hated to be asked her pronouns. She said:

> I waited my whole life to be able to be the person I was meant to be. God made a mistake creating me as a male, and now I am the woman I was meant to be. I embrace my femininity, and dress like a female, do female things, and am just overall feminine-appearing. My name is historically female—Katherine. Every time someone asks me for my pronouns, I cringe inside, because it forces me to acknowledge the choice I

made. Unlike cisgender people who are born in the person they best fit with, I had to make a difficult choice that came with many traumatic hurdles. I know therapists and counselors mean well in asking for a client's pronouns, but for me, I dream of the day someone will just use "she" as my pronoun, and in making that assumption that I'm female, I will have been given the greatest gift.

This was a perspective I had never considered. This person opened my eyes to a new possibility of how some of my clients might feel or experience being asked about their pronouns, and this informed my practice and how I asked questions. This learning opportunity benefitted everyone—it helped me to consider another perspective and include changes in my practice because of it, it may help future clients who feel much like this woman did about pronouns, and I believe it helped the woman to be able to share with me and offer assistance from her experience.

Seek Legal Counsel as Appropriate

All therapists and counselors should have malpractice insurance coverage, and with these policies there usually comes legal advice and consultations or representation as appropriate and necessary. Professional associations in different mental health fields often have counsel available for information or consultation as well.

These services are available for a good reason! And therapists and counselors should use them. Ethics and the law are two very important parts of competent clinical care. If therapists and counselors feel the "sticky," and are not able to navigate via supervision, legal consults are a must.

Define the Client at the Very Beginning

Especially when working with more than one client in the room, such as in cases with a family or couple, it is helpful for therapists and counselors to define—therapeutically, ethically, and legally—who the client/client system is. This will help therapists and counselors avoid sticky situations.

For example, if a therapist is seeing a 40-year-old woman for individual therapy, that person is the client. But if the therapist agrees to see the client with her boyfriend for a few sessions to work on improving their communication skills, who is the client? It is important for the therapist to clarify this to the client(s) in three ways:

1 **Therapeutically:** Is it appropriate for the therapist to be both the client's individual client and the couples' therapist? Does seeing them both create any conflict of interest?
2 **Ethically:** Will this set-up be beneficial to the client and not cause her harm? Will the therapist be willing to speak to either of the clients

individually while she is doing the couples' work? Is it ethical for the female client to not have individual sessions during the time that the therapist is doing the couples' work?

3 **Legally:** Has the therapist opened a separate file for the couples' work? Has the therapist discussed whose insurance she will bill and under what code?

When therapists and counselors define the client/client system for themselves, communicate the specifics of them to the client(s), and act in ways that support the legal and ethical requirements of these choices, they are aligning themselves with best practices. Additionally, doing this at the beginning of therapy helps the therapist or counselor and client(s) avoid possible misunderstandings and sticky situations.

It's About the "How" You Say It

For many therapists and counselors, creating boundaries, being firm about enforcing those boundaries, and making strides to "win" the Battle of Structure in therapy can be difficult. This may be especially true for folks who are conflict-avoidant or "people pleasers," worry about hurting or offending clients, or have insecurities about their abilities. However, having and enforcing these boundaries in therapy is an important part of staying off the ethical "slippery slope."

I encourage therapists and counselors to take the time and effort to discover the stances and "voice" they will use to be able to create these necessary boundaries. For example, consider the following ways that *two different therapists* draw a boundary in a couples' session with an angry husband, Otto:

> **Therapist #1:** Otto, I'm going to ask you to stop talking for a minute. Your tone and swearing isn't helpful to your wife—do you see her crying and shutting down? Do you remember when you first filled out paperwork at our first session? We discussed that I would stop any session where I felt there was abusive language or inappropriate escalating anger? So, if you can't bring it down a notch and speak more quietly and respectfully to your wife, we will need to end for today, okay?
>
> **Therapist #2:** Hold on a sec, Otto, okay? I'm not sure if you are both feeling the room getting a bit hotter, but I find that when there is a certain level of anger in the room, we're not going to get anywhere. When you filled out paperwork at our first session, do you both recall that we discussed stopping the session if I felt that things were getting too angry or escalated? I want to take a minute for the room to cool off a bit, and check in with you both about how this is feeling to you. I think you need to take a little break, Otto, and let me know if you think you will be able to continue the session. Is there something I can help you do to find a healthier place for the anger you're feeling today?

How do you feel about the two therapists' ways of handling the escalation in the session? There are many ways for the therapist to have handled the escalation in the room. However, the most important part is that the therapist takes the responsibility for controlling sessions that may become inappropriate or hurtful or abusive. Beneficence and Non-Maleficence are two foundational principles that come to mind here. Additionally, in aligning with concept of the Battle of Structure and the Fidelity principle, the therapist should follow through on the rules she set up for the therapy (e.g., discontinuing sessions that inappropriately escalate).

Therapist #1 and Therapist #2 had very different ways of setting boundaries in their sessions with the client, Otto, and his wife. Other therapists may have chosen even different ways to manage the session. Therapists and counselors need to find the right fit for themselves that still allows them to ensure that there are healthy boundaries in the room. Remember, ethics tell you *what* to do, but not specifically *how* to do it!

The "Why I Do This" Box

Clinical practice is incredibly important and meaningful work. But it doesn't always feel that way. Therapists and counselors manage the stress, struggles, trauma, pain, and heartache of clients on a consistent basis. They may also deal regularly with paperwork, billing, technology, insurance, and scheduling issues. For many therapists and counselors, the weight of all of this can shroud the beautiful gifts they get from being in this profession.

In a two-part article (Reynolds, 2013), an author describes her "Why I Do This" box. After grappling with the many layers of responding to gift giving at the beginning of her career, the author shares a powerful note that she sent back to a recently terminated client, after deciding to decline a gift card that accompanied a beautiful thank-you note:

> Dear [Client],
>
> I am touched by your kind words and generous gift, but I am returning this card to you for several reasons. My professional association frowns upon the practice of accepting magnanimous gifts. But more importantly, I don't need a gift as a thank you from you—your gratitude in demonstrated in your thoughtful gesture and words. You have worked hard this year at taking your life back and in searching for happiness again. I am so glad for you and it's been an honor to accompany you on your journey. So, go buy yourself something with this gift card that you would never treat yourself to, and enjoy it—you deserve it!
>
> Fondly, [Therapist]
>
> (p. 41)

This therapist note suggests the "why" she does this work. She highlights several things that are the parts of doing therapy that feel good to the therapist or counselor, and make the work worthwhile:

1 Feeling "touched" by a meaningful thank you note from a client.
2 Being the recipient of a client's gratitude for the efforts made.
3 Feeling glad for a client's happiness and successes.
4 Feeling the honor of accompanying a client on their healing journey.

It can be difficult sometimes for therapists and counselors to remember these important gifts to themselves in doing therapeutic work. For this reason, the author shares that she created a "Why I Do This" box. This box contains all the notes, emails, and thank-you letters or cards she has received from clients over the years. When she is feeling overwhelmed at work, feeling frustrated with clinical issues, or forgetting where the good is in this (sometimes) stressful job, she visits the box. It is here, in rereading the heartfelt notes and thank-yous from past clients, that she is reminded of why she does this work. This gives her renewed energy, positivity, and a cognitive reframe that helps center her SOTT work.

Maintaining an ethical and competent practice begins and ends with SOTT work, and this is one way for therapists and counselors to stay in check with themselves and help prevent burnout.

Don't Work Harder Than the Client

I can remember early on in graduate school, many moons ago, a professor once saying, "Don't work harder than the client(s)." I'm pretty sure that I didn't fully understand the statement back then, but I have carried it with me and found it an extremely helpful tool.

It is easy to get caught up in setting loftier goals for clients than what they want or might be capable of. Sometimes, high hopes for a client might follow us home. Overcommitting to change and a healthier existence for clients can burn us out.

Different therapists and counselors have varying amounts of capacity for helping and caring. Indeed, by nature, the practice of therapy is helping and caring! A good best practice for therapists and counselors is to give 110 percent effort in client sessions, and then try to let go of the work when they leave the office.

Another strategy for not working harder than the client is to appeal to the client when the therapist or counselor needs a check-in over the effectiveness of therapy. For example, a therapist might say:

> I feel like I've been carrying more concern over these arguments with your mother than you are. I remember you saying that these fights are the biggest issue you have in your life, and your main goal when we

started meeting was to reduce them. Are you still feeling that these fights are unbearable and are causing you distress? Or maybe I should back off and not keep centering on them if something has changed...?

This is one way for a therapist to check in with the client, to see if the client is as focused on and invested in working towards change.

Professionalism

What does "professionalism" look like? Professionalism is defined by the Oxford English Dictionary as "The high standard that you expect from a person who is well trained in a particular job." Maintaining professionalism as a therapist or counselor can be a helpful part of maintaining an ethical practice. So, what constitutes "professionalism" as a therapist or counselor?

Some of the most important headings under professionalism that I've heard for therapists and counselors include things like competence, maturity, ability to be present, communication, respect, responsibility, and ethics. But there are many other, more subtle, perhaps less focused-on, things that contribute to professionalism.

Dress/Clothing

Some group practices, agencies, hospitals, clinics, schools, or other institutions may have required standards for what professionalism specifically entails. For example, one therapy agency I know of has a dress code that requires their employees to dress in: "Neat, clean, appropriate clothing. Casual and informal wear, such as flip-flops, sweatpants, or tee-shirts with words or pictures on them, are prohibited." This particular agency's standards include both detailed and more general descriptions here. Therapists and counselors who work for someone else may be given guidelines such as these, but what about providers who are in solo practice?

In one study on perceptions of attire by patients in medical settings, the researchers found that the preference is largely influenced by age, locale, setting, and context of care (Petrilli et al., 2015). Although suggested of medical settings, this may be pertinent to therapists and counselors as well. Regarding things like *age*, do you think a therapist's or counselor's dress matters differently to a ten-year-old and a 70-year-old? Remembering that therapists and counselors have rules and ethics to follow, while clients are free to interpret and judge however they wish, might there be perceptions that we want to avoid?

"Professional" will likely be viewed very differently by different people. Therefore, how do you feel about striving to express professionalism in ways that center most on making *every* client who comes to see you feel comfortable and safe? If this is the standard we are using for how professionalism looks, let's take a look at a few more areas to consider.

Language

Swearing is a subject of longstanding controversy, dating back to the days in which prominent figures of the psychotherapeutic tradition utilized it (Williams & Uebel, 2022). There are very mixed reviews on whether the use of profanity is helpful or acceptable or not. However, given the *extremely* limited studies on this topic, it is difficult to really understand the way that swearing, or using a client's less-than-professional language might impact therapy.

There is some evidence that the use of profanity is linked to activity in the limbic system, which is an area of the brain that involves the processing of emotions (Jay, 2000). Therefore, we can surmise that the use of profanity may be indeed memorable to a client, but what is unknown is if that memory is a positive one or not! So, how does a therapist or counselor maintain a competent and professional practice, while still understanding that language, in many contexts, *including* profanity, is a powerful tool?

Therapists and counselors should also view language, and specifically profanity, through the lens of the possible the power dynamics between therapist and client (Williams & O'Connor, 2019). It may land very differently for a client when a therapist or counselor says, "What the fuck?" using a certain intonation, even if the word "fuck" has been used by the client in previous conversations and contexts. Given the power differentials that may exist between therapist or counselor and client(s), would the client(s) feel comfortable telling the provider if the language was offensive or uncomfortable to them?

Regarding profanity and professionalism, perhaps the most appropriate choice for therapists and counselors is to understand the power of the tool of language in general, and proceed with caution when contemplating the use of it in sessions. Consider the two short dialogues between therapist and client, and think about how the choice of words the therapist chooses might feel to the client. Does the language choice of the therapist in each example feel both *professional* and *ethical* to you? Which style resonates most with you?

Dialogue #1

CLIENT: I get so fucking pissed off when my boyfriend says that shit to me. He's so critical and high-and-mighty. He gets pissed off too when I tell him to fucking get out. But I've told him before that it pisses me off and I'm not dealing with that shit anymore.

THERAPIST: So, let me get this right—seems like there is a pattern here where you describe both of you feeling pissed off, and that's followed by feelings of not being heard by each other, and not wanting to deal with that same go-around over and over again?

In this dialogue, the therapist attempts to both use a bit of the client's language, as it obviously carries meaning for him, as well as to create a more therapeutic understanding of the events the client described.

Dialogue #2

CLIENT: I get so fucking pissed off when my boyfriend says that shit to me. He's so critical and high-and-mighty. He gets pissed off too when I tell him to fucking get out. But I've told him before that it pisses me off and I'm not dealing with that shit anymore.

THERAPIST: So, I'm hearing that there's a lot of anger here, for both of you. I also see that there are patterns of feeling unheard, and the frustration with these cycles leading to wanting to give up?

In this dialogue, the therapist attempts to ignore the client's language, and focus instead on the therapeutic understanding of the patterns and feelings of the client and his boyfriend.

The Power of Touch

Similar to the discussion above on the use of profanity in sessions, the use of physical contact between a therapist or counselor and the client(s) is a debate that is ongoing, with very little consensus amongproviders (e.g., Reamer, 2017). In maintaining a professional and ethical practice, exploring the power of human touch in the therapy room is vital.

The tricky part of looking at physical touch in therapy is that physical contact considered appropriate by some people may be thought of as a violation by others (Bonitz, 2008). Gender and power issues (Curvis, 2020), among a myriad of other factors, must be considered when deciding if or how or when to use touch within the therapeutic relationship. There are cultural norms and differences that can contribute to a client's experience of a therapist's or counselor's touch. These need to be considered and respected by the therapist or counselor to maintain ethics in the therapeutic relationship.

Even the tiniest form of physical contact—a pat on the back, a touch of the hand, or even an unusual closeness of physical proximity—can carry meaning to a client. Will the client perceive a fleeting touch by the therapist as a gesture of comfort? Threatening? Suggestive? Uncomfortable? Confusing?

Being explicit and transparent about physical contact from the onset of the therapy (Curvis, 2020) is one way to keep ethics and professionalism at the forefront when considering physical touch in the therapeutic relationship. Additionally, documentation in the case note is an important part of the safety and protection and ethics for both the therapist or counselor and the client.

In short, perhaps the most appropriate and ethical thought on physical touch is that it should not be used as a general rule. However, there may be times when a therapist or counselor thinks that a supportive or caring gesture or hug is in the best interests of the client (Beneficence) or that it is respecting the clients' Autonomy (the right to make choices that are best for them).

Self-Disclosure

When considering the maintenance of professionalism in the therapeutic relationship, another important topic to explore is self-disclosure. Therapist self-disclosure (TSD) usage varies greatly among different psychotherapy orientations (Miller & McNaught, 2020). Most therapists and counselors I know would say that self-disclosure can be a powerful tool, but that it can also be risky, depending on the client's perceptions and comfort with it.

Sometimes, therapist or counselor self-disclosure may not be intentional. A client might discover things about the provider by looking them up online. They may also draw conclusions about the provider's ethnicity from their dress or their surname. A cross worn around a therapist's or counselor's neck or a wedding ring on their finger may unintentionally disclose religious affiliation and marital status. These things can garner lots of different perceptions—for example, connection, judgment, comfort, or discomfort.

Danzer (2019) highlights several possible risks from inappropriate self-disclosure, including lack of attentiveness, too frequent focus on the therapist or counselor, disclosure for personal reasons, poorly timed disclosures, and the possible lack of attunement with the client(s).

Self-disclosure is a choice that should come only after a very personal examination of the motivation of the therapist or counselor in disclosing. This is a *must* for best practices for therapists and counselors when considering self-disclosure in therapy. An important question to ask oneself is "Am I choosing to share this personal disclosure with a client because I think it will help them, or be a useful tool in some way?"

Chapter Takeaways for Therapists and Counselors

1 This chapter highlights the importance of collaboration with others, and checking in with clients in order for therapists and counselors to stay accountable in competent and clinical work.
2 Two best practices for therapists and counselors are (a) printing out their professional codes of ethics for easy access and note taking on them, and (b) making a "date" to regularly visit their state or province website for laws and regulations updates.
3 This chapter highlights the importance of maintaining a good work–life balance and healthy boundaries in order to support a competent and ethical clinical practice.

4 Therapists and counselors should seek out legal counsel when more support than supervision is necessary to navigate sticky clinical situations.
5 "The Why I Do This" box is explained in this chapter, with highlights of its importance for staying positive in practice and avoiding burnout.
6 Professionalism is an important part of best ethical practices and can include things like a therapist's or counselor's choice of dress, use of physical touch, and self-disclosure.

9 Case Vignettes

Many times, it is when something goes wrong in therapy that ethics come into play. Better for therapists and counselors to become "wired" ethically, *before* the onset of any discontent, in order to more quickly and easily navigate dilemmas that might show up.

The chapters of this text have covered a wide range of topics for therapists and counselors to consider when building a competent and ethical clinical practice. The following vignettes will offer more opportunity for readers to engage with clinical scenarios that require some ethical consideration.

In alignment with the rest of the book, each vignette will be followed by a "Sticky," and "Boil it Down," discussion. Remember that there is often *not* one singular way to be ethical. Since ethics are not black and white "*things*," but rather *mindsets*, the vignette discussions are suggestions for *how* to think about things, not specifically what a therapist or counselor *must* do.

Let's follow a therapist, Lindsey, as she navigates a year's worth of ethical dilemmas in her clinical practice. After each vignette, consider the following:

1 How do you feel about Lindsey's choices with the client(s) or clinical situation?
2 What would you have done the same, or differently, if you were Lindsey?
3 Did Lindsey's choices demonstrate competence as a therapist?
4 Was Lindsey's course of action ethical?

Vignette #1

Lindsey sees a husband and wife for relationship counseling. In the second session, the spouses verbally explode at one another, and tell Lindsey they are both sick and tired of the drama, and that they are both in agreement that they are getting divorced. They want to change the direction of the therapy towards navigating co-parenting communication and parenting time. Lindsey begins a new course of treatment with the couple, as well as referring both spouses to individual therapists for support.

DOI: 10.4324/9781003745136-10

While the divorce paperwork is being filed, the couple continues with the relational therapy, focusing on moving forward in their "next chapter." In one session, the wife expresses doubt that her husband is getting individual therapy, and demands that the husband show documentation/proof from the Explanation of Benefits (EOB) statements that these sessions are occurring before he can see the kids again.

The couple requests that Lindsey speak with both of their individual therapists, so that coordination can occur between all three providers on the goals for treatment. Lindsey asks both spouses for a signed release for each of their individual therapists.

Sticky: Should Lindsey have agreed to change gears towards divorce work on session 2? Or should she have explored a possible emotional trigger that may have caused the change of heart between sessions 1 and 2?

Is it legal or appropriate for the wife to disallow visits with the kids contingent on proof of the dad's individual treatment? Is it appropriate for her to demand to see "proof" of her husband's therapy?

Should the therapist talk to both spouses' individual therapists? What does she do with the notes she takes on those conversations? Is it the therapist's responsibility to explain protected health information (PHI) and the ways to disclosure of it to a spouse by the other therapist?

Boil it Down: Lindsey is torn between the clients' right to make their own decisions to divorce (Autonomy), versus what might be in the best interests of the clients (Beneficence). In this case, Lindsey decides that she has some expert power in the therapy relationship (by having a lot of experience with how couples can quickly change course due to triggering events that cause emotional swings), and owes her clients some support and psychoeducation before changing gears towards divorce work.

She decides to first explore if there were activating events that triggered the couple's sudden change of heart from relational work to divorce work. "What happened between session 1 and session 2 that contributed to the big change?" She explains how high emotions can lead to impulsive decision-making, and she asks the couple if they'd like to take a couple of sessions to cool off and address the issues they felt led to the "final straw" before making their final decision on their relationship.

Next, Lindsey ponders whether it is legal or ethically appropriate for the wife to disallow visits with the kids contingent on proof of her husband's individual treatment. She recognizes that if she supports this request, she may be appearing to "side" with the wife. Additionally, Lindsey wonders if it's appropriate for the wife to demand to see PHI from the husband, when asking to see his EOBs.

In attempting to maintain the competent and ethical treatment of her clients, Lindsey seeks support from her supervisor and also schedules a brief consult with her professional affiliation's legal team to find out more about family law and divorce. She worries that with no divorce or custody agreement, and no allegation of any abuse or neglect by the husband towards the kids, the wife cannot legally withhold the children from seeing their father. Furthermore, Lindsey wonders if the wife could get herself into legal trouble for withholding the children.

Lindsey recalls her supervisor telling her once to remember that her clients are often the best experts. So she shares her thoughts with her clients to open up a conversation. Then she proposes that they would be able to use the couple's co-parenting sessions to be a safe space to work through any concerns they have, rather than demanding PHI or withholding time with the children.

Lindsey wonders if there are any ethical issues with her talking to both spouses' individual therapists. She decides that "coordination of care" between the three therapists involved makes sense and is in the best interests of the clients (Beneficence). She has the appropriate releases of information (ROIs). However, she needs to be mindful of what she does with the notes she takes from those conversations. For example, whatever the husband's therapist tells Lindsey, she must be sure that this PHI is never shared with the wife or the wife's therapist. So Lindsey decides to create a separate section of the chart for solely husband's information, and solely wife's information, so that the couples' chart content stands separately. She also knows that she will need to act in compliance with her state and federal laws and rules on the contents of the couples' chart, should it ever be requested by either party.

But how can Lindsey ensure that the couples' two individual therapists do not disclose anything that Lindsey has shared with them to their own individual clients? Lindsey is pretty certain there is no way to ensure this, because the protection of information and its appropriate release is the responsibility of those therapists, over which she has no control. However, to protect herself and the best interests of her clients, she documents that she has confirmed this with both therapists and received their confirmation of understanding and agreement. She might also have the individual therapists sign a release that details the protection requirement of the sensitive information that will be shared between them.

Lastly, Lindsey knows the importance of documentation, and so she notes a summary of her considerations, choices, and actions in the clients' chart. She is careful to type up just the occurrences, and rereads what she has written to ensure she has refrained from leading statements, judgments, and her own interpretations in the notes.

Vignette #2

Lindsey saw a couple for therapy one year ago. The couple had sought out her services when they found themselves struggling a bit with some communication issues. After six months of treatment with Lindsey, the couple reported doing much better, had just gotten engaged, and were ready to end therapy.

A few weeks after termination, Lindsey received an email from the one half of the couple, asking for Lindsey's home address so that they could send her a wedding invitation. The email went on to say that the couple believed that without Lindsey's support and help, they wouldn't have been able to work through things and stay in their relationship. The couple agreed that they could not even imagine not having Lindsey at their wedding, since it was Lindsey, they believed, who got them to where they were today.

Sticky: Should Lindsey attend the wedding? Is it true that Lindsey is the reason the couple is where they are today? Is there the potential for any ethical issues if Lindsey were to attend the wedding? And if she didn't attend, would it devastate the clients, and potentially ruin their day?

Boil it Down: The couple is not her client anymore, so there would not be a multiple relationship at this point. Of course, Lindsey knows that she is not the reason that the couple stayed together. It's not about her—it's about the couple entrusting her to enter their system and help guide them. Ultimately, the couple needed to do the work and decide to stay together. The couple doesn't "owe" Lindsey any "thanks," for doing her job effectively.

Lindsey does believe that the couple would be happy if she attended the wedding, since they were very grateful for her support and guidance throughout the course of therapy. However, Lindsey attending the wedding might bring up ethical issues. How will Lindsey respond if a wedding guest asks her how she knows the bride and groom? If Lindsey attended alone, it might be awkward and uncomfortable—Lindsey wouldn't know anyone there. But if she brought a date to the wedding, her date might ask how she knows the couple. Could she comfortably have a drink or two at the wedding? Would the couple feel obligated to take time away from their special day in order to greet Lindsey and thank her for coming? Would it be appropriate for Lindsey to give the couple a wedding gift?

If Lindsey doesn't attend, she needs to figure out whether to tell the couple the truth about why, or she could just tell them she is sorry, but she has another obligation that day. She doesn't want to disappoint or hurt the couple in any way, but she still wants to act ethically, even though the couple are not her clients anymore. And what about *Lindsey*? Does she have a say, selfishly, on whether she has any desire to go to the wedding or not? Does what she wants even matter?

Lindsey decides that since her profession's code of ethics does not expressly say whether attending ex-clients' wedding would be a conflict of interest, she is free to consider all the layers of the situation and make the best decision she can. So she decides that she will tell the clients by email (thus skirting the request for a home mailing address) that she has a prior engagement that day and will not be able to attend, and that she will be there in "spirit," and be sending her very best wishes for a beautiful day. Lindsey then purchases a wedding card that has just the right sentiment on it. She writes a beautiful and genuine note inside about the couple's hard work and commitment and resilience, and sends it to them.

Lastly, Lindsey knows the importance of documentation, and so she notes a summary of her considerations, choices, and actions in the clients' closed chart. She is careful to type up just the occurrences, and rereads what she has written to ensure she has refrained from leading statements, judgments, and her own interpretations in the notes.

Vignette #3

Lindsey has a newer client who is training to be a massage therapist. The client has to do a number of massages for friends and family in order to get the hours she needs for completing the certification program.

The client offers to give Lindsey free weekly massages in place of paying her fee for therapy because she has specialty training in neuropathy and sciatica, both of which Lindsey suffers from. The client know this because Lindsey has had to cancel appointments on occasion when she has had a flare-up, and self-disclosed her condition to all of her clients in order to be transparent about her ongoing need to cancel from time to time.

Sticky: Lindsey knows that bartering is sometimes allowed in clinical practice. Would there be anything unethical about Lindsey accepting the mutually beneficial offer from her client? Is there any way that accepting the offer might cause the client any harm?

Boil it Down: Lindsey's client is attempting to barter services, which she knows her profession's code of ethics frowns upon, but does not prohibit, unless it could potentially cause harm to the client. Lindsey considers the situation, looking for any potential ethical edges. Would being a massage therapy "client" as well as being the client's therapist constitute a multiple relationship?

Lindsey's client has just gone through an acrimonious divorce and is attempting to reinvent a career for herself, so that she will be able to support herself and her children. Since money is tight, not having to pay for therapy sessions would benefit the client, and since Lindsey's insurance does not cover massage for her conditions, it would benefit Lindsey as well. The client does not have very many friends, and her family lives far away. Therefore, it might be hard for the client to complete the required hours she will need.

The specific specialty that the client is training in is something that is rare to find in Lindsey's area. It might help Lindsey to avoid flare-ups, which in turn would help all of her clients because she would have to cancel sessions less often. Lindsey's professional code of ethics tells her that she must get appropriate treatment for any conditions that may be getting in the way of her being able to do therapy. She thinks that the specialty massages will count towards this mandate.

If Lindsey creates a document of understanding, which includes specifics about how the agreement will work, and the limits of it, she will be doing her due diligence in making sure professional boundaries remain in place, and both parties agree to the understanding of the arrangement.

Lindsey can't think of any ways that the bartering agreement could cause the client any harm. However, Lindsey does think about the possibility that the client could potentially injure her or make her condition worse, especially since she is an inexperienced and unlicensed massage therapist at this point. Would an unintentional injury cause a rupture in the therapeutic relationship? Would it cause Lindsey to want to renege on the bartering agreement? Could the client's feelings be hurt by this?

Lindsey considers the actual nature of massage therapy for a minute. Will she be comfortable being unclothed in front of her client? How might the physical touch between the client and the therapist impact their therapeutic relationship? Where would the massages be conducted? In the therapist's office, or at the therapist's or client's home?

Lindsey decides that, first and foremost, agreeing to this bartering arrangement would constitute a multiple relationship. In addition, there are many potential factors that might create "weirdness" or other boundary crossings within the therapeutic relationship that could be harmful to the client. So Lindsey tells the client she would love to help her out, and is grateful that she is training to do such important work with her specialty area; however, in doing so, it would simply create an unethical multiple relationship and boundary crossing that might negatively impact their therapy together.

Lastly, Lindsey knows the importance of documentation, and so she notes a summary of her considerations, choices, and actions in the client's chart. She is careful to type up just the occurrences, and rereads what she has written to ensure she has refrained from leading statements, judgments, and her own interpretations in the notes.

Vignette #4

Lindsey has a 45-year-old client who is a single mother of two kids. Lindsey discovers that this client's daughter is on a soccer team that plays every Saturday in the field next to where Lindsey's son plays soccer. Although they are on different teams, Lindsey knows there is a chance that the two children may play against each other.

One day, Lindsey is out in her backyard at home, chatting with a neighbor who also has a daughter around the same age who plays soccer. The neighbor mentions that a girl on her daughter's soccer team is having a sleepover birthday party the following weekend. The neighbor mentions the name of Lindsey's client's daughter, and asks if Lindsey knows her. The neighbor then shares that the child's birthday party sleepover will have a drop-off right after soccer, and that if the mother (Lindsey's client) is still at work, her husband and stepson will be home to cover until she gets home.

Since the mother of the birthday girl is Lindsey's client, she knows that her client's husband and stepson are being investigated by child protective services because the birthday girl accused the stepson of inappropriately touching her. Since the report was just filed, it was decided that the family would simply not allow the stepson to be home alone with the birthday girl until further notice.

Sticky: Since Lindsey knows sensitive information about the inappropriate touching allegation by the birthday girl, does she have any duty to warn her neighbor about this, for fear of the potential risk to the minor sleepover guests? Can Lindsey ethically say *anything* to her neighbor that might offer a hint of caution?

Boil it Down: Lindsey had already acted ethically in discussing with her client how they would manage the possible overlap of their children's soccer games and how they would interact if they crossed paths. However, with the new information that Lindsey received from her neighbor, she must consider both mandated reporting and ethical issues that might need to be addressed here.

First, Lindsey reached out to her supervisor to discuss, to ensure she was making appropriate and ethical choices. This was an especially important step, given Lindsey's personal involvement in the situation as both a mother *and* the client's therapist.

Next, Lindsey decided that since the situation contained a lot of unknowns (e.g., Was there *imminent risk* to the sleepover children, given that the stepdad would be present at drop-off?), it was best to utilize her biggest and best resource—*her client*. Lindsey contacted her client and told her that she had heard about the birthday party and that her husband and stepson would be home at the little girls' drop-off. The client confirmed this was true. The therapist then shared that she had concerns about the situation, especially given the current investigation.

The client, although cooperative in the conversation, was adamant that at no time would the girls be left alone with the stepson. Lindsey went a bit further and told the client that she didn't think the Department of Child Protection would want her to be hosting a sleepover with a bunch of minor girls while the stepson was in the home. The client considered Lindsey's take and asked what she should do. Together, Lindsey and the client decided that it would be best to push the drop-off time later when the client was sure she would be home. Additionally, they decided that the husband and stepson would spend the night at a cousin's house, just to ensure both the safety of the girls and the protection of everyone else involved while the investigation was being conducted.

Lastly, Lindsey knows the importance of documentation, and so she notes a summary of her considerations, choices, and actions in the client's chart. She is careful to type up just the occurrences, and rereads what she has written to ensure she has refrained from leading statements, judgments, and her own interpretations in the notes.

Vignette #5

Lindsey takes her daughter out to a late-afternoon lunch after having to pull her out of school early for an orthodontist appointment. They go to a family-favorite Mexican place on the outskirts of town. It's nearly 3 p.m., so the place is pretty empty between the lunch and dinner rushes.

As they wait at the hostess stand to be seated, Lindsey glances to the left, and sees the deserted bar that is attached to the restaurant. At the very end of the bar, she notices a couple embracing and making out. Just as she's about to turn back to the hostess, who has just arrived to seat them, she sees the couple pull away from each other, and she immediately recognizes the man as a client of hers. However, the woman that the man is making out with is *not* the woman (his wife) that Lindsey is seeing for marital counseling.

Sticky: Should Lindsey just go into the next couples' session with the clients and not mention anything about seeing one party out with another woman at a deserted bar in the middle of the afternoon? Is it ethical for Lindsey to say anything about what she saw at the restaurant bar? Can Lindsey disclose the personal information about one client to the other client?

Boil it Down: First, Lindsey needs to do some self-of-the-therapist (SOTT) work, since she is feeling uncomfortable and frustrated, and is experiencing some irritation towards the part of the couple who was out at the bar with someone else. Lindsey's supervisor and her own personal therapist help remind her that *it's not about her*. They help her process her feeling of anger that the one partner has been leading Lindsey along, baiting her into doing couples' therapy, while the party is stepping out on their spouse. However, they also validate Lindsey's belief that something needs to be done here, and that she can't just continue on with the couples' therapy as it is.

At the subsequent session with the couple, Lindsey tries to leave openings for the couple to share any new information, but both seem to be either tight-lipped or in the dark about anything going on other than the couples' presenting issues. The session carries on as it normally does, but Lindsey becomes increasingly more uncomfortable with keeping her newfound knowledge secret.

Lindsey does have a "no secrets" policy in her practice, but as she rereads it, she realizes that it really refers to either client sharing something privately with her. She's not sure whether inadvertently stumbling across the client's hookup at a barren bar in the middle of the afternoon is an appropriate reason to ignite the "no secrets" policy; it just doesn't seem right.

Although Lindsey doesn't normally contact either one of her couple clients outside of their joint sessions, she decides this is an extenuating circumstance and that she should reach out to the partner she spotted at the bar. The partner admits that he has had an on-and-off-again affair for many years, but surprises Lindsey by sharing that his wife knows about the affair. The client tells her that although his wife is unaware of his late-afternoon meet-up with the other woman at the bar the previous week, she does indeed know about their relationship.

Lindsey shares that she feels uncomfortable with the information she is holding, and feels the need for them to discuss iit in the next session together. The client asks Lindsey to not mention the bar incident specifically, but agrees to her sharing that he has told her about the ongoing affair, and that Lindsey has full permission to tell them both that she feels the need to redefine the nature of their work together. Additionally, Lindsey tells the client that she would like to ask the wife about limits and boundaries surrounding this other woman, and that they agree upon being transparent going forward.

Lastly, Lindsey knows the importance of documentation, and so she notes a summary of her considerations, choices, and actions in the clients' chart. She is careful to type up just the occurrences, and rereads what she has written to ensure she has refrained from leading statements, judgments, and her own interpretations in the notes.

Vignette #6

Lindsey sees Couple A for therapy. Couple A refers a new couple to Lindsey, who we will refer to as Couple B. Couple A and Couple B are friendly with one another, and frequently hang out in the same social circles.

While Couple A are making solid progress in their marriage, and trending towards staying happily together, Couple B decides to try a trial separation and take a break from couples' therapy.

At a future session, Couple A tells Lindsey they were out at a community event, where they saw one half of Couple B making out with a member of the band that was performing that night.

Couple B calls Lindsey to restart therapy shortly thereafter, as they are trying to get back together. Lindsey agrees to see Couple B again, but feels awkward about the information she now knows about the "stepping out" of one partner while they were on a break.

Sticky: Is it ethical for Lindsey to continue the couples' work if the husband is not aware of the wife's hookup with the band member? What is ethical for Lindsey to disclose or not disclose? Is it ethical for Lindsey to refuse to see the couple for their reunification work?

Boil it Down: Much like the previous case, Lindsey does a great job of recognizing the "sticky" in the clinical situation. Again, she does have a "no secrets" policy, but it does not address if she finds something out inadvertently, nor does it cover the very sticky situation of finding the information out through another client.

Lindsey feel stuck. If she reaches out to the one partner who was kissing the band member while they were separated, she is bound by the confidentiality of Couple A's information, and therefore cannot tell either party of Couple B that she knows about it. She also can't say anything to Couple A about this, including even acknowledging that she is still seeing them.

Lindsey decides to hold one session with Couple B, and starts off by asking an open-ended question about what happened during their separation and what they each may have learned from it. She shares the importance of transparency going forward if they want to build a solid foundation this time. She asks them each about their commitment to staying in the marriage and their goals for therapy. Regardless of how hard she tried, Lindsey did not get even the tiniest of disclosures about the hookup from either spouse.

After meeting with her supervisor, Lindsey decides she simply cannot hold on to this information in good faith and remain competent in the therapy room. The situation is confounded by her inability to talk with the one partner separately about needing to figure out a pathway for Lindsey not to be a secret-keeper. Doing so would violate the PHI from Couple A.

Lindsey decides she simply cannot continue with the couple and lets them know that a conflict of interest has come up, and that she doesn't feel that she can ethically continue the work with them. They are curious, but Lindsey just explains that the layers of confidentiality of all of her clients do not allow her to say more. She refers the couple to a fabulous therapist in her practice, and all is well.

Lastly, Lindsey knows the importance of documentation, and so she notes a summary of her considerations, choices, and actions in the clients' chart. She is careful to type up just the occurrences, and rereads what she has written to ensure she has refrained from leading statements, judgments, and her own interpretations in the notes.

Vignette #7

Lindsey has taken on two new teletherapy clients in the last week. The first is an eight-year-old boy. The boy's mother reached out to Lindsey, saying that she had heard great things about her work with kids, and hopes that she will be able to help her son's behavioral issues that have accompanied his recent diagnosis of a hyperactivity disorder.

Lindsey's second new client is a 19-year-old female who is at home for the summer while she's out of college for a few months. This client has a history of depression and anxiety, and the client was referred by her high school guidance counselor who touts Lindsey as the "best therapist in town"!

Sticky: Lindsey is wondering if there is anything unethical about taking on the eight-year-old for teletherapy. Is there anything she needs to be especially mindful about? She also wonders about the 19-year-old and the appropriateness of teletherapy for her issues of depression and anxiety. Will Lindsey be abandoning the client when she returns to college in another state, where Lindsey is not licensed, so she will no longer be able to see her?

Boil it Down: Although she is very experienced as a clinician, Lindsey has only recently moved to a solely teletherapy practice. For this reason, she realizes that she needs to be sure she is competent on this platform in a way that will meet the needs of these two clients.

Lindsey decides she needs to do a more thorough assessment of the appropriateness of these two clients before taking them on. She calls the eight-year-old's mom and asks a few questions—"Is the client able to sit still for the full 45 minutes on camera? Have they ever had a telehealth visit with the child, and how did it go?" From the conversation, Lindsey and the eight-year-old's mom decide that they will do a trial session to see if the modality is fitting for the child.

During the session with the eight-year-old, he asks to talk privately to Lindsey, without his mom in the room. The mom agrees to leave, and the child tells Lindsey he wants to use the "chat" feature to type in the things he wants to say to her, instead of just talking which is "sooooo boring." Lindsey agrees, and she and the child type up a great conversation, with lots of goofy emojis to punctuate their discussion.

Later that week, Lindsey and the mom decide the modality works for the child, and that he reported looking forward to the next session. The mom also added that the typed messages between the child and Lindsey were saved as a chat on her computer after they logged off. Horrified, Lindsey apologized, and knew she would have to make the child aware of this feature before they met for the next session. Although Lindsey properly assessed the child client for the appropriateness of teletherapy for his needs, she neglected to fully understand her teletherapy platform before using it. For this reason, she was not able to fully inform her child client of the risks (parents reading your typed messages) of the teletherapy platform.

For the second client, the 19-year-old college student, Lindsey starts off with a phone call to assess the fit of teletherapy with the client. Lindsey makes a thorough exploration of the client's history of depression and anxiety, and inquires about whether she has done teletherapy before. The client has indeed done teletherapy and likes it. Lindsey also explains that she will not be able to continue to see the client when she returns to college. Given that she's not licensed in that state, she wants to be sure the client will not be abandoned.

Next, Lindsey makes sure the client has an adequate Wi-Fi, and private space where she can talk freely with the therapist. The client reports that she does. So Lindsey schedules the first appointment with the client.

Lindsey sees the client throughout the summer, and then transitions to a discussion of termination as the date looms for the client to return to college. Lindsey makes sure the client is set up with the counseling services at her college and emergency numbers in that state, and they schedule for another meeting in a couple of months when she's home for a long weekend.

The next day, the client receives a phone call from her college counseling center, telling her they've been alerted to some concerning messages in her email, and wanted to do a wellness check with her. Feeling angry, violated, and embarrassed, the client has a strong reaction to the person from the counseling center. This, in turn, makes the counselor on the phone anxious, and she threatens to call the local authorities in the client's town. The client gets off the phone and immediately calls Lindsey in hysterics.

Lindsey has the client sign an ROI to speak with the college counseling center, and she immediately calls the center to assuage their fears and let them know that the client is fine. During the phone call, Lindsey learns that all of the college's students' emails are monitored for certain trigger words or phrases that have to do with violence, safety, etc. The counselor explains that the college email belongs to the college and that all the messages on there technically belong to the student.

Lindsey reconnects with the client and explains what she has learned. Lindsey suggests that the client make a Gmail™ account and that the therapy invites, and all other exchanges, will be through the client's personal email instead of through the college's email.

Lastly, Lindsey knows the importance of documentation, and so she notes a summary of her considerations, choices, and actions in both of the clients' charts. She is careful to type up just the occurrences, and rereads what she has written to ensure she has refrained from leading statements, judgments, and her own interpretations in the notes.

Vignette #8

Lindsey sees a client for individual therapy, for support through an acrimonious divorce. At the beginning of one session, the client brings the results of her ex-husband's psychological evaluation report. The client's attorney has shared the document with her. Lindsey knows that the client is in the midst of a difficult custody battle, since this has been a frequent topic of discussion in their therapy.

The client asks Lindsey to read over the report and give her any additional feedback about the test results or the conclusions that the psychologist who conducted the evaluation has made. Lindsey is very familiar with the battery of tests (including the intelligence and personality measures), as she has had some coursework and training on them, and she has occasionally seen these kinds of reports from some of her other clients.

After telling the client that her opinion is not valid for accurate interpretation, and that she would need to consult a psychologist that specializes in testing for any details, Lindsey decides to give the client a brief overview of what the scores may mean.

Sticky: Is it ethical for Lindsey to share her interpretations, given that she is not certified to do psychological testing? Is it in the best interests of her client for Lindsey to share her thoughts, or might this come back in any way to hurt the client? Is Lindsey overstepping a boundary by sharing her opinion? Does Lindsey know if the report was obtained legally by the attorney, given that it contains PHI? And given that Lindsey is not the therapist for the client's husband, does she have any requirement to report the mishandled and inappropriately shared PHI of the husband?

Boil it Down: Lindsey considers her professional code of ethics' mandate that she only practice in areas she is competent in. She wonders, then, if perhaps her sharing the basics of what she knew about the battery of tests and results might have misled the client. This would violate the ethical principles of Fidelity and Veracity. In addition, could Lindsey's thoughts and understanding of the results be considered "practicing" outside of her area of expertise.

Lindsey decides to have a conversation with the client at their next meeting. She explains that she may have overstepped in offering her limited interpretations on the testing results because, at first, she thought it was in the best interests (Beneficence) of her client. After reflection, Lindsey shares that she feels uncomfortable with not knowing if the PHI of the client's husband was legally obtained, and that without his consent, Lindsey really shouldn't be reading it anyway. Lindsey thoroughly explains that she should not have shared as much as she did with the client, and reframes it the following, and more accurate way:

> My training on this sort of testing is limited. And since I am not certified to either test or interpret the results, I can't really comment on anything it contains. Since I do not have consent to view these results, I'm not comfortable looking at anything like this going forward. If there are general questions you want to ask me here that pertain to questions you have regarding what you've read, I'm happy to consider whether that would be appropriate. For example, if you asked me to talk about the possible ways that symptoms of bipolar disorder might present, I'm happy to share the DSM criteria for it. I also want you to know that you've done nothing wrong here, and in my attempts to do what I initially thought was helpful to you, I may have shared outside of an ethical window here.

Lindsey attempted to regain the control of how the boundaries and limits and ethics should be in the therapy room, thus "winning" the Battle of Structure. She made sure the client understood that she did nothing wrong. Lindsey was very clear about the limits and boundaries she would maintain moving forward, and offered a thorough explanation of these to the client.

Lastly, Lindsey knows the importance of documentation, and so she notes a summary of her considerations, choices, and actions in the client's chart. She is careful to type up just the occurrences, and rereads what she has written to ensure she has refrained from leading statements, judgments, and her own interpretations in the notes.

Vignette #9

Lindsey is seeing a 19-year-old young man (Mateo) who is mid-semester away at college, and who presents with anxiety and attention deficit issues. She sees him both while he is away at college and while he is at home, because Lindsey is licensed in both of those states. Although Mateo reported never having been suicidal, he did have to go to the emergency department of his local hospital on two occasions for severe panic attacks.

Mateo is doing pretty well with Lindsey, and he reports feeling a bit less anxious and being able to utilize some of the strategies she has given him. Due to Lindsey's vacation, directly followed by a spring break trip that Mateo is taking with some friends, they will not meet for therapy for a period of one month. Lindsey gives Mateo emergency resources, as well as encouraging him to journal daily so that he can share how the month went with her upon his return.

While Lindsey is away, she receives a text from an unnamed number she does not recognize. The text says: "Hi, my name is Kaela, and my boyfriend, Mateo, sees you for therapy. He told me that if I ever worry about his mental health that I should text you. Can you help me figure out what to do? I'm worried about him. He's not suicidal or anything like that, but I think he's not doing too great…"

At the same time, Lindsey receives an email request from Mateo's mother, asking for referrals and resources for programs and rehabs for Mateo's father, who has been struggling with severe alcoholism, as well as some mental health issues.

Sticky: Does Lindsey need to respond to any of these messages, given that she is away on vacation? What are Lindsey's obligations with the report on Mateo's mental health? Is there any ethical issue with Lindsey corresponding about treatment possibilities for Mateo's dad with his mother? Can Lindsey respond to Mateo's girlfriend's text, given that it "might" be an emergency situation?

Boil it Down: Although Lindsey is on vacation and has covered her bases to not have to work while she's away, she decides that she will take care of these two matters immediately. Lindsey decides that the ethical action here is to ensure her client's safety. Lindsey had appropriately prepared Mateo for their unavoidable one-month break from therapy, but neither one of them could have known that Mateo would have some mental health struggles in between their sessions.

Lindsey decides to take care of Mateo's mom's message quickly first. Since she has a signed release from Mateo to bill his mom for his sessions, she already knows that he is in treatment with Lindsey. The mom's email does not include any request for information about Mateo's PHI, nor does it brush up against any privacy issues regarding Mateo's treatment. Since the mom is simply asking for resources and treatment referrals for Mateo's dad, Lindsey thinks it's appropriate to provide these. So, Lindsey sends along some contact info for Mateo's dad to the mom.

Lindsey feels ethical about this. However, fast-forward to an email she receives several days later from Mateo's mom. The mom's email thanks Lindsey for her help and sharing of resources, and updates her that the dad was able to get into rehab, and that she had an aftercare provider all set up. Although this was great to hear for Lindsey, it also brought up an ethical dilemma for her.

One of Mateo's main sources of anxiety was based on his father's poor mental health and alcoholism. Mateo worried a lot that his dad would die early or lose his job, or something else that would be traumatic to the family. He had tried to talk to his dad with no avail, and Mateo's mom often played a complacent role, telling him not to worry about it and that his father was doing better.

Lindsey knows that Mateo's anxiety would be greatly reduced if he had the encouraging news that his dad was finally away at rehab, but she is unsure if Mateo's mom has shared this news with him. Mateo's mom tends to be tight-lipped and unwilling to discuss the dad's issues with Mateo. Mateo thinks his mom is trying to shield him from the stress of it while he is away at college and can't witness his dad's actions.

Since she believes it would help Mateo's anxiety, it would be in Mateo's best interests (Beneficence) to have this information. However, Lindsey wonders if it's appropriate for her to be the one to share it if the mom has already done so.

Lindsey knows that the mom is not her client, and therefore she has no legal mandate of keeping her information protected and confidential. Lindsey also knows that upsetting Mateo's mother or having her question Lindsey's competence in telling Mateo might give stress to him and compromise their therapeutic relationship. This could be harmful (Maleficence) to Mateo. Additionally, Lindsey cannot tell the mom that she thinks Mateo would be less anxious if he knew his dad was in rehab, because these worries about his dad's health and well-being contributed to his panic attacks. Disclosing this to the mom would be a violation of Mateo's PHI and confidentiality.

So, Lindsey decides to simply email the mom and ask: "Have you told Mateo this news yet? Since you have shared it with me, I don't want to be in a secret-keeping position with him when we meet. Therefore, I'm hoping you'd be willing to update Mateo before I meet with him next so we can discuss this freely?" The mom quickly responds, "Of course. That's appropriate. I will tell him tomorrow."

Now Lindsey needs to figure out what to do about Mateo's girlfriend's text message. She has appropriately prepped all of her clients on emergencies while she's away, has an "away" message on her voicemail with similar information, and has a no-text policy with clients for sharing any information other than schedule changes, etc. However, since Kaela is *not* her client, and is therefore unaware of this information and these policies, and given the seriousness of her message, Lindsey decides, in good faith, that she needs to act on the information Kaela has provided. But she also knows that she cannot contact Kaela, nor can she even acknowledge that Mateo is a client of hers.

Not being able to trust Kaela's layperson assessment of Mateo's condition, Lindsey knows she must try to contact Mateo right away to ensure he is safe and stable enough to wait until their next meeting without intervention.

Lindsey is not able to reach him by phone, so she leaves a voicemail, an email, and a text asking him to please call her ASAP. When she doesn't hear back for an hour, she calls again, telling him that if he can't be in contact in the next hour, she will call his emergency contact (his mom) to check on him.

Mateo calls back right away, a little surprised by Lindsey's call. He is able to convince her that he is stable and fine without any other treatment until they meet upon their return. Lindsey reiterates the emergency contacts and other strategies and resources to get him through any tough times he encounters. She also explains that she cannot contact Kaela, and recommends that if he wants Lindsey to be able to respond to her in the future, she will need for him to sign an ROI. They can decide together what exactly Mateo would like Lindsey to be able to share with Kaela.

Lastly, Lindsey knows the importance of documentation, and so she notes a summary of her considerations, choices, and actions in the client's chart. She is careful to type up just the occurrences, and rereads what she has written to ensure she has refrained from leading statements, judgments, and her own interpretations in the notes.

References

Abrams, Z. (2026, March). AI in the therapists' office: Uptake increases, caution persists. *Monitor on Psychology*, 57(2), 32. www.apa.org/monitor/2026/03/ai-reshaping-therapy.

Abramson, A. (2021, April/May). The ethical imperative of self-care. *Monitor on Psychology*, 52(3), 64–67. www.apa.org/monitor/2021/04/feature-imperative-self-care.

Aggarwal, N.K., Chen, D., & Lewis-Fernández, R. (2022). If you don't ask, they don't tell: The cultural formulation interview and patient perceptions of the clinical relationship. *American Journal of Psychotherapy*, 75(3), 97–104. doi:10.1176/appi.psychotherapy.20210040.

American Association for Marriage and Family Therapy. (2026). *AAMFT code of ethics*. www.aamft.org/AAMFT/Legal_Ethics/Code_of_Ethics.aspx.

American Counseling Association. (2014). *ACA code of ethics*. www.counseling.org/docs/default-source/default-document-library/ethics/2014-aca-code-of-ethics.pdf.

American Psychological Association. (2017). *Ethical principles of psychologists and code of conduct*. www.apa.org/ethics/code.

Aponte, H., & Kissil, K. (2017). The person of the therapist training model. In J. Lebow, A. Chambers, & D. Breunlin (Eds.), *Encyclopedia of couple and family therapy*. Springer. doi:10.1007/978-3-319-15877-8_544-1.

Appelbaum, P.S., & Gutheil, T.G. (1991). *Clinical handbook of psychiatry and the law*. Williams & Wilkins.

Bakhtin, M. (1984). *Problems of Dostoevsky's poetics* (C. Emerson, Trans.). University of Minnesota Press. (Original work published 1929)

Bazerman, M.H., & Tenbrunsel, A.E. (2011). *Blind spots: Why we fail to do what's right and what to do about it*. Princeton University Press.

Békés, V., Aafjes-van Doorn, K., Luo, X., Prout, T.A., & Hoffman, L. (2021). Psychotherapists' challenges with online therapy during COVID-19: Concerns about connectedness predict therapists' negative view of online therapy and its perceived efficacy over time. *Frontiers in Psychology*, 12, Article 705699. doi:10.3389/fpsyg.2021.705699.

Bellg, A.J., Borrelli, B., Resnick, B., Hecht, J., Minicucci, D.S., Ory, M., Ogedegbe, G., Orwig, D., Ernst, D., Czajkowski, S., & Treatment Fidelity Workgroup of the NIH Behavior Change Consortium. (2004). Enhancing treatment fidelity in health behavior change studies: Best practices and recommendations from the NIH Behavior Change Consortium. *Health Psychology*, 23(5), 443–451. doi:10.1037/0278-6133.23.5.443.

Better Outcomes Now. (n.d.). Why Better Outcomes Now?https://betteroutcomesnow.com/why-bon.

Bonitz, V. (2008). Use of physical touch in the "talking cure": A journey to the outskirts of psychotherapy. *Psychotherapy*, 45(3), 391–404. doi:10.1037/a0013311.

Boszormenyi-Nagy, I. (1987). *Foundations of Contextual Therapy: Collected Papers of Ivan Boszormenyi-Nagy, M.D.* (1st ed.). Brunner/Mazel.

Boszormenyi-Nagy, I. (2014). *Foundations of contextual therapy: Collected papers of Ivan Boszormenyi-Nagy, MD*. Routledge. (Original work published 1987)

Bradley, J.W., & Becker, K.D. (2021). Clinical supervision of mental health services: A systematic review of supervision characteristics and practices associated with formative and restorative outcomes. *The Clinical Supervisor*, 40(1), 88–111. doi:10.1080/07325223.2021.1904312.

Briscoe, J. (2020, June 7). What happens when you have an affair with your therapist? *The Guardian*. www.theguardian.com/lifeandstyle/2020/jun/07/what-happens-when-your-relationship-with-a-therapist-turns-into-an-afair.

Caldwell, B. (2025). Your late cancellation policy may be causing late cancellations. Psychotherapy Notes, High Pass Education. www.psychotherapynotes.com/late-cancellation-fee-policy.

Castonguay, L.G., & Hill, C.E. (Eds.). (2012). *Transformation in psychotherapy: Corrective experiences across cognitive behavioral, humanistic, and psychodynamic approaches* (1st ed.). American Psychological Association.

Chenneville, T., Gabbidon, K., Hornschuh, S., & Dietrich, J. (2021). Balancing autonomy and protection in pediatric treatment and research. *Advances in Pediatrics*, 68, 55–69. doi:10.1016/j.yapd.2021.05.009.

Cicchetti, D., & Rogosch, F.A. (1996). Equifinality and multifinality in developmental psychopathology. *Development and Psychopathology*, 8(4), 597–600. doi:10.1017/S0954579400007318.

Cruciani, G., Liotti, M., & Lingiardi, V. (2024). Motivations to become psychotherapists: Beyond the concept of the wounded healer. *Research in Psychotherapy: Psychopathology, Process and Outcome*, 27(2), Article 808. doi:10.4081/ripppo.2024.808.

Curvis, W. (2020). *Professional issues in clinical psychology: Developing a professional identity through clinical psychology training and beyond*. Routledge.

Cybersecurity and Infrastructure Security Agency (CISA). (n.d.). How to communicate securely on your mobile device. www.cisa.gov/resources-tools/training/how-communicate-securely-your-mobile-device.

Danzer, G.S. (2019). *Therapist self-disclosure: An evidence-based guide for practitioners*. Routledge.

Friedman, S. (Ed.). (1995). *The reflecting team in action*. Guilford Press.

Goodman, E. (2010, January 1). Ellen Goodman's last column: Looking backward, looking forward. *The Seattle Times*. www.seattletimes.com/opinion/ellen-goodmans-last-column-looking-backward-looking-forward.

Hassett-Walker, C. (2025). How individuals seeking help for substance use disorder adjusted to virtual 12-step meetings during the COVID-19 pandemic. *Inquiry*, 62, Article 469580251320767. doi:10.1177/00469580251320767.

Hiriscau, I.E., Stingelin-Giles, N., Stadler, C., Schmeck, K., & Reiter-Theil, S. (2014). A right to confidentiality or a duty to disclose? Ethical guidance for conducting prevention research with children and adolescents. *European Child & Adolescent Psychiatry*, 23(6), 409–416. doi:10.1007/s00787-014-0526-y.

Hudgens, V. (2025). Is there such a thing as ethical AI in therapy? Here's what therapists have to say. Psychology.org. www.psychology.org/resources/ethical-ai-in-therapy.

Jay, T. (2000). *Why we curse: A neuro-psycho-social theory of speech.* John Benjamins Publishing Company.

Kafka, J.X., Kothgassner, O.D., & Felnhofer, A. (2024). A matter of trust: Confidentiality in therapeutic relationships during psychological and medical treatment in children and adolescents with mental disorders. *Journal of Clinical Medicine*, 13(6), Article 1752. doi:10.3390/jcm13061752.

Katz, M., Hilsenroth, M.J., Gold, J.R., Moore, M., Pitman, S.R., Levy, S.R., & Owen, J. (2019). Adherence, flexibility, and outcome in psychodynamic treatment of depression. *Journal of Counseling Psychology*, 66(1), 94–103. doi:10.1037/cou0000299.

Knox, S. (2015). Disclosure—and lack thereof—in individual supervision. *The Clinical Supervisor*, 34(2), 151–163. doi:10.1080/07325223.2015.1086462.

Kooperman, D. (2013). When the therapist is in crisis: Personal and professional implications for small community psychotherapy practices. *American Journal of Psychotherapy*, 67(4), 385–403. doi:10.1176/appi.psychotherapy.2013.67.4.385.

Kühne, F., Heinze, P.E., & Weck, F. (2020). What do laypersons believe characterises a competent psychotherapist? *Counselling and Psychotherapy Research*, 21(3), 626–635. doi:10.1002/capr.12343.

Kuo, P.B., Rudecindo, B., Drinane, J.M., Tao, K., Van Epps, J., & Imel, Z.E. (2025). Cultural conversations in therapy: How often clients talk about their identities. *Psychiatric Services*, 76(2), 133–138. doi:10.1176/appi.ps.20230266.

Lum, W. (2002). The use of self of the therapist. *Contemporary Family Therapy*, 24 (1), 181–197. doi:10.1023/a:1014385908625.

McBratney, S. (2019). *Guess how much I love you.* Candlewick Press.

Miller, E., & McNaught, A. (2020). Exploring decision making around therapist self-disclosure in cognitive behavioral therapy. *Australian Psychologist*, 55(1), 33–39. doi:10.1111/ap.12260.

Mullen, P.R., Morris, C., & Lord, M. (2017). The experience of ethical dilemmas, burnout, and stress among practicing counselors. *Counseling and Values*, 62(1), 37–56. doi:10.1002/cvj.12048.

Mulqueen, M. (2019). Who's listening? Smartphones and psychotherapy. Psychotherapy.net. www.psychotherapy.net/article/smartphones-and-psychotherapy.

Muse, K., McManus, F., Rakovshik, S., & Thwaites, R. (2016). Development and psychometric evaluation of the Assessment of Core CBT Skills (ACCS): An observation-based tool for assessing cognitive behavioral therapy competence. *Psychological Assessment*, 29(5), 542–555. doi:10.1037/pas0000372.

Napier, A.Y., & Whitaker, C. (1978). *The family crucible.* Harper & Row.

National Association of Social Workers. (2021). *Code of ethics.* www.socialworkers.org/About/Ethics/Code-of-Ethics/Code-of-Ethics-English.

Norris, D.M., Gutheil, T.G., & Strasburger, L.H. (2003). This couldn't happen to me: Boundary problems and sexual misconduct in the psychotherapy relationship. *Psychiatric Services*, 54(4), 517–522. doi:10.1176/appi.ps.54.4.517.

Oxford University Press. (n.d.). *Oxford English Dictionary.* www.oed.com/?tl=true.

Petrilli, C.M., Mack, M., Janowitz-Petrilli, J., Hickner, A., Saint, S., & Chopra, V. (2015). Understanding the role of physician attire on patient perceptions: A systematic review of the literature—targeting attire to improve likelihood of rapport (TAILOR) investigators. *BMJ Open*, 5(1), e006578. doi:10.1136/bmjopen-2014-006578.

Rapp, A., Curti, L., & Boldi, A. (2021). The human side of human-chatbot interaction: A systematic literature review of ten years of research on text-based chatbots. International *Journal of Human-Computer Studies*, 151, 102630. doi:10.1016/j.ijhcs.2021.102630.

Rapp, D.J., Hughey, J.M., & Kreiner, G.E. (2021). Boundary work as a buffer against burnout: Evidence from healthcare workers during the COVID-19 pandemic. *Journal of Applied Psychology*, 106(8), 1169–1187. doi:10.1037/apl0000951.

Rastogi, M. (2025, November/December). AI in the therapy room: A client's need for informed consent. *Family Therapy Magazine*, 25(6). https://ftm.aamft.org/ai-in-the-therapy-room-a-clients-need-for-informed-consent.

Reamer, F.G. (2017). Ethical and risk management issues in the use of touch. In J.A. Courtney & R.D. Nolan (Eds.), *Touch in child counseling and play therapy*. Routledge.

Reynolds, L.R. (2013, September/October). Gifts, "thank yous," and the "why I do this" box. *Family Therapy Magazine*, 41–43.

Reynolds, L.R. (2013, September/October). Gifts, "thank yous," and the "why I do this" box part II. *Family Therapy Magazine*, 40–41.

Reynolds, L.R. (2016, September/October). Managing multiple relationships once you find yourself in them. *Family Therapy Magazine*.

Reynolds, L.R. (2018, July/August). Assessing the need for increased self-care in therapists. *Family Therapy Magazine*.

Reynolds, L.R. (2019, March/April). Gauging how long the therapeutic relationship is beneficial to the client. *Family Therapy Magazine*.

Rokeach, M. (1973). *The nature of human values*. Free Press.

Salyers, M.P., Fukui, S., Rollins, A.L., Firmin, R., Gearhart, T., Noll, J.P., & Davis, C.J. (2015). Burnout and self-reported quality of care in community mental health. *Administration and Policy in Mental Health and Mental Health Services Research*, 42(1), 61–69. doi:10.1007/s10488-014-0544-6.

Scott, L., & Wendt, D. (2018). Self of the therapist training in couple and family therapy. In J. Lebow, A. Chambers, & D. Breunlin (Eds.), *Encyclopedia of couple and family therapy*. Springer. doi:10.1007/978-3-319-15877-8_642-1.

State of Connecticut Judicial Branch. (n.d.). Juvenile court informational guide: Legal guardian and caregiver privileges. https://jud.ct.gov/juv_infoguide/IJCP_LG_Privileges.html.

Stubbs, J.M., Carothers, H.L., & Jones, M. (2024). Cultural meaning of client gifts. *Tennessee Counseling Association Journal*, 9(1), 70–85. www.researchgate.net/publication/382750236_Cultural_Meaning_of_Client_Gifts.

The Cut Podcast. (2019, January 22). Bad sex, good sex, fiction that makes sense of how we bone [Audio podcast episode]. The Cut Podcast. https://podwise.ai/episodes/7289786.

Tufford, L., & Lee, B. (2020). Relationship repair strategies when reporting child abuse and neglect. *Child and Adolescent Social Work Journal*, 37(3), 235–249. doi:10.1007/s10560-020-00656-6.

Vincent, J., & Sattar, S. (2024, December 5). Increasing rates of phone thefts worldwide pose significant data security risks. Crisis24. www.crisis24.com/articles/increasing-rates-of-phone-thefts-worldwide-pose-significant-data-security-risk.

von Bertalanffy, L. (1968). *General system theory: Foundations, development, applications*. Braziller.

Wilcoxon, S.A., Remley, T.P., & Gladding, S.T. (2013). *Ethical, legal, and professional issues in the practice of marriage and family therapy* (Updated ed.). Pearson.

Williams, I.L., & O'Connor, P. (2019). Power in the counseling relationship: The role of ignorance. *Journal of Human Services: Training, Research, & Practice*, 4(2), 1–37. https://scholarworks.sfasu.edu/jhstrp/vol4/iss2/3.

Williams, I.L., & Uebel, M. (2022). On the use of profane language in psychotherapy and counseling: A brief summary of studies over the last six decades. *European Journal of Psychotherapy & Counselling*, 23(4), 404–421. doi:10.1080/13642537.2021.2001025.

World Health Organization. (2019). Burnout (QD85). In *International statistical classification of diseases and related health problems* (11th ed.). https://icd.who.int/browse11/l-m/en#/https://id.who.int/icd/entity/129180281.

Zarbo, C., Tasca, G.A., Cattafi, F., & Compare, A. (2016). Integrative psychotherapy works. *Frontiers in Psychology*, 6. doi:10.3389/fpsyg.2015.02021.

Zhang, Z. (2019). Price discount and gift choice: Interplay between economic and social value. *Academy of Marketing Studies Journal*, 23(4), 1–10.

Index

For Product Safety Concerns and Information please contact our
EU representative GPSR@taylorandfrancis.com Taylor & Francis
Verlag GmbH, Kaufingerstraße 24, 80331 München, Germany